I0130074

I WAS CASTRO'S PRISONER

An American Tells His Story

BY JOHN MARTINO

JFK Lancer
Publications & Productions
Southlake, TX

Southlake, TX 76092

JFK Lancer First Edition November 2008

Original Copyright © 1963, John Martino
Copyright © 2008, Edward Martino

All rights reserved. No part of this book may be reproduced or transmitted in any form or by any means, electronic or mechanical, including photocopying or recording, or by any information storage or retrieval system without written permission from the publisher except for the inclusion of brief quotations in a review.

The goal of JFK Lancer Productions & Publications, Inc. is to make research materials concerning President John F. Kennedy easily available to everyone. Our prime concern is the accuracy and the true story of the turbulent 1960s.

For additional copies of this publication, please contact:
E-mail: orders@jfklancer.com
Web: www.jfklancer.com

Printed in the United States
Cover design by Sherry Fiester
Book design by Sherry Fiester

ISBN Number 0-9774657-6-4

Acknowledgements

In July 1959, John Martino boarded a plane for a business trip to Cuba. He took along his 13 year old son, Edward, for a holiday.

Unbelievably, he was taken prisoner by G-2 men, Castro's military police, and held captive for 40 months in prison.

During his imprisonment, Martino saw a secret Russian radio communications system established, endured the despair of the Bay of Pigs invasion, and learned of the installation of Russian rockets. Blessed with an almost photographic memory, upon his release Martino shared an eye witness account of Castro's Cuba in one of the most perilous times in history. The original manuscript was in collaboration with Nathanial Weyl and held a dedication to Alan Courtney, radio host with WQAM in Miami.

When John Martino died, his son, Doctor Edward Martino, began researching the events and persons that were so much a part of his father's life. Dr. Martino became familiar with the work of Larry Hancock, author of *Someone Would Have Talked,* and in 2006 made the courageous decision to publicly identify himself and provide a series of remarks about his personal observations in Cuba with his father and of his father's life after his release from prison; including November 1963.

Dr. Martino has provided permission to republish his father's book with the stipulation all proceeds are dedicated to JFK Lancer Publication and Productions' scholarship fund. Each year, JFK Lancer's goal is to help one special student get to college, and one special teacher be recognized. Hopefully, this scholarship will encourage teacher and student participation in the further study of the assassination of President John F. Kennedy.

"The real key to our national future," President Kennedy said, "lies in the young people of our country."

Toward that end, Doctor Edward Martino's gift of funds to help advance the education of students and teachers is greatly appreciated.

Scholarships information available at: http://jfklancer.com/Scholarship.html.

PROLOGUE

On July 23, 1959, my father and I were arrested in Havana. The vast changes in our world subsequent to that event are indeed profound. When I reflect back on my father, I see two John Martinos. One John Martino went to prison; a changed John Martino was released over three years later.

My dad was the "connected guy" who made his money in gambling and bookmaking for most if his life. He had gone to Cuba in the summer of '58 and worked at the Havanna Deauville Casino until the Castro takeover. In July '59 dad took me on holiday back to Cuba and while there he was falsely arrested. This trip was exploratory as dad and some associates were trying to determine if it would be possible to do business in the Cuba after the revolution.

While there, he was falsely arrested. In a misguided effort to display his allegiance to America and exercise an opportunity to demonstrate his faith in our government, he became a political prisoner.

In 1962, when he was released from Castro's main political prison, La Cabana in Havana, he emerged a very changed man. He became fully convinced that Castro would be successful in spreading Communism in our hemisphere. The connected guy who was my dad had become a right wing radical. Before his ordeal, John Martino was not interested in politics and to my knowledge never voted. He lived on the edge of the underworld, making money in spurts; never able to save much, or invest for the future. Our family lived an "easy come, easy go" existence.

After his release, Dad became involved with anti-Castro elements in South Florida. In the summer of 1963, he participated in the infamous "Bayo-Pawley" affair, a raid on Cuba designed to extract Russian officers who claimed to have proof of Russian missiles still in Cuba. He spoke at a number of right wing groups all around the country, still fully convinced that Castro's Cuba would be the base for Communist expansion throughout the Americas. And in the early 1970s, he spent time in Guatemala acquiring weapons and other supplies for the right wing government that was fighting Communist guerillas in the mountains.

Dad never went back to his old life of gambling and bookmaking. He had discovered a purpose for his life and sought to spread the word about the dangers of Communism that thrived so close to our shores. Additionally, Larry Hancock's work well documents Dad's involvement in the JFK assassination conspiracy. I cannot justify my father's actions in the plot, but I do understand the context leading him to his decision to assist the conspirators.

In addition to Dad's politics changing as a result of prison life, his very faith was challenged with surprising results. Once shortly after his release, I came into my parents' room early one morning to find him on his knees praying, a Bible in his hand, and a religious medal around his neck.

This act caught me by complete surprise as he had never been openly spiritual during my youth, and rarely went to church. I still have that Bible and the Eucharist medal that was given to him by an imprisoned priest who was executed for being a counter revolutionary. I still wear the medal as a reminder of my Dad, and of the suffering that many Cuban people experienced in the early days of the Castro regime.

This book was originally published in early 1963 with a limited printing of 5,000 copies. Our personal family copies had long since disappeared when the one I have was "liberated" from a library by a friend of the family and given to my mom. I am happy to make once again this work available to students of history and researchers seeking a better understanding of the context that led to the events in Dallas on November 22, 1963.

As you read my father's account of his imprisonment, remember that his prison experience paved the way for his radical actions. For him, Communism had a very personal face☐a face that executed over 100 men at La Cabana during his confinement.

Prior to his death in 1975, John Martino became the "Someone who Talked". While we never spoke of this matter, I think that he ultimately understood the tragic consequences of that fateful day in November 1963. I only pray that God may have mercy on his soul.

Edward Martino, PhD
Fort Worth, October 29, 2008

FOREWORD

"I Was Castro's Prisoner" is historically significant book that in 1963 was a media sensation in conservative political circles. Martino presented first-hand personal experience to virtually all the evils that had come with the Castro revolution. He offered personal descriptions of ongoing, brutal executions held "against the wall" and related stories of full-fledged warfare against both the capital and professional classes within Cuba. What Martino witnessed and was openly documenting, were the very worst fears of the Cold War: the victory of communism in a capitalist country, and the subsequent destruction of a way of life for Cuban nationals.

It is no wonder that Martino became a local celebrity in Miami, with frequent mention the city newspapers and coverage on both radio and television. With the publication of his book, his exposure expanded nationwide, with speaking tours sponsored by a variety of right wing political groups, including the John Birch Society. It's also no wonder that Martino would be debriefed by the Central Intelligence agency upon his return, and that he would become the champion for, and associate of, many leading Cuban exile figures.

John Martino's influence was far greater than one might imagine simply from reading this book and visualizing radio interviews or speeches to anti-communist crowds. Martino gained the attention of many very influential figures, from Congressmen and former Ambassadors, to militant exile fighters and senior officers at the CIA's huge JMWAVE operations base in Florida. Some of these figures are mentioned in his book, including one senior CIA officer whose real name he should not have known, and who certainly would have been stripped out of this book if it had been vetted by the Agency.

Actually, "I Was Castro's Prisoner" was not fully completed until after Martino returned from a highly covert, sensitive and potentially explosive mission into Cuba. The reason that Martino was on the mission, other than his personal commitment to the exile cause and overthrow of Castro, was the fact that he had figured prominently in influencing the former ambassador to Cuba, William Pawley, to endorse and financially support the mission. Pawley had been so convinced of the mission's necessity, that he lobbied it at the very highest levels of the Central Intelligence Agency and with key congressmen, including Senator Eastland.

Amazingly, Pawley had even managed to get the CIA to allow "LIFE" magazine photo coverage of the mission, which included CIA operations personnel, Cuba exiles from Alpha 66 led by Eddie Bayo and millionaire Pawley. The mission was given active support by CIA ships and aircraft and was designated Operation TILT. Photographs from the "LIFE" photographer clearly show Martino (then well into his 50s) on the mission and in company of exile leader Eddie Bayo. Without doubt, John Martino was a man who put his life on the line over the issues he outlines in "I Was Castro's Prisoner."

However, the TILT mission also begins to open up the first of several mysteries that involve John Martino in events far beyond being simply a spokesperson and activist against Fidel Castro and the communist rule in Cuba. The TILT mission was intended to bring out Soviet missile technicians who were going to swear that Russian missiles were still in Cuba, proving the United States had been totally duped during the agreement that ended the missile crisis of 1962.

Clearly such a result would have inflamed opinion for direct US military action against Cuba, and at the same time it would have politically destroyed the Kennedy administration. Yet it appears that the mission, along with its CIA support, the LIFE photo coverage, and an agreement to bring the officers to testify directly to a Congressional committee, was never communicated to, much less approved, by the President—or by the committee which legally had oversight and approval of all CIA missions into Cuba.

Of course, Martino's attention was focused on his exile companions and the elimination of Fidel Castro—any related political consequences would have been of little concern. Martino's attitude, aims and commitments grew from his "I Was Castro's Prisoner" experience.

A question remains concerning what else the experiences related in the book may have led Martino to participate in—including the possibility that Martino may have played a minor role in a conspiracy that resulted in the death of President John F. Kennedy. Following the death of the President, Martino was prominent among those who provided purported evidence to prove that Fidel Castro had been the moving force behind Lee Oswald.

Martino promoted that story to the press as well as directly to the FBI. Amazingly, the FBI closed out Martino because they could find no significant sources that he might have had within the Cuban community. But later, only months before his death, Martino confided to two long time friends that there had been a very different story, that he himself had served as a courier and had certain details regarding a conspiracy to kill JFK in Dallas.

However, the conspiracy failed, because JFK's death was to have pointed directly to Fidel Castro, thereby forcing the United States into an invasion of Cuba. Martino's remarks, his investigation by the House Select Committee on Assassinations and the decades later corroboration of his role in that conspiracy are covered elsewhere. You will not find the details of what Martino did in 1963 in "I Was Castro's Prisoner"—what you will find, is the reason why Martino acted as he did.

Larry Hancock
Author of *Someone Would Have Talked*
2008

CONTENTS

CONTENTS

CHAPTER 1

ROULETTE WHEELS
AND FIRING SQUADS

My wife, Florence, I made my first trip to Havana in July 1958 for the opening of the Deauville Hotel and Casino. The city was gay, bustling, bursting out horizontally and vertically with new hotels and apartment houses.

Cuba was under General Fulgencio Batista; the revolutionaries were out in the hills, but there was occasional tenor in the streets of the city. Teen-age followers of Castro's 26th of July Movement would throw bombs in police stations or leave them inside buses carrying people to and from work. When the bombs exploded, they would scatter limbs, flesh and blood, and the mangled debris of human beings. In retaliation, the police would sometimes kill suspected bomb throwers and leave their corpses in the streets as a warning to others. We saw very little of this, but we knew it was going on.

We spent about a week in Havana. I installed an electronic protective system for the Hotel Deauville casino. Most of the gambling spots lacked adequate protection and they came to me with the request that I install similar devices. They were quick to realize that this was vital to their business because, when a casino has a crooked croupier; it is for all practical purposes dead.

What the Havana gambling places needed were electronic surveillance systems that would make it impossible for the croupiers to rob the gambling tables.

I agreed to make these installations and drew up a list of the equipment I would have to buy in the States. This was work I had been doing for the previous ten years. With my partner, I set up specialized electronic surveillance and protective systems and installed them, designing the installations, and sometimes, inventing new devices, which I have sold all over the world.

Once I had the equipment, I returned to Havana and proceeded to install it. At this point, I met two people who would play a fateful and malign role in my life, one of them purposefully, the other because of forces beyond his control.

The first of these men was Doctor Gustavo Estevez, the physician of the Hotel Deauville. My acquaintance with him was due to the fact that I had been suffering for fifteen years from chronic colic of the kidneys, a condition that can be extremely painful and that can be arrested, but cannot be cured.

The second was Captain José de Jesus Castano y Quevedo. A powerfully built, intense and strikingly handsome man in his early forties, José Castaño was about six feet one and towered over most Cubans. He was Chief of Operations of Batista's special political police organization, the BRAC, or Bureau for the Repression of Communist Activities.

Castaflo frequented the Deauville casino and we soon struck up an acquaintance. He impressed me as a dedicated professional soldier of the best type. As we got to know each other better, he told me something about his life. He had entered the Cuban Army as a private at the age of nineteen and risen step by step through hard study and superior marks on the competitive military examinations.

By 1940, Castaño was assigned to the Cuban Military Intelligence Service. His business was to ferret out anti-democratic activities. During World War II, this meant concentrating on catching Nazi agents. Thereafter, it was a matter of uncovering the secret organizations of Cuban Communism and of Soviet espionage in Cuba.

A non-political man, Castaño did this work under three different Cuban Presidents, representing two different political parties: Batista, Grau San Martin and Prio Socorrás. He received special training at the F.B.I. Academy in Quantico.

I was told in Cuba that Castaño was regarded by FBI Director J. Edgar Hoover as one of the five men in Cuba who really knew the details of the Red network there. Castaño was an excellent linguist who had taught modern languages at the Military Academy, El Caribe. As the Communist threat to the Americas gained in importance, he set himself the task of learning first Russian and then Chinese in his spare time.

DEAF EARS AND CLOSED MINDS

At the time I met him, Captain Castaño was disturbed and unhappy about his work. The revolutionary movement of Fidel Castro was riding high, on U. S. State Department support and a mawkish American press that could see no evil in the bearded leader of the Sierra Maestra. Castaño told me on several occasions that he knew Fidel Castro was a Communist and that his movement was under Communist control. Castaño said he had tried to get this message to the American people, but the American correspondents in Cuba would neither listen nor examine the evidence. He said he felt like a man shouting from inside a corked glass bottle.

Castaño told me that in 1957 and 1958 he sent documents concerning the Communist nature of the Castro movement to the American Embassy in Havana. He did this twice, under the ambassadorships of both Arthur Gardner and Earl E. T. Smith. These reports dealt with the activities of Castro and his men in the Mexican training camps where they prepared their invasion of Cuba. They detailed the connections of the Castro leaders with Mexican and Iron Curtain Communists and contained actual photographs of Fidel Castro in the company of Russians in Mexico City. As far as Castaño knew, these reports made no impact on the Americans.

In this, Castaño was wrong. Thanks to the testimony of Ambassadors Gardner and Smith before the Senate Internal Security Subcommittee and to Smith's book, *The Fourth Floor*, we now know that both Ambassadors did their utmost to warn the State Department that support of Fidel Castro might mean a Soviet base in the Caribbean. These warnings were ignored, according to Ambassador Smith, because of the activities of middle-echelon State Department bureaucrats who were committed to the Castro cause.

Later, when I was a prisoner of Fidel Castro, I learned more of Captain Castaño's efforts to warn the American people. Julio Garcia, a former officer of the BRAC, became one of my cellmates. He told me that in June 1958 Castaño had called the American reporters in Havana to a press conference at BRAC headquarters.

Castaño showed the group documentary evidence that Fidel Castro and his leading henchmen were Communists. Jules Dubois, correspondent for the Chicago Tribune, who was at the time a defender of Castro and his movement, called the documents a "paquete," that is to say, a bundle of forgeries concocted by the Batista Government. Herbert L. Matthews of the New York Times joined him in this attitude. Captain Castaño pleaded with these people, pointing out that the documents were authentic and that the material had been given to the American Ambassador.

However, Dubois and Matthews evidently considered that they knew better and not a single line of the evidence accumulated by the BRAG was published in any American newspaper. Castaño once asked me what was the use of a free press that gave a little clique of prejudiced reporters the power to slant and suppress the news in the interests of America's enemies. I had no answer to that one.

THE CULT OF DIRT

While I was installing the protective systems, I would commute between Havana and Miami Beach, returning to Florida on weekends to be with my family. The casino job was running smoothly.

One day in November 1958, Dr. Estevez happened to notice my pocket radio receiver and asked me what it was for. I explained that it was part of a radio paging system that we had devised which made it possible for everyone in the system to receive individual calls from a central telephone answering service. I explained that in the United States many doctors, lawyers, salesmen and others used this sort of system to make it possible for their offices to get in touch with them when they were on the street or in their cars.

He suggested that this would be a wonderful idea for Cuba, where the telephone system was still comparatively young and where even physicians had trouble getting phones installed. At his suggestion, we discussed the matter with his father, who was also a doctor. I addressed a meeting of the College of Physicians in Havana, explaining how radio paging worked and arousing a great deal of interest. Accordingly, Dr. Estevez and I set up a company in Cuba for radio paging. We called it Radio Llamado de Cuba, S.A. Dr. Estevez was Secretary-Treasurer. Political chaos was growing in Cuba, and Dr. Estevez assured me that the Revolution was sure to win but that afterwards the country would settle down and there would be a favorable atmosphere for our business venture.

I returned to Miami Beach for Christmas, but was back in Havana on December 27. I stayed over for the beginning of the New Year and, therefore, was in the Cuban capital when Batista and his government fled. By January 2, all businesses were closed; the stores had their shutters over the show windows, and the city looked as if it were waiting for an air attack. At the request of the casino owners and of my business associates, I began moving the electronic equipment out. They had no optimistic illusions about the future and wanted to salvage whatever they could.

Soon the bearded veterans of the Sierra Maestra swaggered into Havana and received a wild, tumultuous welcome. There were already little signs of what was to come. When they saw Christmas trees in the windows of houses, the barbudos would sometimes pound on the doors and threaten the inmates with their automatic pistols. The most noticeable thing about them was that they were not only unkempt, but also filthy. Their clothes were soiled; their faces and beards were dirty; their bodies stank. This was not simply the result of combat conditions, for the fighting had been over for a week now and all the barbudos had had opportunity to bathe, trim their beards and put on clean clothes. It appeared that to be unwashed was the badge of the Revolution. Before the barbudos swarmed into Havana, very few beards had been seen in Cuba. For sanitary reasons, they were unsuitable in a tropical climate and even the old men seldom wore them. Cuban men had generally been fastidious to a fault about bodily cleanliness and neatness of dress.

THE ALAN COURTNEY SHOW

By January 17, most of the electronic equipment had been taken out and shipped home and I returned to the States. A day or so later, I phoned Alan Courtney who has a night radio program in

Miami which reaches about a million listeners. As early as 1957 Alan Courtney was exposing the Red connections of the Castro movement. He was one of the first. His show has guests and the audience participates by phoning in questions and comments.

Naturally, Alan was interested in my impressions of Cuba.

"The situation doesn't look good," I told him. "They are executing a lot of people. Signs are sprouting up like mushrooms, urging people to buy Cuban products and claiming that they are better than American products. I have the impression that this new crowd is cultivating hatred of the United States."

Alan said he was sure the Communists were behind the Castro Revolution. He asked me how I would like to go on his radio show as a guest and discuss it. I told him it would be impossible because I had business interests in Cuba and would have to go back there and try to get along with the people in power.

We compromised finally on his proposal that I telephone in and that he and I discuss the Cuban situation over the phone without his mentioning my name.

I went on the *Alan Courtney Show* last night. At that time, Fidel Castro was riding the crest of a wave of popularity in the United States and all Latin America. Despite the Roman circus trials and the firing squads, it was believed that he could do no wrong. The people had bought the propaganda picture of Castro foisted on them by press, radio and television.

He was a tropical Robin Hood and a new Abraham Lincoln. Personally, I could not visualize Abraham Lincoln with a telescopic rifle in one hand and a brandy and Benzedrine highball in the other, but then I was in the minority.

People began to call in and make adverse comments on my radio remarks. Some argued that I had never really been in Cuba at all. To others, I was an agent of the Batista dictatorship who was trying to tie the tin can of Communism on the tail of an honest Cuban patriot and agrarian reformer.

After a few weeks in Miami Beach, I phoned Alan to tell him I was going back to Cuba and would let him know my impressions of conditions there on my return.

"Fine," he said. "You do that, John."

As I was standing at the ticket counter at Miami International Airport, a United States Marshal asked me if I was going to Cuba. When I replied affirmatively, he said:

"You know conditions are pretty hairy there. If you go to Cuba, you are going on your own." I told him I knew that.

In Havana, the hotels, the casinos and the nightspots had been taken over by the Rebels. In the Hotel Deauville, the fellow who used to clean the swimming pool had suddenly emerged as the business agent of the trade union. That meant that he dictated to all the workers of the hotel and, since the unions were riding high, it meant he also dictated to the management. When I asked what there was that was so special about this swimming pool cleaner, I was told that he was a member of the Communist Party.

In the Deauville and elsewhere, I was soon made aware of a strong feeling of resentment toward the United States. The Cuban air had become poisoned and I no longer enjoyed breathing it. I pulled out the last of my electronic equipment from the casinos and returned to the States. Alan Courtney again asked me to go on his show and I did so anonymously the same way as before. In the course of the telephone interview, I said there must be something wrong in Cuba because a U. S. Marshal had warned me at the airport that, if I went there, I did so at my own risk.

This touched off a barrage of phone calls to the station to the effect that I was a liar and that the incident with the marshal was an invention. They said that I was the sort of person who brought up the red herring of Communism whenever a government was installed anywhere in the world that didn't suit me. The next morning, Alan called to say that he was sorry, but he ran a responsible radio program and, because of listener complaints, he would have to check my story about the U. S. Marshal at the airport.

I told him to go ahead. That afternoon, he phoned: "Johnny, I investigated at the airport and you were absolutely right. That is what they advise everybody going to Cuba."

During the next few months, Cuba was far from my thoughts. I was traveling to New York, Las Vegas and other places, setting up electronic equipment. Around the middle of March, Dr. Gustavo Estevez wrote to ask me what I intended doing about the company we had started in Cuba. I replied that my associates and I would prefer to wait until the dust settled. We felt that the new Castro Government was communistic, but we were prepared to wait and see what it did. I added that I would be in touch with him.

THE DEATH OF JOSÉ CASTAÑO

Around this time, I learned that my good friend, Captain Castaño, had been convicted by a revolutionary tribunal and executed by a firing squad. This was bad and shocking news. It was also the sort of thing that could easily happen during a revolution. On the other hand, Castaño had been one of the bravest and most implacable enemies of Communism in Cuba. His execution fitted in with the general picture that was taking shape in my mind.

It was only much later that I learned what really happened to him. José Castaño stayed on in Cuba because he was a professional soldier and thought it would be cowardly to run away. He had been named chief of the BRAC on January 1, 1959, by the entirely imaginary provisional government of General Eulogio Cantillo, which warmed the chairs of power immediately after the flight of Batista. Forty-eight hours later, Castaño was arrested at his post.

The Communists who headed the new Government in the first days of the Castro regime—Fidel and Raul Castro, Ché Guevara, Carlos Rafael Rodriguez, Antonio Nuñez Jiménez and several others—had every reason to hate and fear Castaño. The details of their subversive pasts were in the BRAC archives, which they had seized as one of the first acts of the Revolution, and in Castaño's prodigious memory. His continued existence jeopardized the success of the Communist plan to continue with the great deception and to make the world believe that Fidel Castro was the agrarian reformer and Lincoln of the Caribbean that Herbert L. Matthews claimed he was.

When Castaño was brought before one of the circus trials that satisfied the thirst for blood of the Havana rabble during the early months of the Revolution, the sentence was a foregone conclusion.

He would be killed because he was a political enemy. But in addition, his reputation as a decent and honorable man had to be shattered so that he would have no followers after his death.

Among others who bore false witness in the trial was Alicia Agramonte y Marrero, an aging actress with a collapsed figure, who was a Communist. Alicia Agramonte accused Captain Castaño of having raped her. The most devastating refutation of this charge was her face and figure. Castaño was attractive to really beautiful women and it is inconceivable that Agramonte could have interested him sexually.

On the basis of this and other perjured testimony, the tribunal condemned Castaño to death by firing squad.

At this point, the attorney for the defense, Dr. Anibal Pacheco, contacted high dignitaries of the Catholic Church and foreign embassies, particularly the American Embassy. The authorities in La Cabana Prison told Pacheco that, unless orders to the contrary were received before five in the morning, Castaño would meet death at the paredón.

The American Embassy pleaded to have the death sentence commuted. Attorney Pacheco saw Fidel Castro at two in the morning. Castro told him that he had ordered Comandante Humberto Sod Mann to tell Ché Guevara to call off the execution.

Having little confidence in the integrity of any of these people, defense attorney Pacheco got in touch with Father Javier Arzuaga, who was the confessor for the hundreds of Cubans executed in La Cabana. The priest told him that Captain Castaño had not confessed as he had been informed at three that morning that his life was to be spared. After receiving that news, Pacheco went to bed and slept soundly.

He awakened to learn that Castaño had been executed at four o'clock, the morning of March 7, 1959. What had happened was that Ché Guevara had assembled a squad of cut-throats, including the notorious American, Herman Marks, and had taken Captain Castaño right outside the gate of the prison. Ché Guevara had personally shot Castaño in the back. When he fell to the dirt, other members of the squad dispatched him. Captain Castaño's widow was not allowed to have her husband's body for fear that the Cuban people would learn he had been murdered, not executed.

I have been told that one of the reasons Ché Guevara was determined to have him killed was that Captain Castaño had managed to get a microfilm copy of the extensive BRAC files on Communism to the FBI in Washington. I do not know whether or not this is true.

CHAPTER 2
PRISONER OF FIDEL CASTRO

In the summer of 1959, a group of Americans asked me to fly to Havana to bid on installing automatic totalizing machines for the Oriental Race Track and flood lighting for night racing. I agreed to go to Cuba and look into the situation.

On the afternoon of July 23, I called Rafael, a Cuban friend who was connected with the track, gave him my flight number and asked him to meet me at Havana airport that night. As I was packing, I decided to ask my thirteen-year-old son, Edward, if he would like to come along.

"That would be fine, Daddy. I have never been to Havana."

While Edward and I were at the Miami International Airport buying our tickets, Jorge Hernández, a Cuban friend whom I hadn't seen for several months, approached me.

"I have been looking for someone who is going to Cuba," he said. "Could you do me a favor?"

"What is it?"

"When you go to Havana, would you call Mrs. Sofia Cisneros—here is her phone number—and tell her that Mrs. Rodriguez has had her operation and is convalescing well."

I suppose I was preoccupied with the problem of the racetrack totalizers. At any rate, it didn't occur to me that it was strange that Hernández should camp at the airport waiting for a potential messenger, when he could have telephoned or wired Mrs. Cisneros. Not suspecting that the message was in code or that I was involving myself in Cuban revolutionary politics, I took the slip of paper with the phone number and agreed to deliver the message.

My friend, Rafael, met us at the Havana airport that night and we drove to the Hotel Comodoro where Edward and I checked in. While the three of us were having dinner, I telephoned the

Cisneros house. A man's voice answered and identified itself as Manuel Cisneros. He established the fact that I was John Martino of Miami Beach and that I had a message for his mother. He said she was not at home and asked me to call back in twenty minutes. I tried again after dinner. Manuel Cisneros said he had been in touch with his mother and they would appreciate it if I could drop by the house with the message around nine-thirty.

"There is nothing confidential about the message," I said innocently. "I can give it to you over the phone."

"My mother would prefer to receive it from you in person, so she can thank you."

"Unfortunately," I said, "I must drive to the race track immediately."

"Splendid. My house is on your way."

The trip seemed to me quite unnecessary, but there was no graceful way out of the situation. Cubans carry politeness to excess and they can easily be offended by our brusque American way of doing things. When we drove up to the Cisneros house, I told Rafael that my errand would not take more than five or ten minutes and suggested that he show Edward the dog track, which was right around the corner.

"Won't you sit down," Mrs. Cisneros said when I had given her the message. "I will get coffee ready."

"That is very kind of you."

She excused herself and disappeared into an adjoining room. As I sat down to wait for the coffee, the front door burst open and four men in civilian clothes, armed with Tommy guns, plunged into the room.

"Don't move," their leader shouted in barely adequate English. "Hands up! Everybody here is under arrest."

Mrs. Cisneros returned to the drawing room and we were searched. The police took my money from my wallet, counted it and returned it. They removed my wallet and hotel key. The leader explained in his gimpy English that they had been ordered to surround the house and arrest everyone in it. We would now have to wait. I had better drink my coffee.

I explained that my son and my friend were at the dog track and didn't know what had happened to us. This made no apparent impression on the policeman. He began to ply me with questions, asking me how I liked Miami, how I liked Cuba, what I thought of Fidel Castro and how many times I had been here.

"If I do any talking," I replied, "It will be when I am taken to the police station and told why I am being held."

We waited for an hour and three quarters. Then more police came in, bringing with them two persons they had evidently just arrested—a woman with blond hair and an old lady. We were put into two cars and driven to another part of town. The cars parked beside a building; five of the guards entered it, taking the blond woman with them. We waited another quarter of an hour.

Then an extraordinary thing happened. Three more cars arrived, carrying fifteen more civilian policemen who were also armed with sub-machine guns. To my astonishment, they disarmed and arrested the policemen who had taken us into custody.

All this occurred in the middle of the street at a time when most of Havana was outside enjoying the night air. Consequently, there was a crowd around us—and a great deal of speculation and argument as to what was happening.

We were ordered back into the cars at gun point, whereupon the motorcade took off and soon was racing at breakneck speed through the streets of downtown Havana. Our destination was the central police station. Once inside, we were taken to the confidential bureau, which served in the early days of the Castro regime as the secret police headquarters.

"Gringo, you are going to see a friend of yours," one of the guards said, spitting the epithet at me so that I could read the hatred on his face. "You are going to see the Chief of Police."

POLICE CHIEF EFIGENIO ALMEIJEIRAS

In this as in other matters, the police were mistaken. I had never met Efigenio Almeijeiras Delgado, Chief of the National Revolutionary Police under Fidel Castro, but I did know something about him. During my three years in Cuban prisons, I would learn a good deal more and, on my return to the United States, I would take the trouble to distinguish between rumors and cold facts. Incredible as it may seem, Almeijeiras was a professional petty thief, who used to operate under the name of "Tomeguin." (This is the name of a small Cuban bird with a pronounced beak that is in the habit of picking up other people's property.) In the winter of 1949, then Lieutenant Esteban Ventura Novo, Chief of the Robbery Division of the Cuban Bureau of Investigation, picked up "Tomeguin" Almeijeiras. He was charged with mugging women and with purse snatching.

It appeared that "Tomeguin" and his gang operated in the Fraternidad Park opposite the Hotel Manhattan. In addition to snatching purses in the park and on city buses, they stole car batteries and peddled drugs. Almeijeiras was a marihuana user. Since it was his first offense, Castro's future Police Chief drew only 60 to 180 days. When he was released from prison, he resumed his former occupation, but changed his area of operations to the Vedado district. He used to snatch the purses and handbags of women who went to the Calixto Garcia Hospital to visit the sick.

He next came to the attention of the police when he got into a fight with a hospital cook, after which a friend of the cook ambushed him and shot him in the leg. This was his baptism of fire as a revolutionary. He was later charged with being a member of a gang that beat up people, for hire, in the city of Havana. Finally, the files of the municipal court of Puerto Padre in Oriente Province, which no doubt have been since purged of the entry, contain a record of the conviction and sentence to sixty days in prison of Efigenio Almeijeiras Delgado and Armando Cubria for pederasty. The two homosexuals were caught in flagrante in a private house.

Alex Rorke, an American news photographer who was arrested in Castro Cuba, cast additional light on Police Chief Almeijeiras. On the Celebrity Table program of radio station WRCA (New York) for November 16, 1959, Rorke characterized Almeijeiras as "a dope addict and a murderer," adding "he murdered his own wife." I have no corroboration of the charge of murder and report it for what it is worth, if anything. However, Almeijeiras' career as a marihuana user, drug peddler, petty thief and sexual deviate was confirmed to me by several different sources during the years I spent in Cuban prisons.

Almeijeiras was part of the criminal element that was attracted to Fidel Castro and to Castro's program of invasion and revolution. He was wanted by the police, had no stake in the existing social order, no loyalty to anything, and everything to gain by violent political change. As I shall point out later, all during his adult life, Fidel Castro has had an affinity with the underworld, associated with criminal elements and perpetrated crimes. The relationship of the professional criminal class and of dope addicts and pushers to the Castro movement is a phase of our contemporary history, which has been ignored by the correspondents.

Almeijeiras trained with Castro's forces in Mexico and was one of the 82 men who landed from the Gramma on December 2, 1956. Of these invaders, all but twelve were either killed or captured by the Batista forces. Almeijeiras was one who survived. That made him one of the immortals of the Cuban Revolution.

PILOT OF THE COUNTERREVOLUTION

I was taken into a large office crowded with policemen. Almeijeiras was a mulatto with a brutish and rather stupid face. He wore a straggly goatee. As I entered the room, he greeted me:

"Mr. F—, we have been waiting for you. We expected you last night."

I flushed with anger as nobody had ever called me that before. Suddenly, I was aware of someone advancing on me from the side.

As I started to turn around, I felt a hard blow on my mouth that knocked me down. I was lying on my back on the floor, looking up at the ceiling. There was the taste of blood in my mouth and I felt sick at my stomach with anger. The police sergeant who had hit me was a powerfully built man who must have weighed about 210 pounds. My own weight at the time was 150.

I got up from the floor and found a chair. I tried to dissociate myself from what was happening to me, to imagine that I was a bystander. I knew that, if I lost my temper, I could be beaten to death here in the police station. That had happened before in Cuba.

They ordered me to take off my clothes and, while I sat naked in the chair, went through the routine of searching my pockets and linings, counting my money and taking my wallet, my ring, my watch and the rest of my jewelry, which they then returned to me.

"All right, wise guy, where is your pilot's license?" I gave Almeijeiras a blank look. I have never flown a plane in my life. "You know what I am talking about. We know you are a pilot. We know all about you. Where is the license?"

"You must be out of your mind," I told him. "You have got the wrong man. You have my wallet, my driver's license, and my credit cards. They will tell you that I am John V. Martino of the Neptune Electronics Company and of Miami Beach."

"That's what you say," the sergeant who had hit me remarked. "You are a Yankee pilot. You are a gunrunner. You're part of the counterrevolution and you have been hired to drop propaganda leaflets on Havana. You are also in charge of the squads that burn the sugar cane in the fields."

I spoke to him in a calm, reasoning tone:

"It is very easy for you to check on who I am. All you have to do is call the airport. They will confirm that I came in by Pan American flight tonight."

The police sergeant apparently had not thought of that. He began by ordering me not to tell him how to do his job and then asked where my plane ticket was.

"It is in my coat pocket, the coat I left in my hotel room. You have the room key. Why don't you go get it?"

They ignored that. Phones were ringing and there was great deal of bustle and disorganized commotion. About half an hour later, they brought in Edward, who seemed to be taking the experience calmly. I was not allowed to talk to him and they took him and my friend, Rafael, into separate rooms for questioning. Meanwhile, the officer who had arrested Edward and Rafael had turned over my suitcase and the papers I had left in my hotel room to Almeijeiras and his assistants.

After going through these documents, one of the police officers turned to me: "These papers are all false. Why don't you tell us the truth?"

"How can you say they are false?" I asked him indignantly. "All you have to do is check their authenticity with your own Department of Immigration. Moreover, I want to phone my Embassy."

This touched off a minor explosion.

"You don't have to tell us what to check and what not to check. You Americans are all alike. The minute you get into trouble you yell for the American Embassy. Well, you are in Cuba now. And it isn't the way it was before when Ambassador Smith was here. We are the bosses of Cuba now and we are going to make you Yankees do what you are told."

At about half past two that morning, I again asked them to call the Embassy for me. I reminded them that they were holding my son who was only thirteen years old.

"Is that so?" the sergeant asked in fake astonishment. "But he knows all about gunrunning and he knows who you are."

When you are exposed to this sort of stupidity, it can be really exasperating. A wall of stubbornness that cannot be penetrated blocks you. I was in the hands of a police department which was being run by a dope pusher and petty crook and which was staffed by cops who acted as if they had learned about police methods from the silent movies.

They finally put me into a cell and I was able to snatch a few hours sleep. The next day, July 24, was devoted to asking me questions, the same questions over and over again. Relays of interrogators alternated with each other, some who spoke English, some who spoke an unintelligible jargon and others who didn't pretend to any English at all. I was supposed to fall into a trap and contradict myself, after which my fabricated story would supposedly collapse like a house of cards.

They showed me a photograph of a pilot in a U. S. Army Air Force flying suit, standing beside a plane. They said that was me in World War II. The resemblance between the pilot and me was only superficial; I had never seen him in my life.

"Please call the Embassy," I said at one point. "You are holding a boy and a sick man. At any moment, I may have an attack and need a doctor."

"When we finish with you, you are going to need much more than a doctor" was the reply.

About five that afternoon, they took me downstairs and threw me into another cell. It had no water, no lights and no bed. I slept on the floor. When I wanted to go to the toilet or wash my hands or get a drink of water, I had to ask the turnkey, who would take me to the bathroom. All they had given me to eat that day was a cup of black coffee and a piece of bread. When I complained that I was hungry, I was given a cold meat sandwich and another cup of coffee.

On the 25th, I was allowed to see my son, but not to talk to him. Edward's clothes were in a mess and he looked worried and upset.

The next day I spent alone in my cell. It was the 26th of July, the day of celebration for Fidel Castro and his forces, the first such celebration since the Rebels had taken power. My jailers were out in the streets and they gave me a respite from the interrogations.

On the 27th, as we were crossing the courtyard, I saw the tail section of a plane and asked what it was doing there. I was told that it belonged to a friend of mine and that they had shot it down the other night. Whatever I was being accused of was seemingly taking shape, assuming specific features.

I saw my son again that day for five minutes. On the morning of the 28th, I was standing in my cell, which was in the courtyard of the Central Bureau, when I heard someone talking in English.

"Are you an American?" I shouted. "Come over here." A man in his late thirties approached.

"I am from the American Embassy," he said.

"Thank God. So they finally told you where I am."

It turned out, however, that the police officers had told him nothing. He was here to see about an American who had refused to pay his hotel bill. I told him who I was and that I had been detained without charges since July 23.

"Yes? What is your trouble?"

The guard broke in to tell him that we were not allowed to talk.

"Go to the Embassy and tell them that I am John Martino and I am in prison here."

The next morning, I was brought downstairs. Edward was there with wonderful news. They had decided to release him and Florence was flying down that afternoon to take him back with her. I had a sudden foreboding about my own situation and I told Edward that it was possible he would never see me again and that he should not forget me.

Florence arrived a few hours later, appearing suddenly in front of my cell door. She had been close to panic and had convinced herself that she would never see either of us again. We started to talk when the prison officials told us that they had taken Edward to the American Embassy.

"Go to the Embassy at once," I told Florence, "and see if he is really there or if this is some trick. You must get him out of the country immediately. And tell the people at the Embassy that I am innocent, but I am in very serious trouble."

She left or rather tried to leave. They held her for an hour for a confrontation with the woman with blond hair, whom Florence had never met in her life. Finally, I saw her leave the police headquarters by a back door and step into a car.

COLONEL VENTURA AGAIN

The next morning, I was taken to the office of the Chief of Police. Almeijeiras showed me the photograph of a dapper, handsome man in uniform with erect, military bearing.

"Do you know this man? He is your friend isn't he?"

I shook my head. "This man is Colonel Ventura," Almeijeiras continued.

I told him that I did not know Ventura and had never heard of him.

"That is impossible. You know his wife, don't you? You were waiting for her."

He told me that the woman with blond hair whom they had arrested was Dr. Serafina Freyre Lãzaro, the wife of Colonel Ventura. The Cisneros family was related to her.

I determined to find out all I could about everybody involved in my own case, and in so doing I gathered a pretty good dossier on the top figures in both revolutionary and counterrevolutionary activities.

Luckily I have a memory that is very nearly photographic; this attribute has been invaluable to me in keeping up with electronic trends, and now it provides me with a veritable filing cabinet of names, dates and events from which this document has been constructed. I believe that without the diversion (sometimes it amounted to an obsession), of gathering together the loose ends of this grim tale, I would have gone plain crazy with worry about Florence, Edward and my young twins, Vincent and Stefanie, and about my chances of ever getting out alive. Part of the case against me, I now realize, was taking more or less intelligible shape.

I was to discover that Colonel Esteban Ventura Novo had been one of the high officials of the Batista police and of the police department under Batista's two immediate predecessors. He was a man who had earned the implacable hatred of the Castro forces and they had reasons, which they considered sound, for wishing to destroy him and to persecute his family.

Since he had served for many years in high positions in the criminal branches of the Cuban police service, Ventura was thoroughly familiar with the murky pasts of many of the top leaders of the 26th of July Movement.

Like Almeijeiras, quite a few of these men had records as criminal delinquents, dope peddlers and perverts. In more recent years, Ventura had been chiefly concerned with smashing subversive movements against the Batista Government. He had arrested many of the Rebel leaders and had recruited several of the most important ones to serve as stool pigeons.

These Judases of the Castro movement fell into two classes. The first group consisted of those who had become bona fide police agents either through fear of being tortured or killed or because of greed. These were mostly small fry and they were killed in the first few days of Castro's triumph.

The second, and much more important, group consisted of Communists within the 26th of July Movement, who were obeying Party orders when they betrayed their comrades to Batista's police. They did this for several reasons. First, as undercover agents of the Batista police, they had a certain amount of protection. The police would not kill them in the streets and, if they were arrested, they would almost certainly be let go as quickly as possible. In the second place, they were able to betray anti-communist leaders of the 26th of July Movement to the police under circumstances which virtually ensured that these people would be killed on the spot and thus eliminated from positions of leadership.

Third, their intimate association with the police gave them knowledge of police personnel, plans and methods, which the Communists were able to put to good advantage. Finally, they betrayed their comrades for money and this money was probably turned over to the Communist Party. The details of this sordid and Machiavellian operation will be revealed in due course. At this juncture, the only thing that need be emphasized is that Fidel Castro and his inner clique of leaders were afraid that, if Ventura revealed these facts, they might be totally discredited in the eyes of the Cuban people and in the eyes of the civilized world.

Ventura himself had escaped. He had flown to the Dominican Republic with President Batista a few days before the Rebels entered Havana. But his wife and son were in Cuba.

The Castro authorities wanted to keep Ventura's family on the island. This was partly out of a petty desire to persecute the families of their enemies—what Goethe once called "the malevolence of littleness." It was also because they believed that Ventura would not reveal what he knew about the Cuban Rebel leaders as long as his wife and son were in Castro's hands.

The irony of the situation was that Castro had no real reason to fear Ventura. When the latter finally got his family safely into the United States, he published his memoirs, but the book fell stillborn from the presses.

The reason was that the Castro propaganda machine had depicted the police officials of the Batista regime as moral monsters and Torquemadas. These characterizations, which were in some cases exaggerated and in others quite untrue, were repeated often enough so that people accepted them as facts. Consequently, the reading public in the West discounted and ignored whatever the former officials of the Batista regime had to say. This attitude was as narrow-minded as if an historian of the Russian Revolution refused to pay any attention to Czarist sources on the grounds that the Czarist political police sometimes committed crimes.

In any event, the accusation that I had plotted the escape of Señora Ventura was a very serious one. To make matters worse, Almeijeiras hated Ventura personally, since the latter had arrested and sent him to prison.

Almost Free I continued to deny that I knew Ventura or his wife or that I had anything to do with plans for her escape. I felt these denials were useless, but I had no alternative. Then, to my astonishment, Almeijeiras turned to me abruptly and said:

"Well, I believe you. I think we made a mistake here. I believe you will be going home very soon."

"Thank God."

After that, there was no more questioning. I spent the rest of the day alone in the cell, daydreaming about going home. Around hail past nine that night, the guard awakened me and I was called from my cell into the courtyard, where a man was standing with a squad of Rebel soldiers.

"Go over there under the light," he ordered. "This man wants to look at you."

"What man?"

"Raul Castro."

I walked under the light. Raul Castro wore his long hair tied in a bun with a blue beret on top of it. His face was pale and his skin smooth. He had the characteristic narrow chest and big hips and he stood with the backs of his hands resting against the hips. He stared slant-eyed into my face.

"Just another gringo," he said and walked away.

I saw Raul Castro on one other occasion, by daylight. Seeing him from the rear, I thought at first that he was a girl. His voice was high pitched. On this occasion, the prisoners crowded into the patio, screamed maricon at him and dared him to come down to the courtyard.

The night after my first meeting with this venomous little pervert, the turnkey took me back to my cell and assured me that I would be released next morning.

But the next morning, the Miami Herald reached the prison with Edward's picture on the front page. The story beneath the photograph told how the Cuban police had held Edward incommunicado for five days, had refused to give him a place to sleep and had driven him to the prison to see the men about to be shot. They told him this was what would happen to me unless I "confessed."

"We are going to fix you once and for all," I was told. At eleven that morning, I was put inside a panel truck, known as "La Lorna," which transports prisoners. My friend, Rafael, whom I had not seen since my arrest, was there and we were handcuffed. He told me that he had been questioned incessantly and mistreated. I asked the driver where we were going: "Catillo de Atarés."

Rafael turned white. He said to me: "That is a place where Machado killed a lot of people."

The Catillo was about fifteen minutes drive from police headquarters. It was a very old structure, high on a bill. Rafael and I were put in a large and clean cell, which was meant to accommodate fifty prisoners, but had less than half a dozen.

I could usually tell when a kidney attack was coming and that night I warned the turnkey that one was imminent. He said that there was a doctor in the Castle who would see me right away. About three hours passed, but no physician arrived. Then the turnkey appeared again and said that the Comandante of the prison would see me.

I was taken into the office of Comandante Carlos Miranda Hernández, a big man with a dark red beard, powerfully muscled and standing a little less than six feet. There were two .45's strapped on his pistol belt. With him was a Lieutenant Roberto Garcia who said he would act as interpreter.

"I understand you are sick and need a doctor," Miranda said. "We want to take care of everybody here. We are going to put you in a special cell and we are sending for a doctor."

After I had thanked him, the turnkey took me to another part of the Castle. He unlocked a cell door and we went down two flights of stairs, after which I found myself in a narrow dungeon with a dirt floor. I started to protest to the turnkey.

"You are being held incommunicado," he said, "and this is where the Comandante told me to put you."

He went up the stairs and locked the door behind him. There was a weak electric bulb in the ceiling and I could see an old, broken-down bed without a mattress. The cell was damp and there were mosquitoes and cockroaches. On the walls, various inscriptions had been carved in Spanish. As I am of Italian descent, I could decipher enough to realize that these were the names of men who had died here. The cell, I learned later, was called "el cuarto de la muerte" (the room of death) because people were executed and sometimes tortured here in the time of Machado.

About five minutes later, the light went out. I was completely alone in darkness and dirt. There was nothing I could do but lie on the rickety bed and pray that someone would be sent to save me. The kidney attack that I had been waiting for came and tore at my guts. I called for the guards, but nobody came to the door. I screamed and I believe I broke down and cried.

CHAPTER 3

THE AMERICAN EMBASSY: PROFILE IN COWARDICE

Finally, daybreak came. I asked to speak to the Comandante and a few minutes later Miranda Hernández appeared to ask me whether I had any complaints. Then, it dawned on me:

"You speak English today, don't you, Comandante? Where did you learn it?"

"I used to work for a drug firm here in Cuba that belonged to the Yankee imperialists."

That was the first time I had heard that expression.

"Comandante," I said, "I am a very sick man and you promised to get me a doctor."

"I will get you a doctor when you start to talk." I was about to remonstrate, but he raised his hand for silence. "You Americans have always had things your own way. You always thought you were the best people in the world. Now we are going to have things our way. Gringo, you are going to have to confess and do exactly what we want you to do."

He left. A few hours later, a young man, who said he was a fellow American, was pushed into my cell. His story was that the police had arrested him and beaten him up because he was suspected of being a friend of Colonel Ventura. I said I did not know Colonel Ventura. That night, I again asked the Comandante for medical attention and requested that he remove the stool pigeon from my cell.

For the next ten days, I was left absolutely alone in my dank, mosquito-infested cell. Coffee and a piece of bread were left for me in the morning and rice and beans for dinner. All the food was cold. They were evidently trying to break me down.

At the end of two weeks of this, an intelligent and friendly young soldier from Santiago de Cuba was put on guard at my cell.

He wanted to practice his English. That night, we had a long talk about politics and the Cuban Revolution. He told me that they now admitted they had made a mistake about me, but they were going to hold me anyhow while the Chief of Police investigated my background. As I understood it, since they already had me in prison, they were looking for justification for keeping me there. The news was not encouraging.

At about three o'clock in the morning, a detachment of guards proceeded to load guns and grenades on a truck. We could hear their voices. The guard, who was called Alfredo, said:

"You see, friend Martino, it is just the way it was under Batista. Fidel Castro is afraid because he lied to all of us who fought under him in the Sierra Maestra. He is sending weapons and ammo into his special hideouts in the Sierra Maestra."

"You had better not talk like that. You might get into trouble. For that matter,

Alfredo, you don't know enough about me to trust me."

He said that he knew a lot about me and volunteered that he was going to Havana tomorrow. Was there anything that he could get for me? Oddly enough, I still had the money they had returned when they took my wallet, so I gave him twenty dollars to buy me food, shaving articles and a change of clothes. I will always blame myself for the events that followed.

That night, Alfredo returned with the things he had bought. As he was about to open my cell door, the Comandante stopped him.

"What is going on here?"

"Comandante, I bought some things for John Martino."

The Comandante went through the purchases and withheld the newspapers I had ordered. He turned to Alfredo:

"Who gave you permission to buy this stuff for Martino?"

"Lieutenant Garcia, sir."

"I am the Comandante here, not Garcia. Give me your gun."

I never saw Alfredo again. Toward the end of 1959, I ran into Lieutenant Garcia's brother in La Cabana. He said:

"They sent that boy to the Isle of Pines. They had a tape recorder and a microphone rigged in your cell. It was a bad day for Alfredo when he said that Fidel Castro was a coward and a liar."

Because he was decent, because he was a boy of integrity and because he treated an American prisoner like a human being, he had been sent to the most hellish prison in the Western Hemisphere. I felt and still feel responsible and, as long as I live, I will never forget him.

CATILLO DE ATARE'S

Built around 1640, the Castle is completely surrounded by a dry moat, about twenty feet wide and thirty feet deep. It stands high on a hill, overlooking the city, and is accessible only by a single road which winds up the hill and which is guarded at the bottom by a sentry in a pillbox. This sentry stops all cars bound for the Castle, inspects them and holds them until he is given a telephone order to let them pass by the Officer of the Day.

On each side of the courtyard, there are cells that plunge down into the bowels of the Castle. Beneath the courtyard, there is a trapdoor for the stairway that goes under the first pillbox and proceeds to a series of underground dungeons—eighteen in all. These cells have practically no ventilation. I have never known anyone to be put in them, but the other ones are bad enough. There are no water or bathroom facilities in any of the cells in the Castle.

THE PERFIDIOUS DR. ESTÉVEZ

One morning, an officer named Captain Contino appeared at the Castle, sent for me and introduced himself as the head of the legal department of the Cuban National Police. When he found I was sick with an incurable kidney condition, he asked me for the name of my doctor.

"Fine," he said when I gave him Dr. Estévez' name. "I will check his hospital and have him sent right up here to look at you."

"You can't be serious, Captain."

"Of course I am serious." He stared at me and evidently concluded that I was pretty seedy looking. "Get yourself a shave and a haircut, Martino."

I complied with alacrity before the permission to use the barbershop could be withdrawn. That night, my old friend and business partner, Dr. Gustavo Estévez, appeared at the door of my cell in the company of the Comandante.

"You are not sick," he said to me. "You are only sorry for yourself."

I was flabbergasted. At this time, I had no knowledge of the fact that Estévez was a dedicated Cuban Communist who placed loyalty to the Party above the Hippocratic Oath.

"If I am not sick, Doctor, you have taken money from me under false pretenses. You have my American medical records and you know you opened a medical file, an expediente, for me in the Cuban Department of Health. How do you explain that?"

"That is what you say." He turned to the Comandante.

"There is nothing wrong with this man. If he says he is sick, give him an aspirin."

That night, the Castle began to fill up with prisoners. All of them were civilians. As the evening advanced, I found I had five guests in my cell that was furnished with one broken-down bed and one crippled chair.

Among the newcomers was Gustavo Alemán, a man of great courage and integrity whom I shall never forget. He escaped Castro Cuba eventually, only to join the Playa Girón invasion and be sent to the Isle of Pines.

"They came to my house early this morning to arrest me," Gustavo said. "They opened fire with a sub-machine gun and almost killed my two little daughters who were in bed.

We are in worse hands now than we were under Batista. At least, under Batista, if you didn't set bombs or commit acts of sabotage, nobody bothered you. But this man is arresting people all over the island because he suspects they may turn against him some time in the future."

Around one in the morning, we were interrupted by the sound of half a dozen cars driving up to the Castle. After that, we heard volleys and we knew men were dying against the paredon. That night, they killed a man in the ditch right beside my cell. We never knew who he was—only that he had been arrested that night and executed without a trial of any sort.

Between volleys, Gustavo Alemán said:

"Martino, you have no idea how many people have been executed in Cuba. And the worst part of it is nobody believes it. While he is causing suffering and death all over the island, Fidel Castro is applauded and even worshipped by millions."

Shortly after I heard my first execution, a group of Rebel officers visited the Castle on an inspection trip. Among them was Huber Matos, who later turned against Communism and was sentenced to twenty years on the Isle of Pines, and the unfortunate and popular Camilo Cienfuegos, who was killed in a contrived plane accident for the same reason.

After the visit, I was told that Atarés would be reserved in future for military prisoners only, that all the civilians would be transferred to the Catillo del Principe, but that I would be kept where I was as a special prisoner held at Fidel Castro's personal orders. When the civilian prisoners were moved, Gustavo Alemán managed to give me his home telephone number. If I got out, I was to get in touch with his wife, Violet, who would help me.

About a week later, my old friend, Rafael was put in my cell. The reason, of course, was that the cell was wired for sound and they hoped that, if we were left together long enough, we would incriminate each other. About four days after Rafael was put into my cell, his lawyer obtained his release on a writ of habeas corpus. He had the distinction of being granted the last habeas corpus writ in Castro Cuba, for the next day a conspiracy against the Castro regime which had been organized by Dominican dictator, Rafael Leonidas Trujillo, was smashed and civil rights were suspended for the indefinite future.

THE ATTACHÉ' AND THE RUSSIAN RADIO

That week, I was moved to another cell, one right next to the Comandante's office, and, as a result of that move, I was able to hear and see Russians in Cuba.

At about three in the morning of my second day in my new cell, as I was lying on my bunk, I heard a motor running and a whirring sound. I wondered what a motor was doing in this old castle, but I fell asleep before I could find an answer. At about five in the morning, the noise began again and shortly afterwards I heard men walking and talking, but I could not distinguish what they were saying.

Since I had been given permission to walk in the patio, I was able to investigate the source of the noise. Inspecting my cell carefully, I discovered that it was partially under the Comandante's office.

That meant that the whirring sound had come either from the office or from directly under it.

Early the next morning, the noise began again. As I was walking back to my cell from the toilet, I looked up and, to my great surprise, saw that a 50-foot radio antenna was now on top of the Comandante's office. In my cell, I waited until the motor started again. I concluded that the antenna was collapsible and could be retracted through the roof into the office by the motor. This opinion was strengthened by the fact that the antenna was never visible by day.

When I heard the men talking again, I grasped my cell bars and chinned myself so that I could look down into the dry moat. There was the Comandante with eight men in civilian clothes. They were talking in a Slavic language, which I believed to be Russian.

Two or three days later, providentially it seemed, I had a visitor from the American Embassy, a consular officer named Wayne Gilchrist. With him, there was another man, a Cuban. When we had exchanged greetings, I asked Gilchrist who his companion was.

"He is a Cuban who works in the legal department of the Embassy."

I was not at all happy about being obliged to discuss a confidential political matter before a Cuban about whom I knew nothing, but there was no alternative. Actually, the Cuban, Dr. Luis Cáceres Rodriguez, Jr., turned out to be a decent, honorable and responsible person.

In Dr. Rodriguez' presence, I told Gilchrist about the collapsible radio antenna and the Russian technicians. The secret character of the installation made me believe that it might be used to relay coded reports and directives between the Kremlin and Fidel Castro and his Communist associates. I considered the matter very important.

"It is urgent that you report this information to Ambassador Bonsai," I said.

"What is the matter with you, Martino?" Gilchrist said. "What is the use of your talking like this? You are only going to get yourself involved more deeply and, if the report is false, you are going to get the Embassy involved."

I told him that I knew a radio antenna when I saw one and that I was not much interested in Gilchrist's personal opinions. I merely wanted the facts reported to the American Ambassador. I added:

"It is easy for the Embassy to check this. You can set up a monitor, pick up the signals and determine their origin."

"All right, Martino, I will report it," Gilchrist promised.

Thus, I informed the American Embassy of the presence of a secret radio installation, manned by Russians, in the Catillo de Atarés as early as September 1959. When I discussed the matter later with Consul Kessler, he informed me that Gilchrist had never reported the matter to his superiors in the Embassy.

Then Kessler added:

"We just can't bother with half-cocked statements like that."

This, and similar experiences, made me uneasy about the conduct of our country's foreign affairs. Actually, I had had little contact with State Department and Foreign Service people and had only hazy ideas of what motivated them. But Gilchrist seemed a typical product of a bureaucratic system that stifles individual initiative and puts a high premium on conformity and buck passing. The average Foreign Service officer, I learned, spends his first ten years doing semi-clerical work and living by the book. In return, he can expect steady upward progress on the bureaucratic ladder provided he never sticks his neck out or swims against the current.

Wayne Gilchrist, as a young man, impressed both Florence and me as singularly passive and skillful at avoiding decisions or unpleasantness, traits he shared with many of the other American Embassy people I dealt with.

He asked me if I wanted a lawyer and I replied that I was informed that, since I was an American, legal counsel could not help me.

"Well then, what do you want? How are you?"

"You see how I am," I said in desperation. "You have eyes in your head. Look at this cell. Tell them for God's sake to try to get me out."

"Well, they tell us they are holding you for investigation. We can't make head or tail of why they are holding you. There isn't a thing we can do."

I asked how my wife was and he replied that she called every day.

"Please tell my wife to write to me at the Embassy. Then, when you come out again, you can bring her letter. I have no objection to the Comandante reading it. Better still, the next time I talk to the Comandante, I will ask him when I will next be permitted to have visitors."

"You know," Gilchrist replied, "we don't have time to visit people who are in jail. Our only function is to look after the welfare of the prisoners."

"You can't be doing a very good job of it," I exploded, "because this is the first visitor I have had in all the time I have been in prison and now you tell me you don't know when there will be a second one."

"Don't get excited," Gilchrist replied. "You are in a strange country and there is a revolution going on. These people are pretty wild. You see those guns?" He pointed to a pyramid of stacked rifles. "They really shoot."

"You sound afraid, Mr. Gilchrist."

"I am not used to all these arms. I have never been in a situation like this in my life."

"As an American Vice Consul, you ought to be ashamed of yourself. You can't even speak Spanish."

"I was sent here and I have to make a living. Besides, I am learning Spanish."

I told him that I thought the Embassy should send people who were able to talk to the officer of the day without an interpreter and that it was shocking that the United States should be represented by untrained and ignorant personnel.

"How am I going to make a living?" he repeated.

That ended the first of Gilchrist's visits. I suppose he meant well, but the impression he made on the prison authorities was negative and, with each of his visits, I felt my position weakened. He would make such tactical errors as to visit me in the morning with lipstick on his face, mussed clothes and a visible hangover. Unkempt and unwashed as they were, the barbudo officials of the prison expected a man who represented the American flag to be as neat and sharp as a British colonial officer.

SHAVING THE BARBUDOS

Vladimir Delgado Torres, the young guard in charge of the upstairs galera, or cell, spoke excellent English. He used to come down to my underground cell to talk or to bring me light novels. He was about twenty-one years old and had spent the last five years of his life as a revolutionary, placing bombs, sabotaging installations and killing people.

He was the nephew of Castro's Chief of Police, the Efigenio Almeijeiras Delgado, whom I have already described, and he had hopes of getting a job in police headquarters.

He told me that they were picking up all the Rebel soldiers in Havana, taking them to the Castle, fingerprinting them and investigating their political pasts.

"We are having a lot of trouble with them," he said. "The order is that we take them to the barber shop and get their hair cut and their beards shaved off. We have to hold them down, sometimes tie them down, in the barbers' chairs. Sometimes at gunpoint. These fellows, you understand, are the ones who fought and starved for Fidel Castro up in the hills. There is a lot of hatred inside them. They feel about their beards and long, straggly hair the way an American soldier might feel about a Silver Star. In protest against the forced shaving, they started a riot, broke up the bunks and set fire to the cushions. We had to send guards down with drawn bayonets and they spilled a lot of barbudo blood before they could restore order."

"What do you do with them when they are shaved and deloused?" I asked Vladimir.

"Most of them are sent back to Oriente to shift for themselves. There is a big change going on—what do you call it?"

"A purge?" I suggested.

"Yes, a purge . . . Captains show up from Havana who never did any sabotage and never worked for the Revolution at all. We are fingerprinting and registering officer cadets and many of the candidates are Havana men, whom I know from the days of the underground, because they worked for Batista or for the earlier governments."

"Well, Vladimir, maybe it is time for the barbudos to go back to their families. The fact that they fought in the mountains doesn't necessarily make them good material for a standing army."

Vladimir replied that, when the Revolution had won, the barbudos had wanted to go home, but Fidel Castro had told them then that they were the true revolutionaries, the men who had been tested in hardship and battle. He said he wanted these men by his side, that they would be the new Cuban army and the new Cuban police. Now they were being tossed aside.

MORE PROTECTION FROM THE EMBASSY

One day the Comandante called me into his office:

"Martino, I understand that somebody called Gilchrist came to see you the other day from the American Embassy and they tell me that this Gilchrist is a person of absolutely no importance. Why don't they send the Consul or the Vice Consul to see you?"

"Well, Comandante, Gilchrist is the one they sent."

"Pick up the phone and call the Embassy. Call Vice Consul Kessler and tell him I was sorry I wasn't in the other day when he sent his boy. Ask him to come down here and discuss your case with me."

I called the Embassy as he directed and said that Comandante Carlos Miranda Hernández would like to discuss my case. Kessler replied that he was too busy to come to the prison whenever I called. When I pointed out that this was my first call, he agreed to come "tomorrow or the next day."

When the Comandante heard the message, he said: "No, that won't do at all. I want him down here tomorrow morning." He picked up the telephone and, to my amazement, Vice Consul Kessler agreed to his demand.

The next morning, Kessler arrived and had a private talk with the Comandante, after which I was summoned to the office. Comandante Miranda Hernández was there; his chauffeur, a Chinese soldier named Roberto Wong, and Vladimir. All of them spoke and understood English. In this situation, Kessler turned to me and asked:

"Tell me, are they treating you well? Are they hitting you? Are they abusing you?"

There was nothing I could say except:

"Of course not, Mr. Kessler." Then I added, in an effort to convey to him that these people understood English, "Why don't you speak to the Comandante in Spanish?"

Kessler apparently didn't grasp the point. He asked me in English whether I was getting medical attention. When I didn't answer, he repeated the question in Spanish to Miranda.

"Of course, he is getting medical attention, aren't you, Martino?"

Naturally, I couldn't tell Kessler in front of the Comandante that I had received absolutely no medical attention since my arrest several months previously. It would have only invited reprisals. Nor would it have done any good. The Embassy at that time was anxious to believe anything Castro told them. Thus, in August of 1959, my wife wrote the then Secretary of State Christian Herter about the way I was being held more or less incommunicado without medical treatment and without being charged with any crime. On August 13, a certain A. C. Donaldson replied for the Secretary of State that "the Embassy understands he has been visited and treated by his personal physician in Havana." This was an outright lie. I had received no treatment and, by August, the Embassy had not sent anyone to the Catillo to find out the facts.

I evaded the question about medical treatment and turned to Comandante Miranda Hernández:

"Whatever happened to Alfredo, the young soldier who bought those things for me?"

The Comandante turned to Kessler:

"This American is a bad one. He tried to bribe the guard to take messages to his friends."

I cut in and said: "That is not so."

The Comandante replied that the guard had admitted it and that he had been tried and sentenced to three years on the Isle of Pines. To my astonishment, Kessler said that he agreed with the Comandante and that they had been wise in sentencing Alfredo.

I asked Kessler why he had bothered to come here at all, since he obviously was determined to disbelieve everything an American citizen told him.

The Comandante told me to shut up. Then, Kessler and the Comandante began to talk about William Morgan, an American who had betrayed many Cuban anti-communists to the police of Red Cuba and a man who had publicly boasted that he would kill American Marines on the Male con in the event of invasion. The Comandante said that Morgan had done a wonderful job in betraying the Trujillo conspiracy and Kessler hastened to add his "me too." In disgust, I requested permission to return to my cell, which was granted.

Later that day, the Comandante came to my cell to tell me that I should show more respect to the American Vice Consul. I replied that I had not known which country Mr. Kessler thought he was representing, the United States or Cuba.

"Mr. Kessler agrees," the Comandante said, "that you should be dealt with by Cuban law. He came to see you only because I sent for him. You should cooperate with the Cuban Government and tell the truth."

"Well, Comandante, I can see you don't like Americans."

"You are correct in that respect, Martino. I have always hated them."

I suggested that he leave me alone in future and he replied that he would be happy to do so.

Alex Rorke, whose radio interview I have already mentioned, also had the privilege of being protected by Kessler. As he told the story to interviewer Ray Heatherton:

"Then a man by the name of Kessler came to the house, whom— he called himself consul at the American Embassy—he looked at me and said, 'You must be having a wonderful time.' I said, 'If you think it is wonderful to have these people who look like trigger-happy delinquents around, who are cocking and re-cocking their guns and exchanging clips all day, and being subject to interrogations night and day, then perhaps it is fun, if you consider it that.'

"Now he took our names and while he was trying to leave, they had a big fight, the Castro agents, amongst themselves, to try and decide whether or not to hold Kessler. Kessler left—never heard from him again. Now . . ."

Heatherton: "And he was an American consul?"

Rorke: "His title was Vice Consul of the American Embassy."

In a talk before the Palm Beach Round Table on January 28, 1963, Rorke described the same incident. He said that he and his American friends were taken before an Embassy official "who, surrounded by Castro officials, said in unfriendly tones: 'I understand you have been giving these gentlemen (motioning to the Castroites) a difficult time. They can hold you as long as they want to and I can do nothing about it."

Strangely enough, Kessler seemed to have the impression that the Comandante was trying to help me. When Florence went to the American Embassy in August 1959 to arrange to visit me in prison, Kessler told her that Miranda Remandez was a humane man. On the same occasion, Gilchrist told her and Kessler that I had informed him I was ready to make a confession. Needless to say, that was absolutely false.

A few weeks later, I became very iffy. One night, I believed that my last hour on earth had arrived and I asked Vladimir to have the Comandante send for a priest. Instead, Miranda Hernández appeared at my cell door and delivered a tirade against priests, nuns and the

Catholic Church in general. I was so sick and, I believed, so close to death that I threw caution to the winds and told the Comandante he was a dirty Communist.

Ranting and pouring abuse on my head, he pulled one of his .45's and shoved the muzzle against my stomach. The two guards managed to calm him enough to get him out of the cell area. There was a murderous look on his face as he left and I was quite prepared to believe Vladimir when he told me later that I had made a mortal enemy.

Fortunately, I never saw the Comandante again. The man in whom Kessler had expressed such confidence was arrested for stealing public funds, convicted and sent to prison in Camaguey. During my years in Cuban prisons, I followed his subsequent career with intense interest. In time, he was released from prison and stripped of his rank. While serving as a private in the Militia, he was killed by the counterrevolution.

CHAPTER 4
SANCTUARY FOUND AND LOST

I believe I owe my forty months in Cuban prisons to the determination during that period of the State Department and the American Embassy in Havana to appease the Castro regime. Readers may find this difficult to believe, but a few paragraphs of background about our Cuban diplomacy and our Embassy in Havana may help clarify matters.

When Franklin Delano Roosevelt became President of the United States, he sent Sumner Welles to Cuba to eliminate the Machado dictatorship and install a democratic government. After accomplishing this mission, Mr. Welles rose to the position of Undersecretary of State. Although he was a man of great knowledge, high intelligence and remarkable gifts in the field of diplomacy, Mr. Welles was in many ways a malign influence. For over a decade, he shaped State Department policies and was responsible for a large number of appointments and promotions. This was particularly true of Latin America. Sumner Welles had a knack for finding talented young men, but they sometimes turned out to be Communists, homosexuals or both.

One of Sumner Welles' brilliant young recruits to the State Department was Laurence Duggan. By the middle or late 1930s, Duggan was Chief of the Division of Latin American Affairs of the Department of State. As such, he helped form and execute our Latin American policies and had major influence over appointments and promotions.

Mr. Duggan was not a homosexual, but unfortunately he was a Soviet spy. In the 1930s, for an unknown period of time, he was a member of the Hede Massing espionage ring, which worked for the Soviet Secret Police (NKVD). In 1948, the FBI questioned Duggan about his subversive activities, but the latter became so nervous and agitated that the FBI special agent said he would resume the interrogation in a few days. Before he could do so, Laurence Duggan jumped, fell (or was pushed) from the window of his office in a New York skyscraper to his death.

At the time of Castro's rise to power, Cuban, Mexican and Central American affairs in the Department of State were handled by one William Arthur Wieland, a friend and perhaps a protégé of Sumner Welles. This man, who was in charge of our Cuban policy during the critical year of decision, was characterized by former U. S. Ambassador to Cuba Earl E. T. Smith as one of the American officials who "were slanting news that way, that were telling falsehoods; that were pro-Castro." Former U. S. Ambassador to Brazil William Pawley, who also had Wieland under him, went even further. He said he believed Wieland to be one of those who "are serving the cause of our enemies." When asked whether he thought he was doing this intentionally, Pawley replied: "I have got to say that he is either one of the most stupid men living or he is doing it intentionally."

In October 1962, the Senate Internal Security Subcommittee published extensive testimony and a report on William Arthur Wieland. It did not find Wieland disloyal to the United States, but held that he had falsified his employment application and personal history form.

"Yet he (Wieland) never told his superiors officially or wrote in any State Department paper—down to the very day when Fidel Castro stood before the world as a self- proclaimed Marxist—what he told friends privately as early as 1958—or earlier—that Castro 'is a Communist' and 'is surrounded by Commies, (and) subject to Communist influences.'"

Finally, "Mr. Wieland became an active apologist for Fidel Castro, even to the extent of openly contradicting intelligence officers who were attempting to brief Dr. Milton Eisenhower (then on an official trip to Mexico representing his brother, the President) respecting communism in the Castro regime." There were Communists in the Embassy under Ambassador Philip Bonsai. According to the testimony of Captain Charles R. Clark, Jr., who was American Naval Attaché in Cuba between 1957 and

1960, two Cuban Communists were on the Embassy staff, but administrative officer Ed Wilson was unable to fire them, although he tried very hard to do so.

American Ambassadors Arthur Gardner and Earl E. T. Smith recognized the Castro movement from the outset as Communist-infiltrated and hostile to the United States. Smith testified that the Chief of the Political Section of the Embassy, John Topping, and the Chief of the CIA Section were "pro-26th of July, pro-Castro and anti-Batista." Smith's Number Two CIA man gave "unwarranted and undue encouragement to the revolutionaries." Captain Clark voiced the usual complaint about CIA men—that they were amateurish and that their cover was terrible. Ambassador Smith had so little confidence in his staff that he never allowed a cable to go out of the Embassy that did not have his signature.

"I wrote practically every political cable that went out," he said under oath. In addition to being ultra-liberal in their political thinking, some CIA men were implicated in a series of conspiracies to murder President Batista, supposedly a friend of the United States, and to overthrow his regime. There was a scandalous involvement of this sort in the so-called Cienfuegos Naval Conspiracy, an assassination plot against the Cuban Chief Executive.

Years later, a CIA man named Earl Williamson met with some of Fidel Castro's agents and supporters at the Retiro Odontologico, a dentists' building. Without the knowledge or approval of American Ambassador Smith, Williamson stated that the United States would recognize the Castro Government as soon as the Rebels overthrew Batista. There was also some discussion of the arms that the CIA was giving Castro surreptitiously.

Williamson's remarks were recorded on tape and given unofficially to Ambassador Earl E. T. Smith. A month or so later, Williamson was quietly withdrawn from Havana and replaced by David Morales, an American of Mexican descent and an intelligent and patriotic public servant. Morales sent voluminous reports to Washington concerning the Communist affiliations of Fidel Castro and his henchmen, which apparently had no effect.

The CIA's myopia was not confined to its underlings in Havana. As late as November 1959, General C. P. Cabell, Deputy Director of the U. S. Central Intelligence Agency, testified before the Senate Internal Security Subcommittee "we believe that Castro is not a member of the Communist Party, and does not consider himself a Communist."

This seems an inexcusable inability to evaluate available evidence and a crass failure to protect the interests of the United States.

When Fidel Castro took power, the friendly Philip Bonsai supplanted the hostile and realistic Earl Smith. Bonsai, ultraliberal, from a distinguished family, precise, a career officer with the reputation of a martinet, had joined the State Department at the time of Welles and Duggan. "He was sympathetic to the ideals of the Cuban Revolution in their early democratic, non-communist form," wrote Herbert L. Matthews. It would have been closer to the truth to point out that the Cuban Revolution had been Communist from the outset, but that certain people were too bewildered or too sympathetic to left wing movements to recognize it as such.

The American Ambassador behaved as if he represented a small country without pride or dignity. At a diplomatic party in Castro Cuba, the dance orchestra played the rhumba, Cuba Si! Yanqui no! A Central American diplomat and his wife left in protest against this insult to the United States, but Mrs. Bonsai danced to the music, while her husband watched with apparent approval. If an Ambassador fails to show respect for his country, others cannot be expected to. In the Bonsai era, Fidel Castro and his clique treated the American Ambassador with undisguised contempt.

THE INDICTMENT

On October 2, 1959, Vladimir told me that I would be moved to the city jail that day and would be brought before a judge who would decide whether or not I was to be held for trial. I was allowed to use the telephone and I called Kessler at the Embassy and asked his aid in getting a lawyer. The Vice Consul replied that he was too busy to run around Havana handling the problems of prisoners.

I suggested to Kessler that he have somebody from the Embassy present when I was brought before the judge. Since I was passing a good deal of blood, I asked him to have the Embassy intercede to have me taken to the Anglo-American Hospital for treatment. Kessler refused to do either of these things. When I asked to speak to someone else in the Embassy, he hung up.

In Cuba, there is nothing resembling our grand jury procedure. The prisoner is taken before a judge who reads the charges. The prisoner is then permitted to make a statement. The judge then has seventy-two hours to decide whether he is to be held for trial or released because of insufficient evidence. If the prisoner is held for trial, he is confined in the Catillo del Principe, one of the worst holes in the Western Hemisphere.

I was taken before the judge of instruction. Nobody was present from the Embassy; in fact, he and I were alone. He handed me a piece of paper and said in English:

"Here is your confession. Sign here."

I looked at him in amazement. I denied angrily that I had confessed to anything.

The judge shrugged his shoulders.

"Read it anyhow," he said.

My so-called confession stated that I, John Martino, had come to Havana three times by clandestine means. I was employed by the counterrevolution to serve as a courier and smuggle people out of Cuba illegally by plane. On my last trip, I had come to smuggle the family of Colonel Esteban Ventura out of the country. I was also a gunrunner, an agent of the Batista exiles in the United States and a counterrevolutionary. When I told the judge that the document was a tissue, of lies and that I would not sign it, he shrugged again, rummaged in his desk and showed me a sheet of paper about six inches square. Had I ever seen this paper before? I said that I had not.

"Let me read you the accusation." The judge said that the paper was the $100 bond of a counterrevolutionary organization known as the White Rose (Rosa Blanca). The treasurer of the group, the former Cuban Senator, Rolando Masferrer, signed it. He said that

I was known to be the head of the American branch of the White Rose. The bond had been found in my pocket when I was arrested.

I told him I had never seen this so-called bond before and that I would not sign a false confession. Sitting there, I remembered that he had said the bond had been found in my pocket. Yet it had never been folded or creased. I made a mental note of this discrepancy, which was to prove important in my defense.

The judge replaced the papers.

"Well, Americano, we are all finished. Why don't you play it smart and cooperate?"

I shook my head. He opened the door and called the three guards. They took me to the city jail, the Vivac in Marianao, explaining that in three days I would either be free or in El Principe.

The atmosphere in the Vivac was casual and friendly. The clerk asked about my case, told me to sit down and make myself comfortable, ordered a milk shake and a Cuban sandwich for me, then strolled out of the jail, leaving me alone and unguarded. When he returned, I asked permission to make a call and he agreed.

I got Gustavo Alemán on the telephone and in a quarter of an hour he appeared at the jail. The guard left us alone in the reception room so we could talk privately.

Gustavo had been released on $20,000 bail. He knew that the Confidential Police were following him and that it was unsafe to use the telephone, but characteristically he was much more concerned with my troubles than his own.

When I told him how I had been let down by the American Embassy, Gustavo said:

"Yes, that figures . . . It is a long story. I don't have time to go into it now . . . What you need, John, is a lawyer. I recommend Dr. Fables. He is a young man, a revolutionary, a person who knows the right people in the police department and a friend of mine. I will leave now and come back later with some food and Dr. Fables."

About an hour later, a thin, stooped man in his middle fifties came into the prison, walked to where I was sitting and removed some pencils and papers from the desk. When I tried to get up to give him my seat, he waved me back. He had heard about my case from the clerk and he told me that the charges against me did not make sense and he was sure that the judge would order me freed in the morning. Meanwhile, there was no reason why I should spend a night in a cell. He took me out to dinner in a restaurant and I had a good meal for the first time in months. Afterward, we talked until late at night and I went to sleep rolled in a blanket in the patio of the prison. "Just imagine you are on a picnic," my host said.

He turned out to be the director of the prison. His name was Medina. He was one of the most helpful and decent people I have ever met. In fact, I can say that, during my long ordeal, 90 per cent of the Cuban people I encountered were sympathetic and helpful. If it had not been for their kindness and sense of justice, I would not be alive today.

My lawyer, Dr. Fables, had at first considered the case against me to be a joke and had even "guaranteed" me my freedom. Then he had searched in the little blue book that he kept in his pocket.

"My God, this comes under Law 425 of the Sierra Maestra." These were the "laws" which Fidel Castro had promulgated when he was a rebel against the government in the mountains. "Anyone found with counterrevolutionary propaganda or selling bonds or raising funds for the counterrevolution . . . Under this charge, you are remanded to custody in the Principe and held there without bail."

Early the next morning, Fables had a talk with the judge of instruction. He returned to the jail to tell me that, according to the testimony the state had, the arresting officer had found a White Rose bond in my trouser pocket.

"Did the judge show you the bond, Fables?"

"Yes."

"Did you notice anything that was out of place?" He shook his head. "Didn't you notice that the bond, which was pasted on cardboard, had never been folded? How could it have been in my trouser pocket?"

"You know, by God, you are right. Why didn't I notice that?   . . . I will take your case and you have nothing to worry about . . . Our first task is to get you into a hospital. We can do that with the help of the American Embassy and you can stay there until your trial."

When he left, I felt greatly encouraged. Later that day, an attractive young woman of about thirty came in. She spoke excellent English, had lived in New York seven years and was married to a New Yorker.

"I am Margaret Medina," she said. "The chief of the prison is my father. He has told me all about your case.

Are you married?"

"Yes, my wife is in Miami."

"Would you like to phone her?"

"I would jump at the chance."

"I have discussed this with my father. Why don't you ask her to collect documents that beyond any possibility of a doubt prove who you are and then fly down here? She should get bank references and that sort of thing, affidavits from reliable businessmen. My father thinks the case against you is fishy. If your wife can bring conclusive proofs, he will talk to the judge of instruction and he thinks he can get the case thrown out."

I told Margaret I could never thank her enough. Florence agreed to do what I suggested; warning me it would probably take a full day to get the documents.

Meanwhile, Medina had been making an investigation of his own.

"Martino, I don't understand this," he said. "All the people arrested with you were released the next day. I am going to look into this case personally and find out what is behind it. I know Fidel Castro. After I have looked into your case, I may decide to talk to him and lay the facts before him."

We went to an open-air concert that night, again talked until the early hours of the morning and again I slept in the patio under the stars.

The next morning, Florence arrived with the documents. She was very excited. After we had examined them, she asked me whether I had received the diagrams of the brush- less generator my partner and I had designed. I shook my head. Florence told me that they had finished with the prototype and tested it successfully at Fort

Monmouth. "I sent all those papers and all the drawings to you at the Catillo Atarés."

"I never received them." This was bad news indeed. We told Medina about it and, that afternoon, he went to the Catillo to get my belongings, including the generator drawings. When he returned, he told me that there were no documents or drawings there that had been sent me by my wife. The thought that these people were not only depriving me of my freedom, but stealing my work, was disconcerting.

While I was in jail that night, I had another severe attack and the officer on guard sent me to the hospital around the corner. The doctor on duty examined me and wrote out an official order, recommending that I be hospitalized for treatment.

Medina returned to the police station later that night with Florence and Margaret.

"I have bad news for you," he said. I have received an order from the Judge of Instruction to deliver you to Principe Prison. That will be tomorrow. Meanwhile, in the morning, Mrs. Martino and I will go to the American Embassy and try to see that you are put into the Anglo-American Hospital instead . . . Now I have a surprise for you. You and your wife will spend tonight in my home as my guests."

"You shouldn't do that," I said to him. "It could get you in trouble."

"Don't worry about me. I know what I am doing. This is my own idea."

The next morning, Medina and Florence went to the American Embassy to see Kessler, who turned them over to Consul General Brown, whom Florence described as a precise man who seemed to be in his late fifties. When my wife explained the situation to him, Brown told her:

"Don't worry. I have talked to the proper people. They are not going to take your husband to the Principe; they are going to send him to a hospital."

"Are you sure?"

"Positive."

"If anything goes wrong, I will come back here to the Embassy," Florence said.

"Do that," replied the Consul General.

Around one o'clock in the afternoon, Chief Medina arrived with the order to have me sent to Principe Prison.

A few minutes later, the patrol wagon arrived and the prisoners were loaded into it. When the guards came to me, Medina said he would take me himself. With one guard, we piled into Medina's car—the Chief, his daughter, Florence and I.

To me, this is the most astonishing thing about my whole story. We drove to the American Embassy, got out and passed through its gates. There I was, a man who had been in prison, a man under indictment for a crime considered so serious that no bail was permitted and a man under written orders remanding him to prison. And here was the director of the prison taking me to the American Embassy where, under international law, I was a free man.

Before we left the Vivac, Florence had called my friend, Gustavo Alemán, and he was in Consul General Brown's office waiting for us. Brown, Kessler, Gilchrist and two other Embassy aides were there. On the Cuban side: Medina, Margaret, Gustavo and the guard.

As we walked in, Brown turned red:

"My God, Medina, do you know what you have done? Why did you bring this man here?"

"For you to help him," Medina replied with dignity.

"You shouldn't have done that," Brown retorted.

"You have broken the law. This man is on American territory and, technically speaking, you have set him free."

Kessler left the office in great excitement to confer with Ambassador Bonsal. Brown said:

"What do you want me to do, Medina?"

"I told you this morning that they were going to send Martino to the Principe prison and not to a hospital. You replied that, if that happened, I was to bring him back here. I have done so. Now what do you plan to do about it?"

"I can't do anything about it," Brown replied. "This man can't stay here. We don't want any trouble with the Castro government.

We can't antagonize them. In fact, we are doing everything we can to cooperate with them."

"You refuse to help this man then?" Medina asked.

"I refuse because I don't want trouble between the Embassy and Dr. Castro."

"I thought you were the American Consul here?"

"Well, I am."

Medina shook his head. "Now I have seen everything," he said. "May I use your telephone? I will call a judge. Martino was sent to a hospital last night and I have an official document here, signed by the director of the hospital, that he should be hospitalized. If I call a judge whom I know, will you talk to him, Consul? Will you tell him who you are and tell him you want to help this man? If the judge talks to you, perhaps he will unbend a bit and sign an order enabling Martino to go to a hospital."

Consul Brown looked flustered. He left the room for a minute or so—to get instructions from Ambassador Bonsai, I supposed. When he came back, he said:

"I will talk to no judge. I will not interfere in this case. The American Government is not going to cause any difficulties for the Government of Cuba. My duty is to get this man out of the Embassy."

"So you will not help him?"

"Absolutely. Those are my orders."

Gustavo Alemán stood up suddenly:

"Whatever else you do, John, don't leave this Embassy. You are free. You are on American soil."

Kessler told Alemán to shut up. Then Brown turned to me:

"Martino, you have to leave. You can't do this to us."

"Why don't you at least try to help him?" Florence said.

"Why didn't you know enough not to bring your husband here?" Brown asked her.

My wife turned on him:

"Didn't you assure me this morning that there was no danger of his going to prison? Didn't you tell me that you had everything arranged and he was going to be sent to the hospital? And didn't you tell me to come back if anything went wrong?"

"Yes, but I never told you to bring him here."

"I didn't bring him here," Florence said. "Chief Medina brought him."

"Oh my God," Brown said and left the room.

Medina, Margaret and the guard left the office and walked down the hail to where they were out of earshot.

Consul General Brown returned to the office and said:

"Martino, I have just talked to Washington and I guarantee you, in the presence of Mr. Kessler here, that, if you give yourself up to custody in El Principe, that tomorrow, by tomorrow night at the very latest, you will go free. I beg you to do this because we don't want any trouble with Castro, because we are doing all that we possibly can to cooperate with him."

I said: "Brown, why should I believe you? You won't even talk to a judge for me."

"I don't have to talk to a judge. Please, as a good American citizen, go to the Catillo del Principe." Alemán pleaded with me not to do it. "Stay in the Embassy," he urged. "You are free here."

"What are you going to do, John?" Florence asked me.

"Flo, the way the Consul General puts it…" Then I turned to Brown. "By the way, where is Bonsai?"

"Mr. Bonsai is not here right now . . . In fact, he just left.

"I'll bet he just left," Gustavo said sarcastically.

Flo turned to me:

"Don't do it, John. Don't let them fast-talk you out of this Embassy."

"Martino, I am pleading with you," Consul General Brown said. "You must leave. Because all the time that Ambassador Bonsai has been here, he has never had the opportunity of really talking with Fidel Castro."

"What?"

"Yes. Dr. Castro won't talk to him. And if you do this thing, you are going to disrupt all our plans. We are trying to negotiate with the Cuban Government. If you do this to us, there will be unfavorable publicity, there will be uproar, and there will be scandal. You are an American. You must do the right thing for your country."

I turned to Flo: "Well, Flo, what can I do? He promises me that I will be out tomorrow night. Then there is no problem."

"I guarantee that you will be a free man at the very latest tomorrow night," Consul General Brown said solemnly.

"It is up to you," Florence said.

So I called Medina.

"I am ready to go with you to the Principe."

"Do you really know what you are doing, Martino?" he asked.

Alemán appealed to me again: "John, don't walk out of this Embassy."

"Don't move," Florence urged.

Brown was sitting behind his desk, white as a sheet.

"I have no choice," I told them. "I am innocent. If I stay in the Embassy, everybody back home is going to think that I have done something wrong, that I am guilty. I know I have nothing to do with the White Rose. The best thing I can do for the Embassy, for all concerned, is to leave."

We walked out of the Embassy. We got into Chief Medina's car and we drove to the Catillo del Principe where I was delivered to the officer of the day.

Consul Brown's promise to get me out of prison in forty eight hours, even with the solemn guarantee of "Washington" thrown in, turned out to be absolutely worthless. The bitter truth was that I would not leave Cuban prisons until more than three years later and I would have no reason to thank either the American Embassy in Havana or the Department of State for that deliverance.

CHAPTER 5

SADISTS AND PERVERTS
OF EL PRINCIPE

The prison of El Principe, where I was to spend the next fourteen months, is on a hill overlooking the central park of Havana and the monument to José Marti. The Reina Mercedes Hospital is on one side and the Palace of Justice on the other. As in the case of Atarés, the Castle is surrounded by a dry moat with a drawbridge and there is only one entrance. El Principe is about the same age as Atarés, but considerably larger.

The entrance to El Principe is flanked by the fingerprinting department, on the right, and the requisa, or room where prisoners are searched on reception, at the left. There are twenty-five galeras, or partially underground cells, each of which sleeps 65 to 100 men, and which face a central, star- shaped patio. On top of the Castle and set apart from the prison is the infirmary, which faces the central park and commands a view of Havana.

The Ministry of the Interior, which supplies the guards, runs the Catillo del Principe. There is also an Army garrison, which is entirely independent of the Interior Ministry.

When I was there, the Catillo housed between 2,500 and 3,000 prisoners and was overcrowded. As a general rule, the inmates were serving short sentences since, in theory at least; those who had perpetrated major crimes were shipped out to the Isle of Pines. However, the Administration of El Principe was flagrantly corrupt and long-term prisoners with influence or money found ways and means of staying there, thus remaining in Havana and enjoying the privilege of having visitors three times a week.

The worst thing about El Principe was that each galera had a chief and second-in-command and these men were almost invariably hard-core criminals, serving fifteen to thirty years for murder.

I Was Castro's Prisoner

Almost always, they were men who had served on the Isle of Pines and, through political connections, had maneuvered their transfer to El Principe.

The prison had a grapevine of informers. The stool pigeons in the prison received such benefits as extra food and were allowed pabellon. This is a system in the Cuban prisons whereby a man is allowed to have his wife visit him every week or so in a special galera outside the prison, where they can be alone for a couple of hours. Naturally, while these women are supposed to be wives, this is not necessarily the case. Prisoners, who are unmarried or tired of their wives, will pay to have girls sent up to see them.

In the Principe, it was easy to buy anything you wanted. Marihuana cost fifty cents a cigarette. Morphine, cocaine and heroine were available, not to mention Seconal, Nembutal and other drugs of that sort. Cocaine is very popular in Cuba.

The prisoners fell into two groups—those who had money or connections and the poor prisoners who had nothing. The first group had steaks and other delicacies brought in from the outside and cooked them on their small electric stoves in the galeras. The poor prisoners had to subsist on the inadequate and deficient regular prison fare: coffee, milk and roll in the morning; a lunch around ten of rice and malanga, a root which is the traditional diet of hunger in Cuba, and in the afternoon around four o'clock, supper of rice and perhaps black beans or a stew. All this food was served cold, including the coffee.

In most galeras, there was a group that ran the card and dice games, another group that controlled marihuana and a third group that sold the more expensive drugs. All this went on with the knowledge of the corrupt guards under the Ministry of the Interior.

The prison is a place where nobody dares to talk. Everybody knows what is going on, but even the doctors and nurses in the infirmary are afraid to tell the truth, because they may be framed and sent to the Isle of Pines. Deportation to the Island—and hence, as a rule, death by hunger, mistreatment, violence or medical neglect—is the dread that permeates the prison constantly like a miasma. The stool pigeons are motivated by fear of the Isle of Pines as much as by greed. The existence of the Island makes everyone, or almost everyone, try to curry favor with the authorities.

There is a prison store, but hardened convicts run it. Constant disagreements and knife fights occur about the amount of money spent by prisoners there. Most of the hardboiled prisoners carried knives, or even machete blades, slipped inside their trouser legs. Since there was no death penalty for common crimes, a man serving twenty or thirty years for murder had nothing to lose by killing again.

Another bad thing about the Cuban prisons was the institution of amnesty. Whenever there was a change in administration, there would be an amnesty and a large proportion of the prisoners would go free. I have talked to men in El Principe who had been sentenced half a dozen times for the same sort of crime. I know men who have committed murder, been released by amnesty, and have then committed a second murder.

To the outside observer, El Principe seemed quiet and orderly, but inside it despicable assaults on young boys and other depravities were the rule. The evil was below the surface. There are workshops there, but nobody works. It is a community of depraved men, run by those who are worse than the rest. The hard-core, long-sentence, degenerate criminals have one visible trait in common—all of them are tattooed. They have the run of the prison because the administration depends on them to know what is going on. They are very dangerous men.

Every three months or so, the garrison in the prison changes, but the guards from the Ministry of the Interior stay. Once in a while, there is an attempted shakeup. The judicial investigators arrive, but the guards and informers have been forewarned and El Principe appears to be a model prison.

THE HOMOSEXUALS

There was one barracks in El Principe, when I was there, which was known as the galera of the fairies. These men would parade around the prison wearing lipstick and sometimes panties and women's hose.

I Was Castro's Prisoner

Other groups in the galeras practiced sodomy. These were old prisoners; generally serving sentences of twenty years and over and, as a rule, tattooed. These bugarrones, as they were called, kept their boys neatly dressed in white clothes and powdered. They acted as if they were married.

About once a week, some prisoner would be sent up to the infirmary because of homosexual difficulties. A boy would attempt or commit suicide because his "husband" had left him. There would be knife fights over boys between bugarrones. The most terrible thing about this institution in the Catillo del Principe was the way young boys were turned into perverts. I have seen boys of fifteen or sixteen who felt lost when they entered the prison for the first time, but were befriended by bugarrones, given special food, protection and a bed in the galera. That night or the next, the bugarrones would try to take advantage of the boy. If he failed, the boy would be taken to the back of one of the barracks, beaten, held down and forced to submit. I have seen boys of sixteen or less transformed in the course of six months into completely depraved and experienced homosexual prostitutes. They had no choice. During my time in the Catillo del Principe, three boys committed suicide, either to avoid becoming homosexuals or because they had succumbed and felt guilt.

ALMEIJEIRAS, ALMEIDA, RAUL CASTRO

One day, Chief of Police Efigenio Almeijeiras visited El Principe, a prison with which he was thoroughly familiar since he had been confined there for purse-snatching in the old days. There was a tremendous disturbance that day with two or three thousand prisoners milling around the star patio. Almeijeiras was safely on the roof with an armed escort.

The homosexuals spotted Almeijeiras and began to scream to him to come up to their galera because his "husband" was still there. I was told that the mulatto blushed through his yellow-brown skin, got into his car and left the prison, never to come back. I learned that during his time as a prisoner in El Principe, Almeijeiras had been housed in the fairy galera and had been a homosexual prostitute.

Let me move out of chronological sequence to finish the Almeijeiras story. He had a strange influence over Fidel Castro. Although he was scarcely literate and much too primitive in his political thinking to be a Marxist, he was a close advisor of Fidel. Listening to El Caballo (The Horse, as Fidel Castro was called by the Cubans) on television, I would sometimes see Almeijeiras stand beside him and whisper in his ear while he was in the middle of his harangue.

Nevertheless, the Chief of the Revolutionary Police became increasingly disillusioned with the course of the Cuban Revolution and most resentful of the increasing power of the Russians in Cuban affairs. Shortly after the failure of the Bay of Pigs invasion of April 1961, Almeijeiras was holding forth one night in the St. John's Hotel, telling everyone who dared to listen to him how. Castro had double-crossed the men who made the landing on the Gramma.

His friends tried to quiet him, but it was useless. Finally, they phoned Fidel Castro who appeared on the scene.

Almeijeiras called him various obscene names and then offered him a "joy stick," reminding him that they used to smoke marihuana together in the Sierra Maestra.

Castro ordered his arrest. Almeijeiras, who was carrying a gun, dared Fidel to take him. At this point, one of Castro's men rabbit-punched him into unconsciousness and he was dragged out of the hotel.

After that, Almeijeiras was sent to Czechoslovakia for political training. When he returned, he was given a nominally important position with the militia. Only the fact that he had been built up as a hero of the Cuban Revolution had saved him from paredón.

Juan Almeida Bosque, the Chief of the Cuban Army under Fidel Castro, had an almost equally checkered career. In 1948, a Fort Lauderdale woman, whose name I shall not reveal, was visiting Havana. She complained to the Cuban Police that her purse had been snatched and two men had attacked her. She was particularly disturbed because the men were Negroes.

The police arrested a well-known delinquent called "White Head." He confessed to the crime, showed the police where he had hidden the stolen purse, and denounced his accomplice. He was placed under $10,000 bail. At his trial, he pleaded that he had been under the influence of marihuana and had not known what he was doing, but he was sentenced nevertheless to serve four years on the Isle of Pines.

There, he got to know Fidel Castro, who at that time had been sentenced to fifteen years imprisonment because of his attempted insurrection at the Moncada Barracks. "White Head" became a revolutionary, joined Castro in Mexico, sailed on the Gramma and, like Almeijeiras, was one of the twelve "immortals" of the Cuban Revolution who escaped capture by the Batista authorities and survived.

This man's real name was Juan Almeida Bosque. When Castro came to New York for the United Nations Assembly meeting and ostentatiously left his hotel for the Hotel Theresa in Harlem, El Caballo never tired of showing the colored people of New York photographs of Juan Almeida and pointing out that in Cuba a Negro commanded the armed forces.

A more significant relationship is that between Raul Castro and Alfredo Guevara—no relation of Ché Guevara. Raul fell under this man's influence at the University of Havana and continues to be dominated by him. An intellectual and the leader of the Communist group at the University of Havana in the late 1940s; Alfredo Guevara wears high-heeled shoes and perfumes himself. He is at present in charge of cultural relations and his department is staffed almost exclusively with sexual inverts.

HOMOSEXUALITY AND COMMUNISM

Before proceeding with this unappetizing subject, it may be worth pointing out that homosexuality is not merely an erotic and psychic characteristic, but a way of life which often has definite political implications. The homosexual is an outcast from society. He is compelled to live a life of concealment and deceit. He belongs to a secret fraternity that protects and advances its members. In the open societies of the West, the homosexual can be destroyed by public exposure and hence is subject to blackmail. In the closed societies of the totalitarian world, his activities are protected by concealment wherever this is in the interests of the state.

These factors contribute to create an affinity between the homosexual international and the Communist International. The homosexual is an ideal agent of revolution in its destructive phases and of conspiracy, deception and betrayal.

THE AMERICAN EXECUTIONER

Shortly after I entered El Principe, the direction of the prison was turned over to two of the worst human beings I ever had the misfortune to meet—Lieutenant Enrique Kammerer Perez and Captain Herman Marks. One of their first acts was to deny all medical attention to the prisoners regardless of their condition.

On one occasion, my wife flew down from Miami and came to see me on visiting day. She had been talking for about ten minutes when a guard came up to us.

"Martino, get your things together. You are going to be freed." He turned to Florence: "Mrs. Martino, go downstairs and wait for your husband. He is going to be released today."

I told Florence not to believe it, but she obeyed the guard's order.

About a quarter of an hour later, the guard came to my cell door:

"Well, you had a nice long visit, didn't you?"

"Whom do I thank for this?" If I could have, I think I would have killed the guard.

"Your good American friend, Captain Marks, I had to obey his orders. Americano, this captain is so bad that he actually enjoys firing the coup de grace into the brains of the men who are shot at the paredón."

Herman Marks had joined Fidel Castro in the Sierra Maestra. He had a record of thirty-two arrests in the United States, including one for rape. In the Catillo del Principe all the guards hated him. At that time they were guajiros from the hills and comparatively decent people.

The hatred grew when he had seven prisoners bayoneted to death in a requisa (or search) in 1960. In one of these cases, a man's back was slit open so I could see his bloody, exposed lungs.

There was also the time when some of my friends were being held in the capilla, or death cell where men are placed to await execution. Instead of being simply kept there a few hours or being held overnight, they remained in capilla for 163 days.

Every day or so, Marks would go into the capilla and point at one of the men:

"Tonight, they are coming for you."

Once when the wife of one of these men came to visit him, Marks told her that her husband had been shot the day before. It was his idea of a great joke. As it happens, that man is alive today.

A man called de Leon, as I recall the name, asked Marks to give him the coup de grace in the heart, instead of the head, as his body was to be sent for burial to his eighty-year- old mother. The American captain promised to do so. However, after the firing squad had done its work, he pumped five .45 caliber slugs into de Leon's face, changing it into a shapeless piece of meat. The body was sent to the boy's mother and, when she opened the casket, she died of heart failure.

After Marks had bayoneted seven men in El Principe, he was transferred to the Isle of Pines and a full investigation of his conduct was started. Instances of his brutality and sadism came to light and there were increasing suspicions that he had been stealing funds from the prison. Accordingly, he escaped in a small boat with a female American writer and eventually turned up in the United States.

On April 10, 1963, the United States Court of Appeals ruled that Marks, who was stripped of his citizenship, could not regain his nationality and that the U.S. was free to deport him. The American Civil Liberties Union then announced that it would ask the U. S. Supreme Court to review the decision and stay deportation. Aliens are commonly deported to the port from which they came. In Marks' case, his lawyer argued, "he would be killed if he returned there." The Marks story was apparently nearing an ironic finale.

CHAPTER 6
TRIAL BY JUDGE FURY

When I first entered El Principe Prison; I was put in Galera 20, which contained the political prisoners. This cell was unusually large and was supposed to house 150 men. However, there were 450 of us there and we were miserably overcrowded. A partial compensation for the miserable physical conditions was the fact that my cellmates—officers, police and civilian officials of the Batista regime—were strongly pro- American and welcomed me as a friend and comrade in the fight against Castro and Communism. Among these men was Joaquin Martinez Sáenz, the former director of the National Bank of Cuba.

His case was typical of justice in Castro- land. He had been accused of misappropriation of public funds and found not guilty by the military tribunal. As soon as he was set free, Castro had him arrested. He would be held in Cuban prisons for years without ever being brought to trial. I entered El Principe on October 5, 1959. At that time the transfer of power to Enrique Kammerer Perez and Captain Herman Marks had not yet occurred. The authorities noted that I had a medical certificate, stating that I urgently needed treatment. Accordingly, they transferred me to the infirmary on the roof of the Castle with a view of all Havana.

While they placed me in the infirmary, they did not go to the extreme of giving me regular medical treatment. Very soon, I became a celebrity of sorts. The common prisoners would swarm around my bed as they had never before seen a real, live "counterrevolutionary," a pilot who dropped incendiary bombs on cane fields and a Batistiano murderer. This was stopped after a few days. Guards were placed at my bed on twenty-four duty with orders to prevent my talking to anyone.

THE DARKENING CLOUDS

From the infirmary windows, one day we saw a B-26 lazily circling the sky and the puffs of anti-aircraft shells exploding around it. This plane, we were to learn later, was being piloted by Major Pedro L. Diaz Lanz, Chief of the Cuban Air Force under Fidel Castro, who had defected because "Communists gave him indigestion." Two hours after the plane had headed northward and disappeared into the sky, we were locked in our cells. We turned on our radios and were informed that an American plane, flown by a Cuban traitor, had dropped bombs on Havana.

At this time, the overwhelming majority of the Cuban people supported Castro. This incident, and the false version of it promulgated by the Cuban Goverment, touched off a wave of hatred of Americans.

Around three in the morning, there was another requisa. All the lights in the prison were turned on. We were moved into the patio, ordered to strip naked and made to stand at attention. Meanwhile, the guards entered the cells, searched everything, ripped the beds apart, confiscated the canned food and other small luxuries and threw our clothes arid our few personal possessions into a pile in the center of the gal- era. In Galera 20, which housed the former officers and officials of the Batista regime, the requsia was rougher and, on the pretext of an attempted riot, two men were shot to death. We were allowed to return to our cells around five that morning.

The next day, Castro called a giant meeting of protest against the "bombing" of Havana. We watched on TV as, before a frenzied crowd, he accused the United States of inspiring the attack and demanded that Diaz Lanz be turned over to what he called Cuban justice. The association of American travel agents was holding its annual convention in Havana at the time. To their everlasting shame, some American delegates spoke on the rostrum with Castro and said they had seen Havana bombed with their own eyes. Whether they were Communists or merely fools, I do not know. However, what they said was a lie. No bombs were dropped on Havana.

The explosion of anti-aircraft shells caused the few casualties that occurred. William Alexander Morgan, a powerfully built soldier of fortune, a hero of the Escambray front of the Cuban Revolution, a veteran of the military stockades of the U. S. Army and a renegade American, added his voice to the hymn of hatred and opprobrium heaped upon his country. Morgan boasted that, if the United States invaded Cuba, he would stand at the Malecón and machine-gun as many Marines as he could take with him. He was to end, as I shall tell later, in a different way, dying with great bravery before one of Fidel Castro's firing squads.

Castro whipped the people into fury and exaltation. He said that he had abolished the military tribunals and the firing squads and he wanted to ask the people whether he should reestablish them. There were roars of "si, si y si." He had his pretext now for the total destruction of civil rights and due process of law in Cuba. He was merely obeying the will of the people.

Two days after the bombing, I was put into another cell with four other prisoners. We were locked in and placed under twenty-four-hour guard. For fourteen months, we would live there under lock and key, never leaving the cell, never breathing fresh air or enjoying sunshine. The only exceptions were when we were taken under armed guard to see our lawyers, to the prison office or to the dentist. The cell was opened only to admit visitors and there were two guards for each caller.

We were not permitted razor blades, nor were we allowed to shave ourselves. Once a week, the prison barber would come under guard to the cell to shave us, but we were not allowed to talk to him. We were given food in the usual way. Since we were sick, the doctor would give us written permission to send out for special foods.

They would play tricks on us. For instance, they would give us water for five minutes in the morning and then keep it turned off all day. Those who failed to fill a cup or tin can would have to borrow drinking water or else do without all day. The cell was left dirty. In fact, it was the filthiest cell I encountered in my forty months of prison life.

For washing, we had a little cubicle three feet square. Since the cell had eight beds in it and sometimes as many as eighteen prisoners, there was almost always a waiting line for use of the toilet.

Since diarrhea was prevalent, this caused a great deal of torment and filth.

They used to bring sick political prisoners to our cell from the Isle of Pines because there were no facilities there for treatment of the really ill. Consequently, I met some of the elite of the previous regime—colonels, comandantes, even a rear admiral. Our doctor was permitted in our cell only once a week and, since he was hardly a sympathizer with the Castro regime, he often had difficulty getting out.

At this time, the sinister change in prison administration occurred. The new director of the prison, Enrique Kammerer Perez, had been with Castro on the Gramma and had been captured and confined in this prison. He knew all the tricks of penitentiary life from the inside and he was an expert at making our lives miserable.

Captain Herman Marks, whom I have already characterized, became chief of the military garrison.He was known as la gota de sangre (the drop of blood) by the prisoners.

A SWITCH OF LAWYERS

Meanwhile, Fables, my lawyer, would come from time to time with more bad news. In October, he had told me that I would have to stay in prison until my trial and that the dockets were so crowded I would be lucky if it came up in February—four months hence. He was in touch with the Embassy officials, the same ones who had given me their solemn assurance that they would have me freed in forty-eight hours. They now said there was absolutely nothing they could do to help me. I was beginning to realize what a sucker I had been to fall for their appeal to my patriotism.

In December, Fables was back to tell me that I would not be tried by a civilian court after all. My case had been made retroactive and turned over to La Cabana Fortress. I would be tried by a military tribunal. This change in judicial procedure had been made possible by the crowds that had demanded blood and corpses when Fidel Castro, Major William Morgan and the speakers from the tourism convention had stirred them up. The military court was the waiting room for the paredón.

"I am sorry," Fables said. "That is the way it is. I cannot defend you because I am afraid."

It is unusual to find a Cuban who is not fanatically brave, practically unprecedented to find one who admits to fear.

"Are you leaving me in the lurch, Fables?"

"I am resigning as your lawyer. I can't help it if I am a coward."

"I suppose not," I said. "Thank you for what you have already done."

The next morning, I had a great surprise. I was asked to come down to the attorney's room for a conference with my lawyer. As they carried me down in a stretcher, I decided that Fables must have had a twinge of conscience or shame or manliness. But this was not the explanation. There, advancing to meet me, with a broad smile on his face, a lawyer's button in his lapel, and his mustache shaved off, was my old friend, Gustavo Alemân.

"My God, Gustavo, what are you doing here?" I exclaimed.

"Hush. Talk to me as if I were your lawyer."

"You are insane to take this sort of risk."

"Well, I found out that Fables won't defend you. I have another lawyer who will come to see you in about a week. He is a good man. A real man. Do whatever he tells you."

"Splendid. How are things with you, Gus?"

"Just perfect. The G-2 is on my tail and I have a fine chance of winding up in here with you. Hence, I am going from here to the Brazilian Embassy and asking for sanctuary.

He left and a few minutes later they carried me back to my cell. Gustavo found safety in the Brazilian Embassy and proceeded from there to the United States. He returned to Cuba as part of the betrayed invasion force of the Playa Girón. After suffering for a year and a half in the prison hell of the Isle of Pines, he was ransomed, together with his comrades, in the winter of 1962-63 and is now back in the States.

I Was Castro's Prisoner

RAFAEL DEL PINO

About this time, Rafael del Pino was brought into my cell. He was the man whose wrecked plane I had seen in the Catillo de Atarés. Del Pino was thirty-thee—the same age as his schoolmate, friend and boyhood hero, Fidel Castro. He was crippled by a bullet in his hip and unable to stand up.

Rafael told me that he had been so devoted to Castro that he would do anything the latter told him, including murder. They had become adherents of the Communist movement together. They had gone to Bogotá together in 1948 to organize riots, street fighting and civil war and to disrupt the Ninth Inter-American Conference. The bloodbath that occurred in Bogotá as a result is history.

When he returned to Cuba, del Pino joined Fidel Castro's band of student gangsters, terrorists and killers in the University. They plotted the murder of Senator Rolando Masferrer, but botched it and killed a bystander by accident. After that, Rafael had to flee Cuba. He proceeded to Miami, where he found work as a Western Union messenger boy and later delivered flowers. He enlisted in the American armed forces and thus became a citizen, saw active service in Korea and returned to Florida to marry, settle down and raise a family. As a hobby, he flew small planes.

Despite the fact that his, home life was happy, the lure of Fidel Castro was irresistible and Rafael proceeded to Mexico to join the band that was being trained for the invasion of Cuba. Together with Fidel and Raul, Juan Almeida and Efigenio Almeijeiras, Rafael del Pino formed part of the small group in Mexico that met apart from the others and planned operations. As one of Fidel Castro's most trusted men, he said he was sent to California to buy arms and made several trips to Hollywood to close deals concerning guns and ammunition with Mickey Cohen, the racketeer.

"When we were in Mexico," Rafael told me, "I used to drive Fidel Castro to the Russian Embassy. I was with him on many occasions when he received money from the Soviet contact in Mexico City."

And I knew about the time Fidel paid $50,000 to a group of men to hoist the banner of the 26th of July Movement on top of the Eiffel Tower.

"Eventually, it became clear to me that I had to leave Fidel Castro. He had plotted to have some of his people in Havana murder the chief of the S.I.M., Batista's service of military intelligence. The attempt was made in front of the Montmartre nightclub and the wrong man was killed. After we got the report by short wave radio that the attack had failed, Fidel was very quiet.

As we were driving back to our training camp that night, he said: 'Rafael, we will have to do something about this. Some day, it could cause us plenty of trouble.'"

I asked him what he meant by that remark and he replied: "The men who botched the job will have to be liquidated."

After that, Rafael said, he decided that nobody was safe around Fidel Castro with the exception of the key Communist and Soviet agents. He was conscious of the growing malignant hatred of Raul Castro and decided there was very little time in which to get out alive.

I heard a different story about the cause of Rafael's break with Castro from an entirely independent source. According to this, one of Castro's sisters was much attracted to del Pino and this fact aroused in Raul Castro a pathological hatred. It was Raul who persuaded his brother to have del Pino killed. Rafael was tipped off about the decision on the very night it was to be carried out. He fled in terror from the training ranch, arriving in Mexico City on foot.

Del Pino's story was that he delayed his flight until he was entrusted with an arms buying mission in California. He proceeded to Florida and appropriated the funds for his own private purposes.

He was one of the first to point out that Fidel Castro was an agent of the international Communist movement. He picketed the White House with a sign, denouncing Fidel as a Red puppet, getting headlines in the world press. He returned to Miami, dedicated himself to the work of the underground and, at great personal risk, flew over Havana and dropped leaflets.

A close friend of his, a former comrade in the American Army, tricked him into going to Havana on the night of July 23. With his friend, he flew into the Havana area to take some people whose lives were in danger, off the island.

When the plane landed on the highway, his supposed friend removed the ignition key, opened the plane door, jumped out and ran, leaving del Pino in the plane. Hidden nearby were Police Chief Almeijeiras and a squad of his men. They opened fire on the plane, using plain and incendiary bullets. Hit in the hip, Rafael tried to get out of the burning aircraft, but fell by the door. Providentially, a policeman, who did not know that the plan was to have Rafael killed then and there, managed to drag him to safety.

Del Pino was convinced that the plot had been to kill him before he could talk. In the prison, there were two or three attempts to murder him. In one instance, a stool pigeon came to him with an elaborate escape plan. A helicopter was to alight on the roof of the prison by the infirmary and carry him off to safety. Obviously, if del Pino had fallen for this scheme, he would have been "shot while attempting to escape."

After his capture, he was held for a while at the Comandancia. On the second night of his arrest, Fidel Castro came to see him.

"Well, I have you back on Cuban soil, Rafael."

"What do you plan to do to me, Fidel?"

"I am going to have the doctors cure you and then I am going to have you shot. By the way, Rafael, what do the Americans think of my government?"

"They think you are a Communist, Fidel."

Chief of Police Almeijeiras came in to tell Castro that people were waiting for him. Fidel turned to his old comrade:

"Well, Chico, the next time I see you, you will be at paredón." Rafael was taken before the military tribunal sick and crippled, to stand trial for treason. The prosecutor asked for death. Del Pino told the court that if he was to be shot, he wanted his body sent back to the United States. He said that he was an American by naturalization and proud of it. He added that he never wanted to see Cuba again.

Probably the publicity Rafael got in the world press made Castro decide against execution. He was given thirty years on the Isle of Pines instead, which is the same as paredon, but much slower and more painful. After this, Rafael was brought to trial before a civilian court, charged with murder—the knifing of an innocent bystander during an attempt on the life of, Rolando Masferrer, which Castro personally ordered! Acquitted, Rafael was taken to the Military Hospital where he was crippled by an incompetent or sadistic surgeon. Finally he was taken to the Isle of Pines on a stretcher. Before both his trials and between sentence and transfer to the Island, Rafael was with us. Most of the time, he was suffering horribly.

BEFORE THE MILITARY TRIBUNAL

My new lawyer, Dr. Francisco Camargo, made an excellent impression on me.

"Aren't you afraid of appearing for the defense before the military court?" I asked him.

"No, I have defended many such cases. I am a lawyer and it is my business to represent defendants in the courts."

At my request, he got in touch with Florence and, on the following Saturday, she appeared during visiting hours with a fat sheaf of documents for my defense, including a certificate from the C.A.A. that I was not licensed as a pilot.

On the night of my trial, December 18, 1959, I was taken to La Cabana Fortress and carried to the theatre where, under Batista, plays had been performed for the Army officers. Florence and Camargo were there. The Embassy had sent two junior people: Gilchrist, whom I had encountered before, and someone called Mullin.

"Where is Kessler?" I asked Florence. "What good will these two do? They don't know anything about my case."

"I told the Embassy that, but they said they were sending Muffin and Gilchrist. Well, here we are."

"Yes, darling, here we are."

There was a representative of the UPI news service and one from the AP, but they told me there was very little they would be able to send out. At about ten o'clock, the theatre began to fill with soldiers and guards and the trial started.

The president of the military tribunal appointed an interpreter for me and said that, since I was too sick to stand up, I might remain seated.

My lawyer opened by raising seven points of law and fact. One involved proof that I was not a pilot and hence could not have been engaged in smuggling Batistianos to the United States by plane. He asked for a fingerprint test of the bond of the White Rose organization. He made a formal complaint that I had been arrested on July 23, whereas the charges against me had been drawn up on September 27. He also introduced proof of my identity, the nature of my business, an account of my first trip to Cuba and so forth.

The tribunal declared a recess. The judges left the courtroom for about ten minutes and then returned. My interpreter then explained that they had rejected all the evidence and points of law submitted by my attorney. The reason given for this rejection was that they would not accept any documents that had originated in the United States of America! With this as the start of the trial, I decided that I didn't have much of a chance.

The first witness called to the stand was a policeman. He testified that he had searched me in the house and that, when he did so, he found the bond of the White Rose organization in my pocket. My lawyer cross-examined him about this bond, and then finally excused him.

The second policeman was a man whom I had never seen before. He was definitely not one of the men who arrested me. He was sworn and proceeded to testify that the White Rose bond had been found in the suitcase in my hotel room.

On cross-examination, the witness stuck to his story. My attorney then pointed out the conflict between the testimonies of the two policemen and, turning to the tribunal, demanded that both of them be held for perjury.

Again, there was a recess. When the judges returned a quarter of an hour later, they rejected this request. My lawyer then demanded that the charges against me be dismissed. The presiding judge merely waved him off with his hand as if he were an obnoxious insect.

I was called to the stand and the prosecutor proceeded to examine me. The first question was whether I had tried to set up a company called Radio Llamado de Cuba, S.A., to compete with the Cuban Telephone Company. I explained patiently what my company was supposed to do, how it got started and why it could never be a threat to the telephone company. I realized that these so-called revolutionary judges and prosecutors were exceedingly ignorant and educated people, so I went over the elementary ground in as simple language as possible.

Then I was asked whether I was a good friend of Pilar Garcia, Senator Masferrer, Esteban Ventura and others. Most of them were former Batista police officials. I did not know them and so testified. Then I was asked whether I had come to Cuba by private plane. My lawyer jumped up with an objection. That had been the original accusation, but it was not contained in the indictment. I could not be tried for anything that wasn't in the indictment. Therefore, any inquiry into private planes and the attempted escape of Señora Ventura was illegitimate.

The judges told Dr. Camargo that he was out of order and directed him to sit down.

He continued to object. I had been indicted for possessing a bond of the White Rose organization. The policemen who had testified to that had shown themselves to be perjurers. Consequently, new accusations were being made against me, not contained in the indictment. The procedure was flagrantly illegal.

The presiding judge told Dr. Camargo to sit down and shut up in exactly those terms.

I was asked whether I was guilty of the charges and I replied that I was not.

"Why do you say that?" The presiding judge asked.

"For the simple reason that I had been set free. I was placed in the American Embassy the day I was moved from the Vivac. If I had been guilty and therefore expected to be convicted, I should have stayed there."

The president of the tribunal started: "What did you say? You were in the American Embassy? How did you get there?"

I made it appear that I had been taken there by mistake while they were trying to get me to a hospital so as not to involve Medina.

"When were you there?"

"On October 5th for three hours."

"Is there anyone who can testify to that?"

"Yes," Gilchrist said. "Mr. Martino was in the American Embassy on the afternoon of October 5th."

The president of the tribunal sat down. The judges whispered together, and then adjourned for another recess. This time, there was no further reference to my having been in the Embassy. Nevertheless, I could see from their expressions that my testimony had shaken them somewhat.

I found out later from Dr. Camargo that, when they recessed, they had wanted to put Medina under arrest and probe the whole incident. However, while still in recess, they received orders from the head of the legal department not to pursue the matter further as it might cause embarrassing publicity.

The next witness was Mrs. Sofia Cisneros, who proceeded to testify in very rapid Spanish which I could not follow and which my interpreter could not keep up with. I protested that I did not know what she was saying, but was told to shut up by the court. Her son then followed her on the stand. I later learned that both of them had told the court that I had admitted to them that I had come with a plane to smuggle Señora Ventura out of the country.

The conduct of these people was an enigma to me at the time. Subsequently, it has been clarified. Mrs. Ventura was expecting a pilot the night of her arrest. The entire purpose of the police dragnet had been to catch that man—supposedly me. Sofia Cisneros was the godmother of Mrs. Ventura. Her son worked in a bank where he changed pesos into dollars for Mrs. Ventura and was accused by her of having cheated her of $12,000.

The police discovered this and put pressure on both of them to give false testimony against me. Finally, I was asked whether

I wanted to make a statement and whether I accused the court of giving me an unfair trial.

"Who am I to accuse anybody?" I replied. "What chance would I have?"

The trial was over. It had taken until three in the morning. I said goodbye to Florence and was returned to the Catillo del Principe. Three days later, I heard on the radio that I had been found guilty and sentenced to serve thirteen years on the Isle of, Pines. Considering my physical condition, I knew that, if the sentence were carried out, I would never leave the island alive.

CHAPTER 7

PROBLEMS OF SURVIVAL

The night of the riot in El Principe, it was raining and very cold. At about eleven that evening, we were ordered out of our barracks and into the courtyard. Those prisoners who did not move fast enough to suit the guards were prodded with bayonets.

We stood in the rain until about half past nine that morning. Meanwhile, most of the prisoners had returned to their galeras, where they discovered that the guards had stolen their belongings. This touched off a riot. The prisoners began to burn their mattresses and smash their bunks. Others got on the roof and began to hurl bricks and bottles at the guards. The latter retaliated with gunfire and then with bayonets.

As the riot developed in intensity, the Chief of Police came to the prison. His car was pelted with stones, bricks and bottles and he was too timid to get out of it. By about ten o'clock that night, the riot was finally suppressed. Half a dozen prisoners had been bayoneted or shot to death and about 150 were wounded.

The sequel to this riot almost cost my friends and me our lives. When one is a prisoner of a totalitarian regime, survival depends on such advantages as a good information service and an attitude of profound skepticism and distrust toward everything.

News of the riot had filtered out by word of mouth and caused a scandal in Havana. To exculpate themselves, Kammerer Perez and Captain Marks spread the false story that the riot had been caused by the political prisoners in Galera 20 and in the Infirmary and was part of a frustrated escape plot that they had hatched.

A friendly guard told me the next morning to be very careful; the prison authorities were going to stage a phony jail break as a means of reinforcing their explanation and that, in the course of the supposed escape, all the political prisoners were to be murdered. I was dumbfounded and, at first, did not believe the report.

Sure enough, the next morning a man who was marked by us as a stool pigeon got past the guard and whispered to me:

"Martino, I am going to give you the key to your cell.

Everything is ready. Tonight, there will be a break. The counterrevolutionaries will seize the prison and everyone will go free." I said that was fine, but, when he offered me the key to the cell, I refused to take it.

"Tonight, when the time comes, you can leave the key by the cell door," I told him.

That night, Glorioso Hernández, a Negro prisoner who was hostile to the Castro regime and was our friend, took me aside. (I can give his name safely because he is dead.)

"Look up there, right over the infirmary, there is a man with a .80 caliber machine gun," Glorioso said. "The minute you people come out of your cell tonight, they are going to open up on you with that. Downstairs, there is exactly the same situation. We have managed to warn them too."

Around eleven that night, the informer who had first approached me came to the cell door and whispered to me to take the key. I said that none of us was interested in leaving the prison.

"Well, I am going to open the cell door anyhow. When the counterrevolutionaries come upstairs, they will know where you are and they will liberate you."

Sure enough, at two that morning the cell door opened. Voices whispered to us to come out, that the escape had been planned down to the last detail and that, in a few minutes, we would be free.

None of us moved. And in Galera 20, the same thing happened. Enraged because his murder plot had failed, Lieutenant Kammerer summoned me and Dr. Joaquin Martinez Sáenz, the former President of the National Bank of Cuba, and accused us of having plotted an escape. Naturally, we denied this false charge and, since he had no evidence, Kammerer had to let us return to our cells.

FREEDOM SLIPS THROUGH MY FINGERS

My lawyer saw me regularly and was very optimistic about my chances. As he defended other political prisoners, he went to La

Cabana frequently. The authorities there indicated to him that they were prepared to review my case, whereupon the verdict would be reversed and I would be set free. I believed him and felt that it was merely a matter of bearing the conditions in El Principe for a few more months.

In February 1960, an amnesty law was passed which freed most of the common criminals. As a result, my good friend Glorioso Hernández became head of the infirmary. There was immediately a drastic change for the better.

Glorioso cleaned out the stool pigeons, prohibited marihuana smoking in the patio and suppressed homosexual activities as best he could.

Glorioso Hernández had been implicated in the gun battle between the leaders of two rival factions of political terrorists in the Cuban police. This occurred on September 15, 1947 under the presidency of the corrupt and devious intellectual politician, Dr. Ramón Grau San Martin. March 4, 1960, a French ship, La Coubre, carrying munitions from Antwerp to Cuba, exploded in Havana harbor. Quite a few sailors and longshoremen were killed.

The funeral of these men was televised. On this occasion, David Salvador, a former Communist, who was the first head of the Cuban Confederation of Labor (CTC) under Castro, accused the United States Government of having had the ship blown up. He ranted and screamed for about half an hour, demanding more firing squads and more blood. This action of David Salvador was one that we would remember when he too fell victim to Castro Communism, became for a while our fellow prisoner and was later wounded seriously in a bloody requisa on the Isle of Pines. Fidel Castro used the La Coubre affair as the pretext for a new campaign of hate against the United States.

The day after the disaster, I was taken down to the lawyers' room on a stretcher between rows of angry prisoners, who called me a dirty Gringo, and worse and who would probably have killed me if it had not been for the intervention of the guards. When I finally reached the office safely, I asked my lawyer why he had come to see me under these conditions of hysteria.

"I have very bad news for you," he said. "You know we had information that Fidel Castro was ready to release you without waiting for the legal review. Your wife submitted a petition on the grounds of your illness and we had a letter sent to Fidel Castro.

"This morning, after the ship exploded, we received this reply."

He handed me a sheet of paper. There it was. My review had been turned down and I had been ordered sent to the Isle of Pines. The sentence meant slow death for an invalid. The logic of the decision was clear. The ship had been blown up. Castro blamed the explosion on the Americans. Therefore, the only Americans he could lay his hands on must pay.

"Don't despair," my attorney said. "I have a friend who is one of the best lawyers in Cuba. He has read the transcript of your trial and tells me that I should file an appeal with the Cuban Supreme Court as we have seven constitutional grounds for demanding your release."

He gave me some papers, which I signed then and there. "I will file these papers in La Cabana and here right away," he said. "They are to prevent your being shipped to the Isle of Pines. If you are sent to the Island, you will surely die."

"What are my chances, frankly?"

"The crucial issue is whether or not they will give me the transcript and exhibits of your trial," he replied, "so that I can prepare a brief for the Supreme Court. If they refuse, we can use legal measures to try to force them. Don't worry about the Supreme Court. It consists of fine, honest men. If your case reaches the Supreme Court, I stake my professional reputation that you will go free."

I thanked him, but urged him not to return to the prison to see me until the wave of hatred against Americans subsided.

ANOTHER BRUSH WITH THE EMBASSY

Shortly after this, the attending physician came into my cell and, after examining me, asked why the American Embassy was doing nothing on my behalf. I replied that I was a simple American and could not be expected to understand the motivations of the Foreign Service.

When the doctor left, he said he would try to do something for me. The following Saturday, I had a visit from Kessler and Mullin.

"Well, Kessler, it has been a very long time."

"What can I say to you, Martino? How are you?"

"You see how I am. Why did you come down here?"

"Well, somebody phoned and said you were in very bad shape . . . Martino, we made a terrible mistake. I wish there were some way we could correct it."

"Have you talked to my lawyer, Kessler?"

"Who is your lawyer?" He asked me.

"You say that you made a mistake and you want to do everything you can to correct it, but you haven't even bothered to find out the name of my lawyer or that he is filing an appeal."

"Please send your lawyer to see me," Kessler said. "The Ambassador and I were talking today about you. We made a bad blunder in your case and now we are going to try to do everything we can to help you."

"That is wonderful, Kessler. After all these months of complete neglect from the Embassy, at a time when I am sick, suffering great hardship and facing a thirteen-year sentence, you say you are going to help me. You said that once before."

At this juncture, Mullin interrupted: "What's the matter with you? Don't you appreciate anything?"

"You make me ashamed of being an American," I told him. "Do you know that the prisoners here have no respect for you American consuls? They say that, if my government was worth anything, it would do something to help me."

"Well," Mullin replied, "if you don't want to be an American, I'll bring you an official document and you can resign your citizenship."

At that point, I lost my temper and told both of them to get out.

A few days later, my lawyer, Camargo, came to see me. He assured me that he had a long talk with Kessler and that the Embassy knew that it had made a mistake and wanted to make amends. He said I was wrong to distrust them.

Camargo added that he had been given all the documents concerning my trial and the trial transcript without any opposition at La Cabana. This was a favorable sign.

"Listen, John, don't get mad at the Embassy. They are going to do their best."

I wondered.

That was in August. I felt sick and fairly desperate. When I had gone to prison, I had weighed 150 pounds. Now I was down to 93.

The following month, I had a joint visitation from Camargo and Kessler. The American Consul repeated, in the presence of my lawyer, that they had made a mistake in my case. He added that they had heard from Washington that I had friends in New Jersey who were concerned about me. They were going to do their utmost to get me into a hospital.

I expressed my thanks to Consul Kessler. I assumed that they had just discovered that one of my cousins was a New Jersey judge. Whether that or some friendlier motive was the reason for their sudden solicitude didn't really matter. I felt encouraged. I believed there was a good chance that they would really try to do something for me.

As the months passed, I got a clearer picture of the way in which the Visa Section of the American Embassy protected Americans. Once when he came for a visit, Glorioso Hernández asked me to talk to the American Consul, about an American downstairs known as Bill Martin. He was an ex-captain of the Air Force in jail on a bad check charge. Martin had no blanket and was suffering from the cold snap.

Accordingly, when John Mullin and Wayne Gilchrist appeared to visit me, I asked if they could see to it that Bill Martin got a blanket.

"Blanket?" Mullin repeated. "The Embassy doesn't have money to buy blankets for prisoners. The only thing we are interested in is their welfare."

"Doesn't their welfare have something to do with whether they are able to keep warm?"

"We don't have any funds in the Embassy to buy anything for prisoners. But I tell you what we can do. I can talk to some of the wives of the staff and perhaps they will have an old blanket at home that they might be able to spare."

"Mullin, don't go to all that trouble," I said, suppressing a rage that almost made me sick at my stomach. "My fellow prisoners and I will see that Bill Martin gets his blanket."

On the other hand, there were occasions when the Embassy staff would practically fall over each other trying to minister to the whims of an American prisoner.

In the latter part of 1959, an ex-US Army Captain, Austin Young, disembarked by boat in Pinar del Rio with a group of Cuban exiles. They were captured in the mountains, accused of launching guerrilla war and sentenced to prison.

While awaiting a thirty-year term on the Isle of Pines, Captain Young and a Cuban friend managed to cut through the wall of their jail and escape. By pre-arrangement, a car was made available and Young made his way surreptitiously to Havana. Here Young stayed at the St. John's Hotel and talked to James Buchanan, a Miami Herald reporter. Later, when Young met me, he told me that he had arranged through his attorney to give his exclusive story to Buchanan and that he had planned to seek asylum in the American Embassy and thus escape his sentence to a slow death on the Island.

Before that could happen, however, Young was arrested at the hotel and Buchanan was picked up as he returned with bandages for the wounded professional soldier. Buchanan was held at the Comandancia. He admitted that he had helped Young, but denied that he was a co-conspirator. He claimed that he had merely acted as a newspaperman after a story. A powerful group of American newspaper editors and publishers came to the defense of the imprisoned correspondent. During the two weeks that Buchanan languished in a comparatively comfortable Cuban jail, Florence went to the American Embassy on two successive days to try to get them to do something for me.

She noticed that there was a great pother about whether it was the turn of Kessler or of Gilchrist to take coffee and sandwiches to Buchanan. The third time, Florence got rather irritated and asked why all this fuss about Buchanan.

"Well, he is in there," Gilchrist replied, "and he doesn't have facilities for getting coffee or sandwiches."

"How about John?" Florence interjected. "He has no facilities for getting anything."

Then, to her astonishment, Gilchrist turned to her and said rather sorrowfully: "You know, Mrs. Martino, I am in the middle of this thing." While I doubt that Wayne Gilchrist is a person whom I could ever like personally, I want to say that I believe that he, Kessler and Brown, were merely instruments of policies of appeasement. The responsibility lay with a State Department Latin American affairs clique, led by such people as Dr. Milton Eisenhower and William Arthur Wieland. It lay with an American Ambassador who was so gullible that he thought Fidel Castro a well-meaning social reformer.

On the Visa Department level, it was essential that James Buchanan be stuffed with sandwiches and coffee because he was an influential writer. Freed, Buchanan was the subject of a TV network drama, dealing with the horrors of Cuban prisons. There was nothing in that worthwhile production that might have suggested to viewers that the State Department lacked zeal in protecting Americans.

To finish with this unpleasant subject of the Embassy staff in Havana, I should like to say that Kessler impressed me as a more decent person than his associates. Just before the United States broke diplomatic relations with Communist Cuba in the last days of the Eisenhower Administration, he came to se me in prison. He said in essence: " You know when we could have helped you, we didn't know who you were or whether you were innocent or guilty. I refrained from interrupting to tell him that it had been his business to find out. This is one of the reasons nation's have embassies abroad."

After that, " Kessler continued, "when we saw that you had been telling the truth, and that you were the victim of a frame-up, our relations with Castro were going down the drain and there was just nothing we could do."

"It is easy for you to wipe the slate clean by telling me this, " I replied. " I am the one in prison. You are free."

After the rupture of diplomatic relations, the Havana Embassy staff was returned to the States via Miami. Kessler made a visit of penance to my wife. He told Florence that he had lain awake many nights, worrying about what he had done in the Martino case. He told her that he now realized that when I reached the safety of the Embassy, they should have kept me there and told Castro to go to hell.

Kessler is dead now, I no longer bear him any ill will. If he needs my forgiveness in condemning me to forty months in communist hell, I give it to him gladly.

CHAPTER 8

MEN WITHOUT FREEDOM

Among the most dangerous potential enemies of Castro Communism was a special group of elite officers of the Cuban armed services. These professional soldiers were feared because of their knowledge of command and weaponry and because of their demonstrated courage. They were deemed incorruptible because, like professional military men in other countries, they had been saturated with the concepts of patriotism and service to country.

Other prisoners had committed the crime of being rich and successful. Still others were civil servants who had been engaged in the suppression of the illicit narcotics traffic, which, as I shall show, was a zone of extreme sensitivity for Castro and his henchmen. Still others were militant enemies of Communism. And still others were in prison because they had incurred the rancor of men who were to be swept by the tides of revolution from the underworld of Havana to the seats of political power.

My good friend Colonel Abel Durañona occupied the bed next to mine in the Infirmary. A graduate of the Cuban Naval Academy and a professional officer of the finest type, he had been sent to the United States by the Cuban Government in World War II and had flown bombers from Seattle to U.S. eastern bases for the Air Transport Command. Later, as a Cuban hurricane pilot, the Colonel used to fly observation planes into the eye of storms. In 1955, he took a PBY into a raging storm and earned a medal for heroism by rescuing four people who had been downed in the ocean in another plane.

Durañona was a short, jocular, powerful man in his early forties, intellectually impressive and with great vitality. He had a great deal of faith in America as did his American wife, Olga, who used to visit him every week in prison. He was arrested on January 1, 1959, the first day of the triumph of the Castro Revolution. At that time, he was the commander of the naval air base at Mariel. However, the real reason for his arrest, Durañona believed, was that back in 1952 he had fired on a boat that was carrying contraband drugs into Cuba. The smugglers were seized, arrested, arraigned and let out on bail. At the first favorable opportunity, they jumped bail, fled to Mexico, joined up with Fidel Castro and invaded Cuba on the Gramma. Once these dope-smugglers-turned-revolutionaries felt the taste of power, they naturally turned on the man who had them arrested and buried him alive, first in El Principe, later in La Cabana.

THE TRANSISTOR RADIO

You must realize that we had nothing to do in the Infirmary. We would spend our time talking politics and waiting all week for Saturday with its possibility of visitors.

"It is an odd thing," Rafael del Pino said once. "When we wake up in the morning, nobody talks to anybody. Then we get cleaned up, and after breakfast Martino goes to the radio and tries to get Key West, and we wait for the news as a group of men, all with the same fate."

We had a broken-down radio in the Infirmary. Some days, we could get Key West. On other days, we would have to listen to Castro propaganda. Then one day, the new head of the Infirmary, Glorioso Hernández, gave a shot in the arm to our morale.

"Martino," he said, "I am going to get you a transistor radio. But you must be very careful. It comes with an earphone. You must lie in bed when you are using it. With this radio, you will get the United States in any sort of weather, without fail."

After that, all we lived for was the Key West newscasts. The first would be at eight in the morning, then at eleven, then again at six, finally at midnight. Almost every night, I would lie awake with the single earphone in my ear and I would get Mexico City, Texas, Miami, and Cincinnati. Sometimes, I would stay awake listening to the Allan Courtney Show. The next morning, when everybody woke up, I would tell them all the news. Our spirits would rise and fall with that report. At about this time, they brought into the Infirmary one of the finest men I ever met. His name was Arturo Hernández Tellaheche and he had been Minister of Labor under President Prio Socorrás. A violent anti-communist and a highly educated man, Arturo was about fifty-five, married and with two children.

One day he said to me: "John, I am in jail because Fidel Castro is an old personal enemy . . . Did you ever hear the real story of the attack on the Moncado Barracks?"

I said that I had not.

"At that time, there were two revolutionary groups—mine and Castro's. We had made an agreement that, on the day of the Moncada attack, my group would ambush Batista at Varadero Beach where he was going to officiate at a yacht regatta. The plan was that we would kill Batista at Varadero, while Castro and his men would launch a simultaneous attack in Santiago. We had everything planned and ready. We had the bazooka with which we were going to kill the dictator. We had the house and our men were there waiting at their posts with the death weapon."

But, running true to form, Fidel Castro broke the agreement. He was afraid that, if we carried out the plan, we would be the ones who would take power in Cuba since we would have killed Batista. Accordingly, Castro jumped the gun by attacking the Moncada two hours too early and his attack failed.

"To make matters worse, our plan was discovered, probably because one of Castro's men talked when he was arrested. I found myself in Cárcel de Boniato in the same cell as Fidel Castro and his brother, Raul. The only excuse Castro could think of was that he had made a mistake about the time. I did not believe him. From that moment, Castro and I became enemies.

"As soon as we learned of the fiasco at Moncada, we got rid of all incriminating evidence. Hence, the police could prove nothing against us and I and the members of my group went free.

"When Fidel Castro took power in Cuba six years later, I was out of politics. I had started working as a salesman and, since I have many friends on the island of Cuba, I was doing very well.

"However, during the Trujillo conspiracy, Castro had William Morgan go to my house, posing as my friend. Morgan offered me the Presidency of Cuba, but I replied I did not want to be involved in any more conspiracies.

"'Don't worry,' Morgan said. 'You don't have to do anything. When we take power, I shall make you President of Cuba.'

"When Fidel Castro sprung the trap at Trinidad, I and many others were arrested. Before the military tribunal, William Morgan accused me of having gone along with the Rosa Blanca conspiracy and having aspired to the Presidency of Cuba.

"For that supposed offense, I am in prison and must serve nine years."

Later, William Morgan confirmed this story of his betrayal of Arturo Hernández Tellahéche and of many others. He did this in a conversation we had only a few days before his death.

Among others brought into the Infirmary was Admiral Antonio Arias, a career naval officer of about sixty. Sentenced to twenty years on the Isle of Pines, he was slowly dying of cancer of the throat. He was finally released so that he could spend his last days at home.

There was also a labor leader named Chichi Mendoza who was in prison because, as a strong anti-communist, he had tried to escape to the United States. Arrangements were made by the underground to have the unfortunate American aviator, Matthew Duke, fly him out of Cuba surreptitiously. One night, Mendoza got a telephone call, telling him to go to a certain point on the highway and wait for a plane. He hid in a ditch beside the road.

The plane came to a landing about fifty yards from where Mendoza was lying and the pilot, Matt Duke, walked out of the cockpit. As he did so, the trap was sprung. As the cordon of police closed in, one of the police officers hit Duke in the mouth, knocking him down. While he lay on the ground, they shot him to death. Then, the Chief of Police emptied his sub-machine gun into the plane so that it would look as if Duke had been killed in a bona fide firefight.

In the confusion, Chichi Mendoza tried to get away, but he was shot down. He was sent to La Cabana and then transferred to the Infirmary at El Principe to have the bullets removed. However, while he was with us he was given no medical care, despite the fact that the slug in his neck was so painful that he found it almost impossible to eat. Finally, rather than have him wither away because of medical neglect, Rafael del Pino held him down while Colonel Abel Durañona and I removed the bullets from his neck and arm with a penknife. After this successful "operation," Chichi Mendoza was shipped out to the Isle of Pines to serve the rest of his sentence.

This was the time when Fidel Castro went to New York for the United Nations meeting to insult the United States. My fellow prisoners, who were strongly pro-American, could not understand why we tolerated him on U.S. soil or, for that matter, why we didn't send the Marines in to liberate Cuba.

In our cell, we had a statue of the Holy Virgin. It must have taken Ramolin two weeks to remove the statue and painstakingly carve out a hollow in its pedestal big enough for the transistor radio. Then he had to reinsert the bottom of the statue and seal it in place with wax. Every night when I was ready for sleep, we would put the radio in the figure of the Virgin and replace the bottom piece.

Kammerer heard, probably from a stool pigeon, that we had a good radio set. When he came to our cell, he saw our broken-down radio and had it taken downstairs for his technicians to examine. They reported that it had no short wave control button and not enough power to reach the States. He was perplexed, but still suspicious.

There were numerous requisas. Yet no guard ever removed the statue of the Virgin and examined it to see whether it was hollow or solid. At that time, the guards were sufficiently religious so that the idea of using the religious statue as a hiding place would not have occurred to them.

Nevertheless, at night I took precautions. I would have the radio under my pillow with the earphone close to my ear, while Adolfo Ferrer, a man with one leg, stood guard. Whenever anyone approached the outer gates of the Infirmary, there would be a scramble to return the radio set to its hiding place. Luckily, during our entire stay in Principe, nobody managed to find the radio and, when we finally left the Castle, we were able to return it to Glorioso Hernández.

DEATH AND A RUPTURED APPENDIX

My lawyer came to see me and told me he was having trouble with my case. The fiscal (or prosecutor) of the Supreme Court was challenging his right to appeal on grounds of unconstitutional actions by the military tribunal. He said he would fight it out and assured me there would be a hearing the next week.

"If the Supreme Court agrees to hear your case, you are as good as free."

I asked him what Washington was doing meanwhile.

He replied that Florence had been in Havana the previous week. She had talked to Senator George Smathers and Representative Dante Fascell of Miami, also to many people in the State Department. She felt she was getting the same runaround. They all told her to wait, that the situation was ticklish and that United States relations with Castro were deteriorating. They said, however, they would do their best to get me into a hospital.

After this and other talks with my lawyer, I would return to the Infirmary where my fellow prisoners would eagerly ply me with dozens of questions. I played a special role in the Infirmary and later in other prison cells, for I represented the United States to them and that was a symbol, in their minds, of an invincible defender of democracy everywhere in the world, of armed and all-powerful justice. Not only because they were my friends, but also because I was "the American," prisoners who did not have enough for themselves would offer me food; they would smuggle in medicine for me, and take care of me in dozens of different ways. I can honestly say that I owe my life to the care and solicitude of my Cuban fellow prisoners.

Manuel Leon, a former rural guard in his late thirties, was brought in from Galera 20 very sick with a serious heart condition. He had been imprisoned because he had a personal quarrel with some of the 26th of July people.

Leon was the first person to tell me about the massacre of seventy prisoners by Raul Castro on January 3, 1959—the third day of the triumph of the Revolution. This occurred on San Juan Hill, made famous by Theodore Roosevelt and his Rough Riders, near Santiago de Cuba. The persons assassinated without any semblance of trial included a dozen newspaper editors and reporters, also Juan Gutiérrez Garcia, who had won fame by organizing a march of the peasants to win agrarian reform in Oriente Province, and a thirteen-year-old boy.

He told me how they took these people—both military men and civilians—from the Casa Boñato prison and lined them up while a bulldozer dug a long trench behind them. After that, Ra6l Castro personally, aided by a squad of twelve men, shot them down with Tommy guns and, as they toppled into the ditch, the bulldozer covered them with soil.

Leon wanted the truth about this and other atrocities passed by word of mouth, so that some day all Cubans would know about it.

Orlando Ortega took me aside and told me he thought Leon was going to die. We collected money and bought the medicines Leon needed and then began treating him, but it was too late. One day, he showed me the photograph of his little daughter in her first communion dress. I could see how devoted to her he was.

"She is very pretty, Leon," I said. "Soon you will see her."

"No, I know that I am going to die. I will never see my little girl again. But there is one thing I am happy about."

"What is that?"

"John Kennedy, the new President of the United States. I know he will come. I know he will send American soldiers here and they will set Cuba free."

The next morning around seven-thirty, he called Colonel Durañona and me to his bed and asked for a glass of water. Then he asked the Colonel to hold his head up.

"Will somebody open the window? I want to see the sun."

They opened the shutters of the window and, as I held the glass of water to his lips, he died.

Manuel Leon was a victim of total medical neglect by the authorities. He had been sent to the Isle of Pines, then returned to Havana for medical treatment and left for six weeks in Galera 20 where he got no attention at all. It was only because Orlando Ortega put massive pressure on Kammerer—I never knew what his hold on the latter was—that Manuel was sent to the Infirmary. But by then it was too late.

Another man who was brought into the Infirmary had fought against Castro in the mountains. He would tell me stories about how Castro bought off the Batista officers and how these men were ready to sell their troops, their weapons and their equipment. He also touched on Castro's use of marihuana and cocaine to corrupt and undermine the Batista army. I was to learn much more about this later on from a far better informed source.

Around this time, my lawyer returned with Kessler and with the splendid news that the Supreme Court had decided to consider my case.

"I happen to know that the Supreme Court is composed of some very fine gentlemen," Kessler informed me. "I have talked to the President of the Supreme Court and I believe your case will get a fair hearing."

When I returned to the Infirmary with this news, there was jubilation and my friend, Adolfo Ferrer, even started to cry.

Shortly after that, they brought Oscar de Tuya into the Infirmary, a man of seventy-two, who had owned a tremendous air freight business that moved cargo from all parts of Latin America and the United States. Before his heart trouble, he had been a robust man, but now he was able to do little more than lie in his bed and cry.

He told me that he had contributed half a million dollars to the Castro Revolution. He had assumed that, since Batista had taken power by coup d'etat, it was his duty to uphold democracy by plotting against him. When he saw Castro destroy the free press of Cuba, he realized that he had supported the wrong man and he began to work against him.

"You knew all the tricks," I said. "You told me yourself that you conspired against Batista for four years without being suspected. And you knew Fidel Castro and his methods. How did you get caught under those circumstances?"

He began by telling me what I already knew, how Castro had taken over Batista's army of chivatos, the stool pigeons or 33-

33's, as they were called, and placed two or three families of these professional spies in each block.

"The system is very efficient," he said. "Every time a car or a stranger comes to any house anywhere in Havana, the so- called Defense Committee, led by chivatos, knows about it. If it is a car, they take down the license number. If it is a stranger, they learn his identity . . . The names of strangers who come to call or people who come to houses late at night, of meetings of any sort—all this is reported to the G-2. The visitors and their hosts are followed. The net is narrowed and then the arrests are made. This is the system that Comandante Ramiro Valdés was taught in Russia. It is being installed in Havana and spread all over the island."

They brought in a former sergeant in a tank battalion, Felipe Ramirez, about whom I shall have much to say later on for he became my good friend and saved my life. He was a little bit over five feet tall, but weighed around 200 pounds and was normally a man of great physical strength. He had two beautiful children, Julieta and Felipe, who visited him regularly in prison.

This man was an appendicitis case. He had not been hospitalized until the appendix actually broke. He lay in the Calixto Garcia Hospital and fought desperately for his life. Thanks to God, he won and was returned to the Infirmary and later moved with me to La Cabana.

WE MOVE TO LA CABANA

Around this time—it was the winter of 1960-61— President Eisenhower broke diplomatic relations with Cuba. The next clay, January 2, 1961, there was the first big invasion scare. Gun emplacements were installed all over the Castle; we could see anti-aircraft guns on the tops of buildings, and we had a report from Galera 20 that they were installing cannon on the Malecón.

At nine-thirty on the morning of January 3, Fidel Castro inspected the Catillo del Principe personally and ordered that it be evacuated. The guards came upstairs and gave us American Army uniforms with a large "P" on the back, which we were to wear. I suppose that these uniforms had been given to the Batista government as part of our military aid program and were worn by his stockade prisoners.

The scuttlebutt was that we were to be shipped to the Isle of Pines. This was a terrible blow for me as my appeal was coming up and there seemed to be an excellent chance that I might be released. Hardly anybody ever gets back from the Isle of Pines.

The guard tried to reassure us with the story that there was a hospital on the Isle of Pines, but I knew this was not the case. Glorioso came to my cell door and I saw that he was crying. He told me that, if I were sent to the Island, I would have a very bad time. He was being transferred to the prison at Matanzas. He asked me to write him, as soon as I reached my destination, as he had friends among the common prisoners on the Island and he would get word to them to try to see that we had decent treatment.

I promised. I thanked him and slipped the transistor radio into his hand. Then we got our personal belongings together and went downstairs—I was carried on a stretcher —and waited to learn our fate.

The men were coming out of Galera 20. They were tied together by a long rope, which bound the wrists of each man and then passed to the man behind and tied his wrists. They moved forward in single file. We sick people were waiting in a special room where we could see everything that was happening. The prisoners were being loaded on buses, forty at a time; then, when they were full, the buses moved out into the hot dust of the day.

A guard approached with a rifle with fixed bayonet in his hands.

"I ought to run this through your guts," he said. "The Americans are going to invade and I guarantee you will be one of the first to die."

Orlando Ortega approached, carrying a tray.

"Why don't you leave this man alone?" He told the guard. "This is a poor, sick fellow. Can't you see that he isn't even able to walk?"

The guard walked away. Orlando stooped and gave me an injection: "This will keep you until you go to where you are going."

"Orlando, what do I do about my medicine and my treatment on the Island?"

"Don't worry. You aren't going to the Isle of Pines. I just got the word from Kammerer. But don't tell anyone except Colonel Durañona. They are taking you and some of the other sick people to La Cabana Fortress. Somehow, I will get medicine to you there tonight and I will tell your lawyer where you are."

This was an immense relief.

"You will be all right in La Cabana because I have friends there."

They carried my stretcher into a bus and we began the half hour ride to where I was to live through some of the most horrible days of my life.

CHAPTER 9
THE COCAINE REVOLUTION

As the buses left the prison and turned into the street, we saw a large crowd of women and children, who waved handkerchiefs, screamed and cried as we passed. They were the families of the political prisoners in Calera 20 and they had been notified of our move to new places of confinement by that mysterious and incredibly swift means of communication—the grapevine.

We proceeded down the Malecón where we could see tanks, gun emplacements, and the militia feverishly tearing up the streets and digging trenches. There were very few civilians to be seen. Then we passed through the tunnel and came to the entrance to the Fortress where the guards were expecting us. The seven buses, having driven through Havana at breakneck speed, stopped at the gate, because the road ahead up to La Cabana was too narrow. Now the 240 political prisoners from Calera 20 dismounted and marched, flanked by about a hundred guards armed with sub-machine guns, up the narrow, winding road that leads to the prison compound. We waited in our bus. Soon a lolita, or small station wagon, came down from the prison and took the fourteen of us who were sick to our new place of confinement.

LA CABANA FORTRESS

To get into La Cabana, one must go over a drawbridge that straddles a dry moat. Beyond is the forbidding, moss- covered stone mass of the Castle, its turrets ringed with guards and its tremendous gates also protected by armed men. We passed inside, then through another, more modern steel gate and through the office, where we were registered, processed and checked off against a list.

The Fortress overlooks Havana and, in the old days, it was said that whoever controls La Cabana dominates the city. This was true because the Fortress stands high on a hill, where its gun emplacements can traverse the harbor entrance, the bay, the city itself and, in particular, the Presidential Palace. As one passes through the gates, the first cell to the right is Galera 22 for the military prisoners of Fidel Castro. These are officers and soldiers held for infractions of military law and generally serving from six months to three years.

Behind this galera are the capillas (little chapels), small cells used for punishment and to house the prisoners awaiting execution. In other words, when our fellow prisoners were brought before the military tribunals, we would, as a rule, never be able to speak to them again. A handful would be acquitted. Those who passed into Galera 22 would be doomed to execution. It would mean that they were being put into capillas immediately after trial and that night they would almost certainly be put to death. To get into the capillas, one must pass through Galera 22. As I would soon learn, many horrible things happen in this galera.

Beyond the galera for military prisoners is the office which is headquarters for the officer of the day, who directs the guards, opens and closes the cells, issues orders over the public address system and generally runs the prison. It is in this office that prisoners and, for that matter, sometimes suspects picked up on the streets are interrogated.

The staff in this office consisted of four political prisoners who would all play significant roles in my story. An ex-Air Force helicopter pilot who had been trained in the United States, named Juan Más Machado, was in charge of records. He had fought the Rebels in the mountains and had been in prison since January 1, 1959.

Jorge Rosell, a lawyer, serving ten years for allegedly conspiring against Fidel Castro, took care of the mail. The commissary was in the hands of Juan Alegria, a former captain in the Cuban police force. In 1954, Alegria had arrested a common thief. In time, this man joined the revolutionary forces in the Sierra Maestra and, when the Revolution took power, he accused Alegria of having framed him. The ex-captain was serving five years in consequence. The fourth prisoner-clerk, Clemente Hernández, ran the storeroom.

Eleven galeras, numbers 7 through 17, are entered from the patio. They are all underground—dark, dank and with a musty smell. One goes down a flight of stairs to get into them. They have no windows. The only source of ventilation is an aperture at the back of each galera, which is barred. Some four feet from this aperture, there is a twelve-foot-high railing, which prevents the prisoners from approaching the source of ventilation. Standing in the patio, one can look up to the roof and see four .30 caliber machine guns, one over each corner of the courtyard. Ten armed guards pace the roof and scan the skies and the land approaches to the Fortress with binoculars.

There is no access to the roof from inside the prison compounds. The galeras are 120 feet long. Each had fifty beds with the exception of Galera 14, which had only seventeen beds. This galera, the one to which I was assigned, housed seventeen men, of whom twelve had been under sentence of death for many months and were subject to execution at any moment. While our galera left much to be desired, it was much lighter, cleaner and better equipped than the others. Under previous Cuban governments, it had been reserved for officers who had been sentenced by courts martial and thus it had better light fixtures and even a faucet on the wall with the legend "ice water." Of course, the faucet did not work and there was no ice water, but then one cannot have everything.

MEN WAITING FOR DEATH

Of the twelve under sentence of death, four had belonged to the narcotics squad under the Batista government. Of these men, the most important was Orlando Jáuriga, who had been head of the Cuban narcotics squad for fifteen years and was an expert in tracking illicit drugs. He is colored, around fifty years old and stands well over six feet. He has worked closely with the narcotics bureau of the U. S. Secret Service and has the arrest of a large number of dope pushers to his credit.

With him and also under sentence of death was Cipriano Mauri, a Navy man who had switched to the drug detail, highly educated, famous for his memory of faces and, incidentally, the chess champion of La Cabana Fortress. The third member of the narcotics squad scheduled to die was Mariolito Hernández, an undercover agent of the narcotics bureau who was feared by all peddlers.

Like Cipriano Mauri, Manolito is a white man. To keep his wife and three children from starving, he ran a little stand in the galera with odds and ends for the prisoners to buy. The last of the four men of the narcotics squad was Santiago Linares, a highly respected Negro, who had been a policeman for twenty-five years and had eleven grandchildren to worry about. This meant that practically the entire narcotics squad was incommunicado and under sentence of death. I was bewildered to hear this and asked the reason.

NARCOTICS TRAFFIC

Orlando Jáuriga told me that he and his associates had tried to arrest one of the top figures in the illegal narcotics traffic in Cuba, but their prey had opened fire and, in the course of a running gunfight, had met death. The dead dope pusher had a brother who was a big wheel in the 26th of July Movement. On the day Castro took power, January 1, 1959, the brother charged Jáuriga and his associates with murder. They were tried by a revolutionary tribunal, convicted and sentenced to death.

This was no doubt the pretext for the arrests and I am sure Orlando Jáuriga was sincere in believing it to be the real cause. But, in my opinion, the fundamental reason for silencing these men was to suppress the close connection between the 26th of July Movement and the use of and illicit traffic in drugs. The elimination of efficient and honest narcotics agents would help the Castro Communists later on when they tried to use the illicit export of drugs to both stupefy Free World populations and increase their take in dollars and other hard currencies.

As long as Castro and his henchmen were able to suppress the cocaine aspects of their Revolution, continued deception of world opinion by unscrupulous or gullible journalists would be possible. Men of the stamp of Herbert L. Matthews of the New York Times, whose articles had so skillfully covered the brutal face of totalitarian despotism in Cuba with a fake veneer of idealism and popular aspirations, would continue to command some degree of public respect and attention. As late in the game as 1961, Matthews could write in his "The Cuba Story": "In its idealism—and there has been and still is genuine idealism behind it—the Cuban Revolution is an expression of the aspirations and the needs of the masses of the people in Latin America." To leave Mr. Matthews and return to the narcotics traffic in Cuba, the underlying fact in the Cuban situation, with which everybody who really knows the country is familiar, is that the use of marihuana and cocaine are widespread.

To an almost incredible degree, these drugs are habitually used by the masses and, in particular, by the Negro masses. However, it is not confined to them. Thus, the Italian gangster, Lucky Luciano, who had been deported from the United States, was invited to Cuba about a decade ago by people close to President Carlos Prio Socarrás.

The plan was to transform Cuba into the center for all illicit narcotics smuggling in Central America and the Caribbean. Under President Prio, Cuba was wide open as far as marihuana and cocaine were concerned and there was an influential clique of users and dealers surrounding the President. One of these men, known as "Aguacate," procured dope, not only for the ruling clique of Cuba, but also for a wild film star with an international reputation, who recently died in the arms of his underage mistress. Cuba is, as far as I know, the only civilized country that has recently had as its Chief Executive a known cocaine user.

Fidel Castro, when he was being palmed off on a gullible world as the Robin Hood of the Sierra Maestra, worked closely with Prio Socarrás and his little gang of cocaine users and pushers. As I have shown, his movement had among its "immortals" petty criminals and marihuaneros such as Efigenio Almeijeiras. The man who prepared the hideouts and mountain trails for the invaders on the Gramma was a certain Crecencio Perez.

To Jules Dubois in his eulogistic biography, Fidel Castro, this Perez "was a man respected and beloved by the farmers of the Sierra Maestra." Actually, Crecencio Perez was a smuggler of contraband goods, including narcotics. The Sierra Maestra was a refuge for men wanted by the Cuban law and a base of operations for the smuggling of cocaine and heroin.

A disillusioned lieutenant of Fidel Castro, whom I knew in prison, had very interesting reminiscences about the guerrilla forces in the Sierra Maestra. To protect him, I am suppressing his name and telling this story out of chronological sequence.

"You know most of Batista's soldiers were what they called in those days casquitos," he said. "They were almost all colored boys, aged around eighteen to twenty-four. You know a lot of the Negroes in Cuba and, for that matter, a lot of the rest of us, we have one vice."

He gave me a crooked smile. "We like to smoke marihuana and many of us use cocaine. You know coke is very different from H. The heroin and opium are fine for Anglo-Saxons and Chinese. They give you dreams. But that is not for Latins. Cocaine builds up sensitivity. It is an irritant. It is, ...what do you call it?"

"An aphrodisiac?" I suggested.

"Yes, a sex potion. It means you want it more and you can do it better.

"To get back to Fidel and the rest of us, you know that Almeijeiras was a marihuariero."

I nodded.

"He was always weeded up and so was Fidel. I have personally seen Fidel weeded up so high he didn't know where he was. We all smoked. There wasn't anything else to do. We were up there in the mountains, isolated. We would keep puffing away on the marihuana until we got blind. We had women up there too . . ."

I asked him how marihuana and cocaine played a part in their operations.

"Martino, it was easy to get the stuff. We had connections in Mexico for the cocaine and in Oriente, where in certain parts, the marihuana grows wild.

"We did what many others have done. The Chinese Reds used the same tactics. We would see that the Batista men, the ones who were users, got plenty of marihuana and cocaine. It was one crooked deal after another. I was part and parcel of it. I did it to get what I wanted and, if they had cut me in with the top group, I would have been satisfied and I wouldn't be here. As a human being, maybe I am no great bargain."

"Let's get back to the marihuana," I said.

"There was one trick we used over and over again. Maybe you Americans have used it too. We would approach a little village. Through our spies, we would know the ones who were against us. If there weren't any, ordinary peasants would do. We would go to their farmhouses and kill them. Then we would drag in the bodies of Batista soldiers, men whom we had first stupefied with marihuana and cocaine and then killed. We would leave the corpses of the soldiers and peasants together and then we would come in like avenging angels.

"That would be enough to make the other peasants believe that the Batistianos were the killers and the sadists, the people who were slaughtering old women. And we would seem to be the heroes.

"Fidel at that time had American newspapermen with him. I don't know if these people really knew what was going on. Somehow, I doubt it, because Fidel is a genius at deceit. Anyhow, our atrocities would be photographed and they would appear in the U.S. press as cold proof that Fidel was the hero and Batista the son of a bitch."

"Did everybody know of these things?"

"Of course not. We had lots of idealistic kids who came up into the mountains to join us. Do you think they would stand for that sort of thing? Why, this was what they thought they were fighting against. It's the old story. The majority is fighting and dying without knowing what it is all about; the clever ones know the score and try to stay out of danger. We had many fine, idealistic boys up there. And we also had a lot of thieves and criminals, men marked by the police. You would probably call them the scum of the earth."

So much for that particular anonymous witness.

I learned later that, in the early days of his regime, Castro was controlling narcotics honestly and the Cuban authorities were working in cooperation with Interpol and the U. S. Secret Service. Then Castro developed closer relations with Communist China and, at the same time, his shortage of dollars and other foreign exchange became more desperate.

Huge shipments of opium, heroin, morphine and cocaine were sent into Cuba by the Red Chinese regime. These were many times in excess of Cuban total consumption, both legal and illegal. As noted, the Cubans are cocaine users, but avoid opium, morphine and heroin. Moreover, they believe that cocaine, unlike opium, morphine and heroin, does not cause physical addiction. In other words, a man may have a psychological need for cocaine, if he is already a user, much as a man may need tobacco or alcohol. But he is not physically a slave to the habit, as in the case of heroin. Whether this distinction is real or not is beside the point. It is believed to be real by almost all Cubans, including the experts in the former narcotics control bureau.

These narcotics stockpiles are, I believe, being accumulated as part of a diabolical plan to poison, debauch and stultify the people of the free Latin American Republics and of the United States. Just as drugs were used to demoralize the Batista Army, they are designed to serve as a weapon for the demoralization of the Free World. The fact that hundreds of Communist students come to Cuba from Latin America, Europe, Asia and the United States gives Castro a made-to-order mechanism for narcotics smuggling. The fact that this is occurring on a dangerous scale is indicated by the increase in the arrests of dope smugglers from Communist Cuba by U.S. authorities.

I learned that thousands of acres of fertile Cuban crop land are being devoted to opium cultivation under the supervision of Red Chinese experts. At present, Castro is smuggling Chinese opium and heroin into Mexico, whence it is beng flooded illegally into the United States. American gangsters cooperate with the Cuban Communist in this operation. In 1962, it is estimated that Red China reaped $200 million in foreign exchange from world-wide heroin smuggling.

By the end of 1963, the first Cuban poppy crop will be harvested and processed in a heroin pant which is big built by Red Chinese specialist. The extent and geographical diversification of the Cuban poppy plantings suggest that Operation Heroin is a major element in Castro's over-all planning.

The atmosphere of La Babana seemed entirely different from that of El Principe. Here we are allowed to walk in the sunlight of the patio. Our visitors were not harassed and humiliated. There was no evidence of sadism or malicious imposition of hardship. Here we were not subjected to mental torture whenever possible, and cooped up like animals.

I made the comment to Dario Valdes.

"Don't let it fool you," he replied. " This seems like a drastic change from where you have been, but this prison is deadly. Here is where they shoot people. You don't know how many stool pigeons and informers there are here. Don't talk politics and, when people come from other galeras to talk to you, just pretend that you don't understand Spanish. If I know they are all right, I will give you a sign."

CHAPTER 10
THE AMERICAN PRISONERS

In those days, La Cabana was run by Manolito Fernández, an old comrade of Fidel Castro, but nevertheless a decent human being. The food was tolerable; the policy toward visitors was liberal, and conditions were better than they would ever be again.

A typical day would start with a loud-speaker announcement at six-thirty, after which we would file into the patio, while a detail of three men, one carrying an iron bar, searched the galeras. The man with the bar would tap the steel railings in the rear of the galeras to see whether the prisoners had tried to saw through it. This procedure would be repeated two or three times each day.

Breakfast was at eight, lunch at ten-thirty and supper four hours later. Guards and prisoners enjoyed a siesta between one and three every afternoon. We were free to stroll in the patio and visit the other galeras until nine. At ten, lights went out. Guards prowled the patio and the rest of the prison compound, armed with sub-machine guns and alert for unauthorized movements, while we slept or tried to sleep.

La Cabana had less than 700 inmates at the time and there was plenty of space to move around in. We in Galera 14 had a good deal of privacy. The other prisoners hesitated about visiting our cell, partly because of respect for the privacy of the twelve men under sentence of death and partly because we were considered an elite group.

Manolito Fernández permitted our lawyers to visit us every day. Moreover, these talks were private and could last as long as half an hour.

There were five other Americans in La Cabana when I arrived there. I soon struck up a friendship with Johnny Gentile, a small-arms expert who had been in trouble with the police in the States. He had come to Cuba, married a Cuban girl and become involved with the counterrevolution when the militia killed his brother-in-law. Johnny was an Ohio boy in his early twenties, tall and always smiling. He had fallen into water way over his head and was drowning. I felt sorry for him.

Our medical attention was provided by a shifty-eyed, grey-haired mulatto of about forty, called René Dubuté. This man turned out to be a vicious human being and a blackmailer. He was a prisoner himself and was serving four years for having allegedly signed fraudulent death certificates for Rebels who were victims of the Cuban National Police. In La Cabana, Dubuté fawned on the guards and was generally believed by the other prisoners to be a dangerous informer.

After I had been in La Cabana for a few days, Dr. Dubuté visited me in my galera.

"American, I have your case file here. Did you get your injections last night?"

I said that I had and thanked him.

"You know I am the doctor here?"

"I thought the captain was the doctor," I replied.

"The captain has been working in the office all morning. He is much too busy to come to the galeras. Moreover, I take care of the sick prisoners here . . . Do you have money?"

"Why do you want to know that?"

"It costs money to stay here. Only the sick people can stay here, those I certify as sick. I have lots of expenses. Those that help me with my expenses stay here; and the ones that don't help are sent to the Isle of Pines. Well, what do you say?"

"When my lawyer comes to the prison tomorrow," I told him, "I will have him deposit money in the office for me. How much do you want?"

"I like to play cards and gamble . . . For a start, you could plan to lose, say, $10 a week."

"That's pretty high, isn't it, Dubuté?"

"It is up to you. You can always go to the Island."

I told him he would have to wait until my attorney came. After that, we could discuss it further. He patted me on the shoulder: "I think we are going to get along fine," he said.

When the doctor had gone, Dario Valdés approached me and asked me what Dubuté had wanted. I decided that the fewer people who knew I was going to pay blackmail, the better off I would be. I said it was nothing, just a discussion.

THE THREE AMERICANS

There were three young Americans in La Cabana. They had been tried the week before I arrived in the prison and were now awaiting word of their fate. I first met the oldest of them, Daniel Carswell, an electrical engineer from Eastchester, New York, on the day I entered La Cabana. He was naturally distrustful and refused to discuss his case except to say that he was surprised that the fourth American involved, a dance instructor named Mario Nordio, was not in the prison.

A few days later, the other two boys in the case came into my galera to talk briefly. The youngest, Edmund Taransky, a New York electronics technician, was a short, frail blond man in his early twenties, who was obviously worried and the sort of person who did not belong in international intrigue. The last of them, Eustace Danbrunt, was a husky, heavy-set, chain-smoking veteran of the Korean War. At the time he was picked up, he had been studying to become an electrical engineer.

After a few minutes of cautious exploratory questions, the two boys, with their confederate, Daniel Carswell, left the galera. When they had gone, Brigadier General Sanchez Gómez came over to my bunk to ask me what I thought of them. I replied that I didn't know.

"We have means of getting news here," the General said. "The grapevine tells us that the three boys have been convicted and sentenced to ten years each on the Isle of Pines. And the other boy, Mario Nordio, has been given a suspended sentence and deported to the United States. You can draw your own inferences about Nordio

The story we have is all mixed up, in fact, rather incredible. Perhaps, since you are an American, the three boys will tell you the truth."

"They don't trust me," I replied.

"They ought to, Martino. You and they have the same lawyer."

The next day around ten o'clock, I was called on the loudspeaker. My friends helped me to the office. There was my friend and lawyer, Dr. Camargo.

"I have very good news for you. The Supreme Court will hear your case on the 16th of this month. After talking to a large number of lawyers about the case, I am convinced you will go free."

"I am told the new Supreme Court takes orders from Fidel Castro," I replied.

"This is a clear matter of constitutionality . . . By the way, did you meet the three Americans? And have you heard any news about their case?"

"You mean you are their lawyer and you haven't been told?" Camargo shook his head. "They have been convicted and are getting ten years apiece. The other one, Nordio, has been set free. That is as sure as death."

This information, together with the fact that it had been withheld from him, disturbed Dr. Camargo a great deal. We agreed that I would say nothing to the boys about their fate. He told me that he had got a new medical expediente—number 302—for me and that he would buy me a month's supply of medicine in the morning. I was not to forget the number of the expediente under any circumstances. I arranged with him to have money made available to me in the prison, but, of course, did not tell him that I needed it to pay off a medical extortionist.

That evening, Carswell came to my galera and invited me to have dinner with Danbrunt, Taransky and himself in their galera that night. He apologized for having distrusted me and said that Dr. Camargo had straightened him out.

"We have steaks, tomatoes and lettuce and we also have tea," Carswell told me.

"You do?"

"Oh yes. We have been getting food from the outside. The Embassy sends it to us."

"That is very nice."

"Doesn't the Embassy take care of you?" I shook my head. "I thought the Embassy took care of all the Americans."

"Well, now you know different," I replied.

There was another American prisoner in La Cabana, a man of much more importance than any of the others. His name was William Morgan and he had been one of Castro's chief lieutenants in the period of the guerrilla war. He was an adventurer and an expert in betrayal.

Oscar de Tuya, the old gentleman who had owned the huge airfreight business, was a close friend of William Morgan and kept urging me to meet him and consider him a fellow American in trouble.

"Oscar," I said, "I don't want to know William Morgan. I heard him boast on television that, if the Marines came to Cuba, he would wait for them with his men on the Malecón and kill as many of them as he could. He was mixed up in the Trujillo conspiracy. As far as I am concerned, he can't be trusted and, in addition, I consider him a traitor to the United States."

However, this was not the end of the matter. After an excellent dinner with the three Americans, I returned to my galera and was immediately buttonholed by Ra6l, the police officer under Prio, the man known in the prison as "little forty-five."

Raul, it appeared, was also a friend of William Morgan. I was doing a fellow American an injustice in refusing to meet him. Moreover, he was waiting right out in the patio to talk to me and he was a friend of mine, even though I didn't know it.

When I said that I still didn't want to meet Morgan, Rail disappeared, obviously for a conference with his friend, and reappeared in about half an hour. He had an involved message from Morgan. William Morgan had given Raul details of a business conference I had in Atlantic City in 1947. These details had been known only to me and to a New Jersey business associate. This New Jersey friend had gone to Cuba to try to get me released from prison and had approached Morgan, who was then a big wheel in the Castro Revolution. He had told Morgan about the 1947 incident so that Morgan could prove to me, if the occasion should arise, that he came to me from my friend. After hearing this, I agreed to meet him. Since it was getting late, Rail said he would arrange it for the next day.

That night, they called up the case of Dr. Julio Yebra, Ronald Condon Gil, Cesar Fuentes and two other boys in the case, whose names I don't remember. These men were accused of having plotted to assassinate Fidel Castro. When they were arrested, arms and an electronic device capable of exploding a bomb by remote control had been found. Dr. Julio Yebra considered that the death sentence was inevitable and promised that he would defy the court and the dictatorship when he came up for trial.

In the office, the five prisoners were given the indictment to read. When they returned to the galeras, we learned that they would be tried for a crime that carried the death penalty. We felt very sad about it.

Julio Yebra was an attractive young man in his middle twenties who spoke fluent English, German and French. He had been a revolutionary, an activist in the 26th of July Movement and an ardent believer in Fidel Castro. It was Yebra who had engineered the spectacular escape of Dr. Armando Hart, a Communist who later became Castro's Minister of Education, from the Palace of Justice.

After this exploit, Julio Yebra had to flee to Spain, where he was living quietly as a university student when Castro took power. It was while he was in Spain that he began to realize gradually what was really happening in Cuba. He decided it was his duty to return to his homeland and exterminate the man who was betraying it.

That night, Yebra told me that his trial was set for the same day as my hearing before the Supreme Court—the 21st of January. He told me that a lawyer would be useless in his case and that he intended to use the court as a forum from which he would speak the truth.

The next day, Raul came into my galera, bringing William Morgan with him. The soldier of fortune was an exceptionally powerful man of medium height whose handshake almost crushed my bones. He was blond with deep blue eyes. He sat on my bed.

"I have no hard feelings toward you, John Martino."

"Oscar de Tuya had no business reporting to you what I said about you," I told him.

"I don't blame you," Morgan replied. "You know who I am and you know my record. If you kept on refusing to talk to me, I would understand it. However, the other Americans talk to me and I have felt bad over the past two or three days that there is an American here who had that feeling against me.

I suggested that he get to the point.

"Look, fellow, I tried to help you. I did everything I could. And I didn't do it for money. I did it for this friend of yours, who is also a friend of mine."

He claimed that he had gone to see Raul Castro about me and that he had been told not to bring up my name again. He said he had waited five days and then made an approach to Camilo Cienfuegos, one of the chief heroes of the 26th of July Movement and a man who was on the outs with the Communists. When Cienfuegos told him to stay away from the Martino case, he had told my friend to forget about me, as the situation was hopeless for the time being.

"You mean to tell me you really don't know why you are in jail?" Morgan asked me. I shook my head.

"Some day I may tell you. Not now. There is a chance I may go free. Not a very good chance, but there is a slim hope. If I get out of here alive, I will be a real lucky man. But I think they are going to have to shoot me. Anyhow, as long as there is a chance, I am not going to tell stories and get into deeper trouble."

Time passed. A few days later, Dan Carswell was back in my galera. This time, he wanted to talk about their case. He asked me what I knew about it and I replied only what I had read in the Cuban press and heard Raul Castro say on the radio.

"That part is true," Carswell said. "They actually caught Danbrunt, Taransky, Mario Nordio and me in an apartment just above the Chinese News Agency."

"What were you doing there?"

"It is a long story. A member of the American Embassy had come to the States. He invited Danbrunt and me to do a little job for him."

"Oh, are you used to doing that sort of job?" I asked. He didn't answer.

"Where does Taransky fit into the picture?"

"When we were on the way down to Cuba, we ran into Taransky at the Miami Airport. I knew him from around Boston. He was going to Cuba anyhow and we invited him to come along with us, pointing out that all of our expenses were paid and that, after the little job for the American Embassy, we would have four or five days to enjoy ourselves."

"That is a very strange story," I said.

"Well, that is how it happened. When we came to Havana, we were supplied with the equipment."

He explained that they went into Nordio's apartment on the floor above the Red Chinese news agency. When the Cuban G-2 broke in, they were caught with two tape recorders, an electric drill and about sixty feet of cable with a microphone.

"What were you going to do with all that, Dan?"

"We had drilled through the floor, which is the ceiling of the Chinese agency, and we were about to lower the microphone into the next room so we could put everything that was said there on tape."

I was dumbfounded.

"You are supposed to be an electrical engineer and an electronics expert," I said. "How could you and the other men get caught in that room with that Rube Goldberg equipment?"

"What do you mean?"

"You acted like a completely ignorant amateur. Haven't you ever heard of a wireless microphone?"

He apparently knew nothing about modern equipment. I explained to him that, if I had the job to do, I would have installed a wireless microphone in the Red Chinese news agency. Then from a distance of perhaps two or three buildings away in another office or another apartment, I would have installed an automatic tape recorder.

This would not need anyone to tend it. So that, even if the police found the microphone and traced the tape recorder, they would have the equipment, but they would have no one to arrest.

"I never thought of that," Carswell said.

"Well, you can't be much of an electronics engineer," I said. "Either you are liars or you are playing some sort of a double game."

After hearing Carswell's story, I felt sure in my heart that these three boys could not have been CIA agents. They might possibly have been tricked into believing that they were working for the CIA, whereas in reality the plan was to see that they got caught, so that Castro could exploit the scandal to the discredit of the United States. The CIA under Allen Dulles had certainly acquired an unenviable reputation for stupidity and incompetence. Yet, it seemed incredible that any intelligence agency of any modem government could use such crude, bungling methods and such obsolete equipment.

My final question was why they had planned the operation in a way that risked four men, when it was only necessary to risk one. If Carswell had wanted to use equipment that was twenty years out of date, perhaps that was his privilege. But why did he expose the others to danger?

The other two came in and joined us. I said that Carswell had already told me their story.

"Well, that is it," Danbrunt said. "They caught us red-handed."

He too was supposed to be an electrical engineer. Taransky, the electronics technician, sat there looking dazed as if he had been hit on the head by a mallet.

They asked me whether I thought they would be sent to the Isle of Pines. I told them frankly that their case was not as hopeful as mine, because they were not sick and had no constitutional basis for an appeal. I have often wondered about these three boys, about who really sent them into that trap and why.

They were technically incompetent for the job and they were not experienced or intelligent enough to be exposed to that sort of danger. Whatever the real story behind their tragedy, I am convinced that the three of them who were sent to the Isle of Pines are honest Americans who believed they were serving their country.

THE DEATH OF DR. YEBRA

My lawyer came to see me the day before my hearing to assure me that in two or three days I would be free. On the 21st, as I have already said, Dr. Julio Yebra and his group were put on trial. Yebra came into our galera, spick and span, his uniform freshly starched.

"Julio, where are you going?" I asked.

"I came here to say goodbye to everybody," he replied smiling. "I am going to trial, and tonight they are going to shoot me."

"Be careful up there," I said. "Keep under control. There is just a chance that you will get out alive."

"I told you what I am going to do and that is the way it will be."

We shook hands. He walked out and went to his trial.

When the men go to trial, it is the last time that those who will be condemned to death enter the patio. The prisoners are brought back from trial handcuffed and under armed guard. Those destined to die are taken into Galera 22, which houses the military prisoners, and then are put into capillas at the rear of the galera.

That day, four of the five came back from trial and into the patio. We could see Dr. Julio Yebra turn around and wave to us. Handcuffed, he was taken into capilla.

The other four had crowds around them as they told their story. Cesar Fuentes came into our galera, and then broke down. When the evidence of what had been found in Julio Yebra's room was presented, the President of the Tribunal asked him whether, if he were ever free again, he would make another attempt on the life of Fidel Castro.

Yes, he replied. Castro had proved himself a traitor to the Cuban people and to the Revolution. If freed, he would not rest until he killed him.

The court then condemned him to execution that night. The other four were given thirty years apiece on the Isle of Pines.

That night, I knew I would hear my first execution at La Cabana. The prisoners were put to death behind our galera.

One can always hear everything that happens. If one stands very close to the railing, especially on moonlit nights, one sees the moving silhouettes of the firing squad and the man tied to the pole. We would listen to the executions and we would hoist one man high against the railing. He would observe the shadows and report to us what he had seen.

The night was ominously quiet. Around ten-fifteen, we heard a jeep come in and, when it stopped, men walking around it. They were the firing squad. Ten minutes later, they took Julio from capilla. He proceeded to the jeep, handcuffed, but walking erect. They put him in the jeep, and then drove out the front gate and we heard the jeep go around the side of the castle and then stop.

Our observer told us that the firing squad seemed to be in position. He could hear the sound of men's feet and could barely make out that they were tying Dr. Yebra to the paredón. His hands were tied behind him.

We could hear Julio talking. He asked permission of the lieutenant in command of the firing squad to give the orders for his own execution. The lieutenant hesitated for a moment, and then agreed.

In a loud clear voice, Dr. Julio Yebra cried:

"Viva Cuba Libre! Viva Cristo Hey!"

Then we heard him shout: "Preparen!"

The next command was: "Apunten!"

Then in a resonant voice, "Fuego!"

There was a burst of rifle fire and Julio was down. The lieutenant walked up to him and pumped four bullets into his head—the coup de grace or tiro de gracia.

In our galera, there was complete silence. I asked myself how our twelve friends felt, the men who had been condemned to death and had been waiting in the cell for over a year, knowing that at any moment they could be called to the paredón.

The next morning, we were called out to conteo as usual. But there was none of the usual gabble and horseplay. As I learned later, the rule was silence after an execution.

We learned that Dr. Yebra's mother had been permitted to talk to her son the night of the execution. The conversation had taken place in the office and she had said goodbye to him without breaking down.

She then talked to the prison governor, Manolito Fernández, a man who was always sympathetic to suffering and who felt every execution himself. She told Manolito that she understood that her son had voluntarily sacrificed his life for his country and she hoped and prayed that his would be the last life spent in that manner. This brave woman was given the body.

Earlier, she had gone to see Minister of Education Armando Hart, the man whom Dr. Julio Yebra had rescued from prison at great personal risk. Hart refused to do anything for his old comrade, insisting that Yebra had been a traitor to the Revolution, a man who had sold out to the Yankees, a vendepatria and a wretch who deserved death.

There would be many more executions in La Cabana. They took place in a way that is different from the accepted procedure. In civilized Western countries, the firing squads consist of eight men. Four fire live ammunition and four fire blanks. This is so no individual need feel absolute responsibility for inflicting death. They fire a volley on command and, at these short distances; they don't have to be marksmen.

In Communist Cuba, the firing squad consists generally of eight ragamuffins from the Militia. All have live ammunition. They fire in a straggling way, as it suits them. These men are among the world's worst shots and a coup de grace is always necessary.

When Captain Herman Marks commanded firing squads, he would haul the victim up by his hair and then fire .45 caliber bullets into his head. He would leave the execution grounds with his hands spattered with brains and blood. Recently, I have been informed by Cuban refugees, Congolese women have become part of the firing squads in La Cabana and El Principe.

CHAPTER 11

THE ISLE OF PINES:
A CUBAN INFERNO

About two nights after the second execution, I woke up at three in the morning, lay on my bunk and smoked. Unexpectedly, a guard unlocked the doors of the galera and opened them. I nudged Dario, who was lying on the bed beside me.

"It looks like a cordillera," he said.

The cordillera (or chains, so-called because the men are tied together and march in single file) meant the assembling and transport of prisoners to the dreaded prison on the Isle of Pines.

About half an hour later, the officer of the day began to call off names on the loudspeaker of men who had been convicted and sentenced to the Island. They were given fifteen minutes to get their belongings together and report to the office "for transfer to another prison."

These cordilleras are always announced in the pre-dawn hours when men's morale is at its lowest ebb. The prisoners sit on the edge of their bunks in despondent expectation.

Many have filed appeals; many have hopes that some Rebel friend outside may be able to save them; many are counting on connections they once had with the Government; many have been paying more blackmail than they can possibly afford—and all are praying that they will not be sent to the Island, from which there is hardly any possibility of a return.

The reading of this list goes on and on. To add to the torture of uncertainty, the list is not alphabetized and therefore no man knows whether he is safe until the reading comes to an end.

In this tremendous cordillera, three men were taken from our galera: Ernesto Mestre, Rear Admiral Antonio Arias and Oscar de Tuya, who had become a good friend of mine.

They had also called four of the six Americans in the prison: Dan Carswell, Eustace Danbrunt, Edmund Taransky and Robert John Gentile. The only two Americans now left in the Fortress were William Alexander Morgan and I. There was much confusion. All the prisoners were awake by now, of course, and many had gone to the galeras to say goodbye to their friends for the last time. The loud speaker blared a second time. The men were ordered to hurry. They were wanted in the office.

I turned to Dario Valdés:

"Dario, how is it that they didn't call the name of Cesar Fuentes? He was sentenced in the same trial as Julio Yebra."

"Maybe he has influence," Dario said, "or perhaps he is too sick to go."

"But they called three men who are really sick—Mestre, de Tuya and Arias."

"That's the way the ball bounces. You hope and pray that they won't call you and then the time comes, the moment of truth. Don't get in trouble with Dubuté."

The warning was for me. The antagonism between Dr. Dubuté and me was already visible. I resolved to try to quench it.

Dan Carswell and the other Americans came into our galera to say goodbye. They were visibly shaken, but they kept their self-control. They gave me their wristwatches, their portable radios and some other personal belongings, such as rings and other things of value. On the Isle of Pines, you are not permitted any personal possessions and, if you go there with them, they are taken from you as you enter the prison.

"I can't understand this," Danbrunt said to me. "I was told we were not going to be moved, that they were going to keep us here for a while and that then we would be set free."

They met their fate with courage, like real soldiers. We shook hands. In Cuba, people get into the habit of hugging each other. Everyone there gave them an abrazo.

The loudspeaker ordered us back into the galeras, so the guards could lock up the cells. The men destined for transportation were milling around in the patio, frantically urging their friends in the galeras to take notes and messages to family and friends on the outside. They begged us to send telegrams to their wives or mothers that they had been sent to the Island.

The line was ordered to move out. It formed at the railing and disappeared for a moment as the men moved single file through the office. There, each man was tied to his neighbor with a long rope; the hands of each prisoner were first tied behind his back. There were forty men in each group, forty men to each rope.

They were loaded on trucks, each of which had a strong military guard. The cordilleras don't go to El Principe as they used to in the old days. They proceed directly to Camp Columbia, now known as Ciudad Libertad, and there by airplane they are taken to the Island. We understood later that this cordillera had a great deal of trouble. The flight should have taken an hour, but was three days in transit.

Many of our friends were gone now. There was an atmosphere of tension and despair. The prisoners were silent and morose, the guards nervous. For two or three days after a cordillera leaves, there is a depressed air throughout the prison. Little by little, the depression lifts. New men are continuously being brought in and others are awaiting trial. It is very much like an infantry unit in combat, where one must learn to accept the procession toward disappearance and death as the normal way of life or else lose one's ability to function.

THE PRISON ON THE ISLAND

Julio Sanchez Gómez told me that the official records showed that there were only prisoners on the Isle of Pines under Batista. (Under Castro, in January 1963, there would be 5,325 politicals incarcerated there.) The political prisoners were not kept in the circulares, but in the "pavilions," small apartments for prisoners whose conduct was exemplary and in which the prisoners might receive their women. In addition, under the former regime, each political prisoner was entitled to his radio, newspapers and books. They were allowed to be with their women at certain times and there were doctors and medical specialists in attendance.

When Fidel Castro was Batista's prisoner on the Isle of Pines, following his ill-fated attempt to overthrow the Cuban Government on July 26, 1953, he had his own library, was given writing materials and was allowed to write subversive tracts for publication. He had his private nurse, a man named Antonio Gil, who was doing thirty years for murder. Gil has since been set free, licensed as a doctor and is today one of the medical men in attendance on Castro. In addition, Fidel Castro had been assigned a jeep and driver.

A guard who had been on the Island when Castro was confined there told me that the chief of the prison once decided to surprise Castro and had his son, Fidelito, brought out for a visit. Told that the Chief had a surprise for him, Castro appeared in his jeep.

"Here is your son," the Chief said, in the presence of the guard who told me the story.

Castro leaned down, gave Fidelito a peck on the cheek and then proceeded to complain to the Chief that newspapermen had come to see him, but had not been allowed to take pictures. All this time, he ignored the boy. When he had finished with his complaint, Castro drove away in his jeep, leaving his son behind in tears.

When he took over in Cuba, one of Castro's first acts was to order the execution of the Chief of the prison and of his four-man military escort.

THE GREEN HELL

The prison today has four circulares, or round buildings, six stories high and of reinforced concrete. Each of these floors has ninety-three cells, built to house either one or two prisoners each. They now house three or four. Although an adequate number of toilets was originally installed, all but one to a floor have been ripped out and sent to the Soviet Union on arms ships from Russia that would otherwise be returning empty or in ballast. The result is that there is only one toilet for every 800-odd prisoners. Since the food is often rotten, a large number of the prisoners suffer from diarrhea. Waiting in line for the toilet becomes impossible and they are obliged to use the floors of the cells or corridors. With a virtual absence of paper, the men in the circulares live in indescribable conditions of filth.

Dr. Guillermo Ara, who was one of the four political prisoners released by Castro in the last days of 1962, a man of about six feet who shrank from 168 to 104 pounds during sixteen months, described the food there in an article in the Diario de las Americas for January 6, 1963. What Dr. Ara has to say is the substance of what dozens of returned wretches from the Island, men sent back to Havana because of incurable or terminal illness, reported. I quote Ara, because he is not only accurate, but also eloquent:

"There one is born again every day, because the life of a prisoner is worth nothing. Every twenty-four hours brings a renewal of tension, torture and painful hunger. Dogs are privileged characters in comparison with the political prisoners of the Isle of Pines.

The day of tortures begins very early—at five. At this hour, they serve every galera with what they call breakfast, a piece of bread with 'coffee,' which is a dark liquid that smells like anything but coffee. That is to say, dark water and bread. Milk is something to dream about. For two years, none has been served the prisoners."

Lunch and supper consist of boiled macaroni, cassava or pumpkin. This is served without any fat or salt. The pumpkins and macaroni are often spoiled and their smell makes that inescapably clear.

This diet is one of starvation. Men become emaciated to such an extent that their ribs can be seen through their skin. Strong, powerfully built men, such as some of the Cuban aviators convicted of "war crimes" on Fidel Castro's personal orders (after a previous trial in which a Rebel tribunal had acquitted them) have shrunk to walking skeletons.

In addition, the prison diet is designed to kill because it is qualitatively insufficient for human health. There are no proteins, no protective foods, no fats, no sugars, no dairy products and none of the vitamins necessary for healthy life. Because of vitamin starvation, some of the aviators I have just mentioned are slowly going blind.

There is no running water. In the morning, a water truck is brought in and each man is allowed a pint daily for drinking. For washing, they use salt water piped in from the ocean.

This prison was never finished. Consequently, there are no cell doors. The cell structures are doughnut-like. There are no windows, but merely apertures closed with a grating of steel bars. Hence, the rain pours in. On the inside, these openings look out to a circular stairway and to a tower that rises in the center above the roof of the circulars. There are also grated openings, facing outward, away from the skin of the doughnut, but to use these is dangerous, since the guards often fire at these apertures without warning.

The prisoners are never allowed out of the circulares for air and exercise. During their entire period of incarceration, they are confined inside the circulares. The only physical movement possible for them is from cell to cell and from floor to floor within each circular.

There is a commissary, but, on the Island, there is nothing to buy, not even tobacco. The prisoners are allowed to write one letter a week, which must be on one side of a single sheet of paper. Mail is received on the average once every two months. From the summer of 1962 to January 1963, the American political prisoners on the Isle of Pines were not allowed to send any mail or to receive any mail or packages.

Visiting rules change, depending on the political situation, much as they did at La Cabana. However, here things are immeasurably worse and, in good times on the Island, visiting days are limited to once every three months.

There is supposed to be an infirmary on the Island, but this is a malicious joke. It resembles a galera at La Cabana. This so-called hospital has no equipment at all; its doctors are the medically trained prisoners, and the only medicines available are the packages sent in by the families and friends of the political prisoners. By late 1962, these packages were regularly pilfered by the guards, and prisoners considered themselves lucky if they got half of what their families managed to collect for them at great hardship and toil in a land where virtually everything needed by human beings is in short supply.

The guards on the Isle of Pines, as elsewhere in Cuba, are simply the former common criminals. The overwhelming majority of these offenders are Negroes. In fact, when he ordered their freedom, Fidel Castro spoke of the injustice of imprisoning a poor Negro, who might have merely stolen a chicken because he was hungry. Actually most of these common criminals were long-term, casehardened offenders— murderers, rapists, sadists, perverts. In addition to being naturally cruel, many, if not most of them had a strong racial resentment toward the whites that had formerly ruled as their superiors. When their latent hatred was not strong enough, the Communists would fan it with lying propaganda. This is a calculated stage in Castro's race war. It has no rational limits. The alternatives he is presenting to the white officials, managers, professionals and intellectuals are either total subordination to the Communist movement or slow extermination.

In addition to psychological torture, prisoners who commit the slightest infraction of the rules are placed in special punishment cells. These pigsties are scarcely large enough for one man, but seven to nine prisoners are crowded in each of them. Men are put in the punishment cells completely naked. They are doused with cold water and the floor of these cells is almost always covered with water. The prisoners must move their bowels in an open hole in full view of the rest. The only water for bathing and washing one's plate is a thin trickle over the open latrine.

Following the Playa Girón invasion of April 17, 1962, Castro ordered every circular mined with 2,000 pounds of dynamite or plastic explosives. The guards told the prisoners that, in the event of another anti-Castro armed movement, the first act of the government would be to blow up the prison.

Castro has always feared an American attack on the Isle of Pines and for that reason has turned the Island into a fortress. Before the Russians took over in late 1962, there were about 16,000 militiamen stationed there. The Island was seeded with gun emplacements and protected by tanks and Migs.

The requisas in the Isle of Pines prison are incredibly brutal. The circulares are first surrounded by tanks, assault cars, machine guns and ordinary troops. At a signal, the military open fire on the apertures of the circulares that face outward. This always causes a large number of wounds and, because of the requisas; there are prisoners who have lost eyes, legs and arms. When this preliminary fire is over, the prisoners are sometimes forced out of the circulares at bayonet point, which causes more wounds and even death.

When the prisoners are outside, the black guards proceed with their search and, in the process, steal anything that is of value to them.

Standard operating procedure in a requisa is to force the men to stand closely packed together in lines and more or less at attention. This is required during the whole period of the search, which may last twenty-four hours or more. Men fall out of line and faint. Sometimes, their comrades are allowed to pick them up; at other times, they simply lie there in the dirt. A guard may tell a prisoner to stick his tongue out, to look up at the sky or to turn his head and, if he doesn't move fast enough; the guard will club him with the butt end of his rifle.

During the whole procedure, there is no food or water for the prisoners. The men stand in burning sun or heavy rain unprotected. Regardless of weather, the requisa goes on.

There have been two hunger strikes on the Isle of Pines. The first was caused by hunger. The politicals stayed on hunger strike for seven days in protest against the fact that they were served only one meal, consisting of a plate of macaroni or a broth. The second strike was in protest against the fact that two prisoners, who were planning to escape, were viciously beaten and tortured.

Despite the fact that both strikes were lost, the morale and solidarity of the political prisoners is reported unbroken at the time these lines are written—that is to say, in May of 1963. One of the hunger strikes was smashed by bringing up tanks, which blew open the doors of the circulares with the fire of their heavy guns. The prisoners were forced out of the cells at bayonet point. Those who were slow or resisted orders were viciously stabbed. In this requisa, seven men were bayoneted to death. Among those bayoneted was David Salvador, the first head of the Confederation of Cuban Labor (CTC) under Fidel Castro and a man who was my fellow prisoner in La Cabana.

Some 250 men were wounded in this search. There was no alcohol in the infirmary, no bandages, nothing with which to suture wounds, no sulfa or antibiotics. The victims were left untended. The wounds festered. I was told that about 10 per cent of the prisoners on the Island had tuberculosis and that fungus conditions were rampant.

The director of this prison is a Guatemalan Communist and a confidential agent of Jacobo Arbenz, the former Red President of that country. This man, who is called Tarrau, is a lieutenant in the Castro Army. He does not dare to appear in the circulares without his guard of from thirty to forty heavily armed men. Tarrau had the prisoners who plotted an escape beaten and tortured before his eyes and in the presence of the others.

Not all of the Cuban political prisoners on the Island suffer under these abominable conditions. There are exceptions. When I returned to the United States, I learned from Cuban exiles that one of them was Major Huber Matos, the hero of the Cuban Revolution who broke with Castro on the issue of Communist domination and was sentenced to a long term on the Isle of Pines.

I was informed that Huber Matos employs unprecedented privileges; that he has a room of his own, eats special food, has unique visiting privileges and is allowed to go about in the uniform of an officer of Castro's Rebel Army.

Another enjoying the same special privileges was David Salvador, the anti-American labor agitator who was so active in the Castro blood purge. He even has his own television set.

This is in sharp contrast with the sanguinary vengeance Castro inflicts on those of his close associates who broke with him decisively and completely.

Many Cubans suspect that Matos is being held in reserve in case Castro decides to "liberalize" his dictatorship by including some "anti-Communists" in the Cabinet as a means of getting U.S. support. Certainly, Matos is being built up by leftwing American writers, such as the former Communist, Theodore Draper, as a hope for anti-communism in Cuba.

The condition of the Bay of Pigs invaders in the Isle of Pines prison was better than that of the rest of the politicals. Since there was a chance of selling them for ransom, they were kept in reasonably good physical shape.

By contrast, James D. Beane of Franklinville, North Carolina, charged with counterrevolution, is lame and unable to stand on his feet. My friend, Robert Geddes Morton, the former head of the Pepsi-Cola Company in Cuba, was suffering from severe tuberculosis when he was sent to the Isle of Pines. He was finally released in February, 1963. I was shocked to learn that this man I had believed to be in his fifties, was actually only 31!

The 5,000 or so Cubans and Americans, imprisoned on the Isle of Pines, are being slowly murdered under conditions of unspeakable brutality and slow torture. The liberation of these prisoners and of other fighters for Cuban freedom, held elsewhere on the island, is a duty for all of us who believe in justice and liberty. Their emancipation, however, should be the result of the application of force—economic, political or military—against the Castro dictatorship and not the result of payment of ransom.

THE WOMEN'S PRISONS

There are two women's prisons: Guanajay in the province of Havana and Baracoa in Oriente province. The female guards are the former inmates—common criminals and all of them colored. Many of these women guards are notorious for being hardened Lesbians.

The women prisoners are forced to wear dungarees, shirts and boots and are not allowed to wear any female adornment at all. There are farms attached to the prisons where the politicals are worked like beasts of burden. Guanajay has close to 2,000 women prisoners and Baracoa about 5,000.

In July 1962, at the same time as on the Isle of Pines, there was a hunger strike on Guanajay. News of this came through relatives of the women prisoners who had passed the word along to our visitors and other sources of information. The strike was in protest against a requisa that had lasted two days.

THE PRISON SYSTEM

According to Communists in La Cabana, who discussed the situation with me, there were from 75,000 to 150,000 political prisoners in Cuba in the fall of 1962. This amounted to from 1 to 3 per cent of the entire population.

The Cuban prison system is closely modeled on Soviet practice. The stages of imprisonment are characterized by progressively increasing severity. Thus, when a person is arrested, he is generally first taken to the city hail, where his family can visit him and bring him food. From this place of temporary detention, he may be sent to the G-2 headquarters, which should under no circumstances be confused with the G-2 torture farms. Here things are considerably tougher, but the prisoner can still have visits twice a week from female members of his family and can still receive food from the outside. The third stage may be La Cabana or El Principe, both of which are considerably worse than the G-2 headquarters. Once in La Cabana, the prisoner generally faces two alternatives: execution or shipment to the Isle of Pines.

The Communist rehabilitation program, which I shall describe in due course, is patterned on the same theory of progressive change, except that here the direction is reversed and, with each advance in indoctrination and obedience, there is a further step in improvement of material conditions and freedom.

The same strategy was applied toward visitors. On the first occasion, they would be treated with consideration. The second time, especially if the prisoner—husband or son— had been recalcitrant toward authority, the visitors would be treated with roughness or brutality. The women would be stripped naked and searched by Lesbian guards, who would pinch and feel them. They would be made to jump in the air naked with their legs spread apart so that anything they had concealed could be detected. This was done to children visitors also. The problem did not arise in the case of men visitors, for, as a rule, none are allowed in Cuban prisons.

When the prisoner reaches his final stage of degradation, the Isle of Pines, every obstacle is placed in the way of would be visitors; they are subjected to every possible inconvenience and molestation; they are treated like enemies of the state, and, at best, they are able to see their men three or four times in a year.

PHOTO MARYFERRELL.ORG

John Martino, whose statements initiated Larry Hancock's book *Someone Would Have Talked,* was an anti-Castro activitist in the early 1960s. An electronics expert, his expertise was in gambling machines used in the Havana casinos run by organized crime. Martino was arrested in Havana in July 1959; he spent three years in prison before his release. When he returned to Florida, Martino became heavily involved with Frank Sturgis, Eddie Bayo, and other anti-Castro activists.

EUGENIO MARTINEZ -JOHN MARTINO-EDDIE BAYO-RENE LOMALRU
PHOTO JAMES RICHARDS COLLECTION LARRY-HANCOCK.COM

In the spring and summer of 1963, Martino was heavily involved in the Bayo-Pawley raid (aka Operation TILT) TILT was an operation initiated to smuggle out of Cuba two Russian officers who, supposedly, wanted to defect and alert the world to the presence of Soviet missiles remaining in Cuba after the Missile Crisis. A team was landed but never returned.

CHE GUEVARA AND FIDEL CASTRO

PHOTO WWW.ARGENTOUR.COM

Ernesto "Che" Guevara was born in Argentina in 1928. He trained as a physician before becoming involved in social issues. After converting to communism and traveling to Cuba, Guevara became Fidel Castro's chief lieutenant. Guevara was notorious for his unwavering dedication to the cause and the resulting harsh discipline to those in opposition.

PHOTO BY JASON HO

Immediately after the collapse of the Batista regime, Castro put Che Guevara in charge of La Cabaña prison. Hundreds of prisoners were executed at La Cabaña Fortress prison at his direction.

CHAPTER 12

THE DEATH OF WILLIAM MORGAN

On February 1, I was taken to the office by my good friend, Cipriano Mauri, for a conference with my lawyer. The minute I stepped inside, I could read on Dr. Camargo's face that something was terribly wrong.

"Well, John, I have bad news for you." Everybody in the office was being very courteous and attentive toward me. I realized that the news must be very bad indeed.

"I know it," I told Camargo. "You are no poker player."

"Your appeal was turned down. This is one of the most tragic things in the judicial history of Cuba. The members of the Court are unanimously in agreement that my seven reasons for stating you are in prison illegally are valid. You have a just case. You were tried in violation of your constitutional rights. You were deprived of due process. You were brought to trial for one thing and then convicted for another alleged crime, which was never charged against you in the indictment and which you never committed. You are being kept in prison in violation of law. The Supreme Court validates all these points. But their decision is that they have no jurisdiction over the military tribunal and therefore must uphold your sentence. Only one judge dared to vote for you. The rest have become puppets of Fidel Castro. Some day, these men will pay. If it is the last thing I do, I will see that they pay a terrible price for what they have done to the law."

"Doctor," I said, "There is no use. Just forget about it."

"Did you know that there was a cordillera the other night and that they took the three American boys to the Island?"

"My God. And I had their case up for an appeal. It looks as if an American can no longer get any sort of justice in Cuba."

He was shaken and agitated. I warned him not to say anything that could get him in trouble and he left me with tears in his eyes.

Cipriano Mauri helped me back to the galera and, as we walked, I told him what had happened. In the cell, they were all waiting for the news. When I gave the verdict to Dario Valdés, he picked me up in his arms and carried me over to my bed. The others grouped around me, expressing their sympathy, their anger and their grief. They took the blow as if it were their lives, not mine. Soon the whole prison knew and men crowded into the galera, pressing toward my bed, shaking my hands.

"You don't have to be careful now," Dario said. "You can talk to anybody and say whatever you think. That is one small consolation. Now there are only two alternatives. Either the Cubans will overthrow Fidel Castro or the United States will have to come down here and clean out these scorpions. You are going to be here as long as the rest of us and I have the feeling that very few of us will get out of here alive." About a quarter of an hour later, William Morgan came in, sat on my bed and expressed his sympathy.

"It can't continue this way," he said. "This man is finished. I know the Cubans and I also know what is going on outside I believe there is going to be help, but it had better come fast, because I have the feeling that they are going to take me out and shoot me pretty soon."

HUNGER STRIKE

The next two weeks were uneventful. In the batch of new prisoners that the G-2 had brought in were a group of students and their leader, a young man of great bravery named Luis Alfaro. These students would have been Rebels, but they were too young to have fought with the 26th of July. Now they saw the country turning toward Communism and they were disillusioned and bitter.

After they had been incarcerated for about a fortnight, they staged a hunger strike. As a reprisal, we were all locked up in our galeras.

On the third or fourth day of the hunger strike, Manolito Fernández announced on the loudspeaker that he did not want to punish everybody, because not all were guilty. He asked the men who were discontented to come into the patio and state their grievances, adding that their hunger strike would only make conditions worse for everybody in the prison. He ordered the galeras opened up and the student leaders came out to confer with him. They told him they were striking in protest against the executions, which was obviously something beyond Manolito's control. After talking to them for a while, he convinced them to call off their fast and prison conditions soon returned to normal.

During this time, I had been paying Dr. Dubuté his ten dollars a week and I was being treated fairly decently as a result. Then William Morgan suddenly came down with an attack of kidney colic. He was in terrible pain. Dr. Dubuté came to see him in his galera to give him an injection, supposedly to relieve his suffering. However, Morgan knocked the syringe from his hand, called him an informer and added that he suspected that the injection was poison and that Dubuté wanted to curry favor by murdering him.

The news raced through the prison. About ten minutes later, Dubuté came into my galera with a group of men carrying William Morgan. They laid Morgan on the bunk next to mine. Morgan turned to me:

"Martino, you have medicine to kill pain, don't you?"

I nodded assent.

"Do you know how to give an injection?"

"Yes."

"Will you give me some of your medicine? Shoot it into my arm yourself, because I don't trust this dirty son of a bitch. He is one of the worst men in the prison and I think he is trying to kill me."

"What are you talking about, William?"

"Will you do as I say?"

"Of course," I replied.

Dubuté left the cell and returned with a syringe. I inserted an ampoule of my own medicine and gave William Morgan the injection. They carried William out, but Dubuté stayed behind.

"You Americans are all alike, aren't you?" He said to me in Spanish. When he had left the cell, Dario shook his head:

"Now you are going to have a problem with him, Martino."

"It might as well be now as later," I replied.

But things were not going to come to a head quite that fast. When the showdown was finally reached, Dubuté almost got me killed, but I am happy to say that I think he killed himself in the attempt.

SIX AMERICANS ON A PLEASURE TRIP

That night, there was a sensational story on the Cuban radio. Six Americans had come to Havana on a yacht, the official propaganda said, to wage counterrevolution under the direction of Senator Rolando Masferrer. The radio was full of this and, sure enough, the next morning the six Americans arrived in La Cabana Fortress as prisoners. These boys were brought into my galera by Comandante William Morgan.

They were Donald Green of Clover, South Carolina, James D. Beane of Franklinville, North Carolina, and four others named Thomas L. Baker, George R. Beck, Alfred C. Gibson and Leonard L. Schmidt. They told me that they had come to Cuba in a yacht that they had entered Havana harbor openly, tied up at a wharf and asked for mooring instructions. As soon as they were docked, Castro's Marines had swarmed aboard and placed them under arrest.

"We had a bit over $6,000, which these Cubans seized," Donald Green told me. "When they arrested us, they took us down to their G-2 and made movies of us. Then we were accused of being counterrevolutionaries before a group of newspapermen and now here we are."

I turned to Smitty, a kid with blond hair probably in his middle twenties.

"Are you kidding me with this story, Smitty? Are you yachtsmen? Do you spend your time sailing around the Caribbean? Where did you fellows meet?"

"We met in Miami," Smitty said.

I never knew whether their arrest was a frame-up or not. There wasn't enough time to talk. This was one of the cases that the Castro government evidently wanted to expedite. The very next morning, the six American boys were summoned out of Galera 12 to the office and given indictments for trial that afternoon on the charge of counterrevolution, which carries the death penalty.

Just before the trial, Smitty and Beane, the young man from South Carolina, came in to see me and to get my opinion as to their chances.

"Well, if they are trying you this fast," I replied, "it looks very bad, because this prison is where they shoot people. The only thing you can do now is pray. Is there any one thing they know that they can use against you?"

"We are all Army veterans," Smitty replied.

I thought that might explain the whole thing. I asked them if they had a lawyer and, to my relief, they said that Dr. Camargo was defending them.

Later that day, Dr. Camargo told me that he had been asked to defend the six Americans by the Swiss Embassy, which had been representing American interests in Cuba since President Eisenhower broke diplomatic relations. He was fully aware of the risk to himself:

"I don't have any choice, do I, Martino? I can't let these boys go to trial with a defense attorney appointed by the military court. If I do that, they won't have a chance. The trial has been postponed. It is scheduled for tonight. I will do my best to see that they are not shot, but I don't think I will have much luck."

"Is there any way of saving them?" I asked.

"Our only chance is international pressure," Camargo replied. "This case is getting widespread publicity. I know that Mexico, Brazil and a few other left-wing countries friendly to Castro have begun to complain about the executions."

Betrayal in the American Embassy

That same afternoon, a man named Dr. José Reposa came to see me in my galera. He was sixty-eight, white-haired, but strong and in good physical condition. He sat on my bed and began to talk to me in fluent English. He explained that he had not come to see me earlier because, as long as my appeal was up, he didn't want to do anything to prejudice my chances.

Dr. Reposa was a retired dentist. He had also been a deputy in the Cuban Congress in the time of President Grau San Martin. He had been in La Cabana for quite some time awaiting shipment to the Isle of Pines.

"What," I asked, "a man of your age?"

"Really, I am very lucky. The law says I am too old to be shot. Since nobody over the age of seventy can be kept in prison, my sentence expires in two years.

"When I tell you my story, you will find it hard to believe."

"Try me, Doctor."

"I was educated in the University of Pennsylvania. I have my family and many friends in Philadelphia. For many years,

I was the head of the Cuban delegation to the American Dental Association when we had our conventions. So you can see I am very pro-American."

"I am glad to hear that," I said.

"When all this trouble started, I was very friendly with a certain person in the American Embassy."

He gave me the official's name.

"Naturally, having many friends in the Embassy, I did my best to inform them of certain matters concerning which they had asked me for reports."

"What has that got to do with your being arrested?"

He looked at me and smiled:

"Mr. Martino, I love the American Government and the American people, but something very strange happened in my case. When I went to trial, they presented enough evidence to execute me. They put into the record every visit I made to the American Embassy, the floor I went to and the time I spent there. And, to make matters worse, I was arrested just after I had left the Embassy for the last time. I blame my arrest on somebody in the American Embassy."

"I find that hard to believe," I said.

"You know the last American Ambassador, Mr. Bonsai, was very naive. In addition, he was a left-winger, who tried to curry favor with Fidel Castro. The people working in your Havana Embassy were, with some exceptions, almost as bad as Mr. Bonsai.

"Don't you know that the employees of the American Embassy—that is 60 to 70 per cent of them—were Fidelistas and spies?"

"Are you sure?"

"Positive. Later on today, I will let you talk to three other gentlemen, who are in prison here and who were arrested for exactly the same reason. They were fingered and informed on by someone in the American Embassy."

Later the same day, he introduced me to three other men who told me substantially the same story. And later on, in my confinement in La Cabana, I would hear the same sordid story of treachery and betrayal within the American Embassy. If the reader is skeptical about this charge, let him remember the testimony of the former U. S. Naval Attaché in Havana, which I have already summarized. This man stated under oath that patriotic officials in the Embassy were unable to get two known Cuban Communists off the payroll.

As for Dr. Reposa, I am sorry to say that he did not survive his two years on the Isle of Pines. He was bayoneted to death in the same requisa that cost Salvador his life.

"THE SIX OF US WERE BORN THIS MORNING"

That night, the six Americans went on trial. They came back and were placed in capilla. We knew now that they had been sentenced to death.

This created a sensation in the prison. Everyone crowded into my galera. They kept asking me again and again how it was possible for the American Government to permit Castro to shoot these men. There was nothing I could say to them. The last thing I wanted to do was to disillusion them about the United States or about the new Administration of President Kennedy, from which they expected so much. They would shake their heads and straggle out of my galera.

There was so much commotion in the patio that night that they closed the galeras at six, stationed extra guards in the patio, and ordered lights out and absolute silence at seven. We kept anxious vigil. At ten-fifteen, the death jeep came in as usual, but the man who was watching for us told us that the firing squad had not left the vehicle. The jeep turned around and went out. We waited all night, our observer glued to his post, but nothing happened. We were afraid that the boys had been taken out during the night to the old paredón at the entrance of La Cabana Fortress. That morning, the word came to us that the six Americans were still in capilla. The men who brought food into the capillas informed us later that the boys were still alive.

Around nine in the morning, they were released and came into the patio. I cannot describe the reaction of the Cuban prisoners. There was cheering; men jumped in the air; the Americans were surrounded by a swarming mass of hysterical prisoners, who pounded their backs, embraced them or even broke into tears of joy. I asked Smitty what had happened in capilla.

"Well, you know we were accused of coming to Cuba to start a second front in the Escambray Mountains. Of course, if we had wanted to do that, we wouldn't have come into Havana. The fact that the charge didn't make sense was irrelevant. I guess the order had come down to give us the works and we were all convicted in very short order and sentenced to die that night.

"Well, Johnny, when we were put into the death cell, we were scared to death and the only thing we could think of was to play cards. These colored guards were staring at us and making dirty remarks about what was going to happen to us, but, sure enough, one of the Rebels brought a deck of cards. We sat there and played all night, arguing and swearing at each other, while the guards and Rebel prisoners came and stared at us and scratched their heads and said that all Americans were loco."

"Why did you do it, Smitty?"

"We figured it would occupy us and make the time pass and prevent us from sweating with fear. We never expected to come out alive. By this time, we thought we would be dead. The six of us were born again this morning."

But it was not too much of a rebirth. At four o'clock the next morning, there was a cordillera, which took about 120 men, among them the six Americans. They were sentenced to thirty years on the Isle of Pines. When they arrived there, Castro showed his hatred of Americans by having them kept in solitary confinement for six months. In the winter of 1962, when I was a free man again, I learned from Mrs. Beane that her son, James, was being held incommunicado, that she could neither write to him nor receive letters from him and that he was too lame to walk.

The following week, there was visitor's day and a prisoner escaped. This man was slight and had a baby face. When his visitor came—I forget whether it was his mother or his wife—the other prisoners crowded around him, while he changed into boy's clothes. We all held our breath as the visitors left, taking with them the "little boy," who had shaved carefully before making the attempt. The danger to the plan was that informers among the prisoners would find out what was happening, but we had managed to seal them off while the change into boy's clothes occurred.

After the conteo the next morning, while the prisoners were drinking their coffee, the loudspeaker ordered us back into our cells. Then there was another conteo. This time there was a roll call. They verified that a man was missing and that his name was Aruca.

Normally, when a prisoner escapes, the chief of the prison is removed. We held our breath to see whether this would happen, but fortunately Manolito survived. After keeping the galeras closed for a week, they were re-opened. Visitors were now subjected to strict search. None were allowed inside the galeras. A detail of some 200 Rebel soldiers erected a barricade with heavy wire that cut the patio in two sections. Under the new regulations, one section was our exercise yard; the other was for visitors. Whenever a man escapes from a prison, the rest suffer. Nevertheless, a successful escape is always a matter of triumph.

About ten days later, three of the leaders of the electrical workers union were brought into La Cabana. This was a militant labor organization, which had won excellent conditions for the workers under the regimes of Grau San Martin, Prio Socarrás and Fulgencio Batista. The Castro regime had wiped out these gains and imposed an unwanted Communist leadership on the Cuban Federation of Labor

(CTC) and was now destroying the independence of the electrical workers union. Consequently, a large number of skilled workers in the power industry went into opposition and resorted to extremely effective sabotage.

Fidel Castro, the great advocate of a "dictatorship of the proletariat," now had a chance to show his true colors. The electricians were brought into prison at five that afternoon; by seven o'clock they were put on trial, and by half past ten that night the firing squad assembled for them.

A boy named Ignacio, who was waiting to be shipped to the Isle of Pines to serve a ten-year sentence for counterrevolutionary activities, went into the capilla to talk to the trade union leaders who were to die that night.

The officer of the day was a gigantic mulatto, about six feet three, known to us as Emilio. He was one of the most vicious and depraved human beings I have ever known. He was from Marianao and had a record of marihuana peddling. Emilio went into the capilla to prepare the men for execution.

"Are there three men here or four?" He asked.

The boy, who was almost frightened to death, explained that he was in the capilla, but that he was not to be executed.

Unfortunately for him, he got into an argument with Emilio and with the head of the firing squad. They said to him:

"We have decided to take you along. There will be one less gusano" (that is to say, worm) "to fight the Revolution."

Ignacio was put to death merely because he happened to be in the capilla when the other three were taken out and because, when he protested, he angered these two militiamen. He was the last of the four to be shot.

We had heard the firing squad execute four men and we discovered next morning that Ignacio was not in the capilla. By the end of breakfast, the whole prison knew what had happened. We shook our fists at the guards on the roof and called them assassins.

There were protests by the defense lawyers. There was an investigation of sorts and blame was assigned to the captain of the firing squad, but not to Emilio, who remained one of the two officers of the day at La Cabana.

Executions at our prison were not announced until days or weeks later, at which time a small item would appear in the papers. However, we almost always had full details the next morning of who had been put to death and where the previous night. We were given this information at great risk by our friends within the garrison, who were secretly opposed to the Communist regime.

We had another way of getting information. Men would be designated to pick fights in the patio. The punishment would be to be put in capilla on bread and water. We would see that this was done whenever we knew that there were men from the underground among the military prisoners. These underground elements in the military barracks could easily mix with our men in the capillas and brief them on what was happening elsewhere in Cuba.

That is how we learned that there were bloody riots among the prisoners on the Isle of Pines immediately after the invasion at Playa Girón and that a savage requsia took place there in which five men were killed and the infirmary was filled with wounded. Considering the fact that La Cabana was considered virtually incommunicado with the outside world, our system of receiving detailed, prompt and accurate information was remarkable.

THE WILLIAM MORGAN STORY

With Morgan when he was arrested was another Comandante, a man named Carreras. He stayed in the rear of Calera 7, morose and brooding. I never saw him and don't know what he looked like. One day, Morgan was called to the office on the loudspeaker. When he returned about an hour later, he sat on my bunk and said:

"Well, John, it looks like this is it. My trial is for tomorrow night."

"Willie, what do you think?"

"I don't have a chance. I know they are going to shoot me.
"Don't talk that way, Willie. You were a Comandante. You were a friend of Fidel."

"I was a friend of Fidel," he said with a strained laugh.

"I will be back later. I want to have a long talk with you."

The whole prison was agog with the news that Morgan and Carreras were actually going to stand trial. Not even the most zealous of the young Rebels believed that Fidel Castro would shoot these two men, who had played such a big role in the Cuban Revolution and who were so popular with the people and the armed forces. Morgan had a knack for making friends. He was always laughing, a lover of practical jokes, a man of enormous physical strength and bursting energy. In the prison, he exercised like an athlete and marched like a soldier.

"Well, this is the evening of the day before I die," Morgan said when he came into my galera after supper that evening and sat on my bed. "Let us have the long talk I promised you."

"What shall we talk about, William?"

"You don't think much of me, do you?" He asked, giving me a penetrating stare.

"Well, William, many things have been said about you. After all, you were one of the main factors in betraying the people in the Trujillo conspiracy."

"That is a long story. I am going to try to explain it to you.

"William, you don't have to explain anything to me," I said. The fact is that I liked William Morgan personally, but there was not much in his brief life—he was thirty-three at the time—that an American could cheer about. When the civil war was raging in Cuba, Herbert L. Matthews of the New York Times apparently wanted to build Morgan up and characterized him as a freedom fighter, "a veteran of the U. S. Army in World War II, and adept at judo."

Jules Dubois, who was equally color blind concerning Castro and his movement, called Morgan a "former paratrooper."

The facts were less romantic. Morgan never saw service in World War II; he was never a paratrooper, and his military service with the U. S. Army was neither a credit to himself nor to his country. After a grammar school education, he had worked for the Army as a truck driver. Right after World War II, he enlisted, at which time, although he was only eighteen, he already had a police record in his native Toledo, Ohio. As a private in the infantry of the Army of

Occupation in Japan, Morgan was court-martialed on November 7, 1947 for having been A.W.O.L. on two occasions. Convicted and sentenced to three months at hard labor, he overpowered his guard; stole the latter's clothing and weapon and made his escape.

Naturally, he was captured and rearrested. A general court-martial tried him on January 15, 1948, found him guilty of escape and robbery and sentenced him to five years at hard labor, which was reduced to three years by a board of military review. Thus, he spent most of his military service—which so impressed Dubois and Matthews—as a prisoner in the Federal Reformatory at Chillicothe, Ohio. He was put in solitary confinement there on several occasions for attempted escape, fighting, refusal to work and threatening arson. He apparently rounded out his confinement at the Federal Reformatory in Milan, Michigan, where he was eventually released on April 11, 1950.

Joining the Cuban Rebel forces in 1957 or 1958, Morgan saw service in the Escambray and emerged as Fidel Castro's chief cloak-and-dagger man and one of the most spectacular confidence men and double-crossers of our day. In August 1959, he carried out two major agent-provocateur operations for Castro with conspicuous success. He convinced Dominican dictator Rafael Leonidas Trujillo that he was able to organize and lead a military insurrection that would overthrow the Castro regime. Reportedly, he got $200,000 from the Dominican political boss and, with Castro's connivance, lured Dominican mercenaries and anti-communist volunteers into a carefully prepared death trap. A few days earlier, he had betrayed the leaders of the White Rose society, the militant anti-Castro organization with which I was supposed to have been connected, to the Cuban secret police. As a result, 4,000 suspects were arrested and the backbone of what was at that time the most effective anti-Castro organization in Cuba was snapped.

"There is nothing to explain, Willie," I said to Morgan. "I saw you on television when Fidel Castro paid you your reward for betraying the people in the Trujillo conspiracy."

"Yes, he really made me look like a Judas, even to the Cuban people, didn't he?"

I shrugged: "How could you go on television, knowing that you were to receive this money?"

"I want you to believe me. I had no idea of what was going to happen. What I was told was that Fidel Castro and I were to talk about the Trujillo plot and how it was smashed. There I was. Before I could do anything about it, Fidel Castro was making his speech and he took out this money and gave it to me and said that was my reward for exposing and betraying the Trujillo plotters.

"From that moment on, I hated him, because I realized he had made me into a Judas in front of my friends and in front of the whole world. He made it look as if I had done it for money. My wife could never get over it. After that, my real friends tried to understand."

"Well, what do you want to tell me about it?"

"I guess I trapped many people. I did it on my own. It is hard to explain, but Fidel Castro has a strange hold over people. I believed everything he told me. As far as I was concerned, he could do no wrong.

"The story of the conspiracy is this. I was approached early in 1959 by someone about a plot to overthrow Castro. At that time, there was much turmoil and confusion; there were still lots of Batista people at large. When the approach was made to me, I made one of my biggest mistakes—I told Fidel Castro.

"Fidel was very much interested. We sat down and talked it out. I agreed to pretend to go along with the plot to find out what was really behind it.

"As the negotiations developed, I found that the people behind the conspiracy were Batistianos. I reported this to Castro. He and his advisors decided that I should pretend to join the conspiracy so we could lure these former Batista henchmen to Cuba and destroy them. Castro felt this would increase his personal prestige and would also give him a pretext to kill more of his potential enemies. He felt personally insecure and afraid and he wanted to put the firing squads back to work.

"I became more deeply involved. I went to Miami personally to work out arrangements with the Dominican Consul there. On my return, there was a key meeting to perfect plans with Fidel, Raul, Ché Guevara and others present.

Fidel said: 'Listen, William, while we are about this matter, there are a few other people we must get out of the way.'

I asked him what he meant by that.

"He explained that in Cuba there were many influential and popular people who had held office in the governments of Grau San Martin and Prio Socarrás. There were also big businessmen and others who would make trouble. He said:

"Willie, this is what you must do. You must approach certain people and try to lure them into the conspiracy."

I interrupted Morgan:

"William, I heard a story to that effect from someone I met in prison."

"Who was that?"

"Arturo Hernández Tellaheche, the former Minister of Labor under Prio."

"That part is true."

"Do you mean to tell me that man is in jail because you approached him and offered him the Presidency of Cuba, as he told me?"

"Yes. I did that sort of thing to quite a few people."

He went on to describe what had happened at Trinidad. One plane had come down and the Castro forces had wounded the pilot and co-pilot and quite a number of Batista people. There were two planes. Only one landed. The other got away. He admitted that he had played a very important role in the betrayal, but he claimed that he had not done it for money.

"Fidel Castro doesn't trust anybody. Right after the Trinidad plot, when he cut the ground under me by offering me money, he also took away my command. He left me with my escort of ten men, but the job he gave me was running a frog farm out in Pinar del Rio.

"Look what had happened to me. From being a glory boy and a big military man of the Revolution, I was chopped down to just a Comandante without any command. He did the same sort of thing to all of the Comandantes that weren't Communists or considered reliable by the Communists. Now, I realized that I was just a Commander on paper and that I didn't really have any power at all."

"When did you start plotting against Castro?"

"Later," Morgan continued, ignoring my question, "I realized I should have gotten out of Cuba. But the Cuban press was still making a lot of me and I seemed to be a big man down here. Also I was having trouble with the American Government, which had taken my citizenship away from me, and I felt very bitter about that."

What had happened was that, two weeks after Morgan's act of betrayal in Trinidad was splashed over the world's press, Representative Francis E. Walter had demanded that the State Department revoke Morgan's American citizenship. The legal basis for this was a provision in the Immigration and Nationality Act that forbids Americans to serve in foreign armies. Walter was the chairman of both the House Committee on Immigration and Naturalization and the House Un-American Activities Committee. He was a power to be reckoned with and the State Department hastened to comply with his request.

To continue with Morgan's statement to me: In the early months of 1960, he started to conspire seriously with groups in Santa Clara and Las Villas provinces. At that time, he had a small band of followers who agreed with him that Castro was turning over Cuba to the Communists and that something must be done to stop him.

"I was one of the first men to start a patriotic fighting front in the Escambray Mountains," Morgan said. "I made two or three clandestine trips into the United States to get arms and managed to get substantial amounts to the guerrilla fighting forces."

"How long did this go on, William?"

"For quite some time. Nobody was wise to what I was doing. Or at least so I thought."

"A man like you, who knew all about underground methods of work, how did you get caught?"

"That is the worst part of the whole story," he said. "I had a boy with me in whom I had the utmost confidence. I had picked him myself and made him my chauffeur. He delivered plenty of arms for me to the groups in the Escambray and, as a matter of fact, he went there and fought as a guerrillero.

"All the time he was doing this, he was an agent of the G-2. When the time came, he prepared the trap and sprang it. This boy is the one who is going to send me to my execution."

"And you were never wise to him?"

"Absolutely not. Because he did everything I told him to. He seemed completely in earnest. He went into the mountains and stayed there to fight. So I trusted him with my life."

"Tell me, William, do you think you have a chance?"

"Absolutely not. But I had counted on help earlier. You know there is really going to be an invasion, don't you?" I shook my head. "Men have been infiltrating into Cuba for two or three months now. They are working closely with the CIA. When Pardo Liada said that the counterrevolution is already in Cuba, he was telling the truth.

"But Fidel Castro knows this also. That is why they are scheduling my trial. Castro wants to eliminate anyone who can take power from him and that is why they are going to shoot me."

I told him I was sorry it was ending this way.

"I had no choice. I had to make amends for my terrible mistake. It is hard because of my family. My wife is now in political asylum in the Brazilian Embassy. I have two beautiful daughters."

There was nothing to say. I told him I hoped it would be God's will that he escape from the trap.

"It is impossible. There is one more thing. Are you sure you don't know why you are in prison?"

When I shook my head, Morgan reminded me that I had spoken against Fidel Castro and the Revolution on the Alan Courtney Show in Miami in February 1959.

"My God, how did they find that out? My radio appearance was by telephone and I didn't reveal my name."

"Don't you remember, there was a lot of argument about your statement that a Federal Marshal had warned you about going to Cuba? That made them investigate. That gives you an idea of how many people Fidel Castro has working for him in Miami. They checked the people going to Cuba and, by a process of elimination, decided it was you.

"Then to make matters worse, you talked on the international telephone without realizing that everything you said was monitored. Batista had this system operational and Castro simply took it over. Moreover, they found out you were a friend of Lieutenant Castano. There were stool pigeons in the Deauville Hotel who had worked for Batista—you probably knew who they were—and the same people informed on you. When you left the airport that night, you were suckered right in."

"But, William, why did they accuse me of being a pilot?"

"That part is very confusing. They were actually waiting for del Pino. There was much confusion that night; you will recall there were two arrests. When they accused you of being a pilot, they made a mistake. But that was the accusation and they had to leave it that way or let you go.

"Later on, when they had you on ice, they were ready to release you. Then your wife and son talked on the Miami radio, attacking Castro's Cuba. You realize that cooked your goose, don't you?"

"William, we were told to do that by the American Embassy."

"Well, maybe the Embassy made an honest mistake. It was about that time that I tried to do something for you, but there was too much resentment because of that radio show. Your case had become dangerous for me."

I asked William if there was anything I could do for him.

"If you ever get out of here alive, which I doubt," Morgan said, "try to tell people my story. I am not asking you to say that I was innocent, since I have been guilty of many things. But I tried to make up for my mistake and I am paying the penalty. I am paying with my life. Even though they took away my citizenship, I risked my life working for the United States to destroy Castro."

I promised to do what I could. We shook hands, and then he walked away. William Morgan had many friends. And, even though he was in and out of the galera several times after that, I never talked to him alone again.

"I Kneel for No Man"

That night, after they locked us into the galeras, we had "no idea that anything out of the ordinary would happen, but, at half past one that morning, they called Comandante William Morgan and his codefendant, Comandante Jesós Carrera, to the office. The man who was watching the office for us reported that Morgan and Carrera had been put in capilla. We spent another bad night because we believed they were going to shoot both men without trial.

In the morning, however, we learned that they were still in capilla and would be held there until trial. Around four that afternoon, William Morgan went to his trial, marching jauntily and singing "As the Caissons Go Rolling Along" at the top of his lungs. The trial lasted for six hours and, when it was over, the two men were put into capilla again and the grapevine told us they would die that night.

Around eleven o'clock, the man who was watching for us informed us that a woman and two little children had come into the office. He said that Morgan had then been taken from the capilla and led into the office, where he spent about half an hour.

The prison electrician was called into Morgan's death cell to fix the light. When he got there, William told him to give all of us his greetings and that he would try to let the world know what had happened at his trial. Shortly before his execution, a priest was sent in to him. We know that Morgan did manage to smuggle two letters out.

Early next morning around half past two, the firing squad arrived. The first man they took out was Jesus Carrera. We knew from our observer in the back of the galera that Fidel Castro, Raul and other big shots were attending the executions in person. Either they wanted to be absolutely sure that their most dangerous enemies were dead or they came to indulge their cruelty and thirst for vengeance.

Jesus Carrera was shot to death. Five minutes later, they took William Morgan out of capilla. As they brought him to the paredóu and tied his hands behind his back, a voice, which our observer could not identify with any certainty, asked him to kneel and beg for his life. "I kneel for no man," Morgan replied in Spanish.

Then another voice said something we could not understand and we heard William Morgan cursing them. One of the riflemen shot Morgan in the right knee. He fired again and put a bullet into Morgan's left kneecap. Then Morgan fell, for naturally he could not stand with both knees shattered.

The next stage was to put a bullet in his right shoulder and then another in his left. With Morgan writhing on the ground, the captain of the firing squad—I do not know his name—walked up to the tortured man and emptied a clip from his Tommy gun into his chest. When he was finally dead, they smashed his face with five .45 slugs.

This was confirmed to us by a member of the garrison who was an eyewitness of the execution. The priest, Father Dario Casado, who saw the body, agreed with this account.

Morgan's body was given to his sister-in-law, the woman who had come to see him with his two little children just before his execution. Father Casado, who was imprisoned a month or so later and who then slept next to my bed, saw the corpse and told me that Morgan's face was completely gone and that there was hardly anything recognizable about him.

William Morgan was buried the night of his death in the Colon Cemetery. Many of his friends came and saw how his body had been mutilated. This created such a scandal that the practice of giving the bodies of men executed by firing squads to their families was stopped.

The morning after the execution, when we had finished our coffee and were in the patio, a tumult began in the courtyard. Prisoners began shouting, "Bandits, Killers, Assassins" at the guards on the roofs. For the first time, the prisoners openly damned the Revolution. Many of the men in the patio were crying because the story of the brutal way Morgan had been killed was being circulated. The rumbling, which almost rose to the pitch of a riot, was a tribute to William Morgan's popularity. Whatever the verdict on Morgan's life, his death was that of a man.

CHAPTER 13

BACKWASH OF INVASION

Now that the invasion was approaching, the infiltrating of counterrevolutionary agents was being accelerated and sabotage was of much more frequent occurrence. Since I was an American, this meant that I was considered a much greater danger to the authorities from a security standpoint.

For some time, I had received no mail, no packages or visitors. I learned that this was the result of standing orders; the Swiss Embassy had tried to get parcels to me, but had been refused at the prison, and that my mail was sent to the G-2. Since I was not allowed to write letters, I was being held incommunicado.

On April 2, we learned that we were going to have a distinguished guest in our galera—Comandante Humberto Sori Marin. This man had been with Fidel Castro in the hills. He was a lawyer who had dedicated his legal training to the cause of human injustice. Sori Marin was the author of the infamous laws of the Sierra Maestra. Among other things these laws inflicted the death penalty on any Cuban who had run for public office on any political ticket in the 1958 elections. Moreover, they permitted any member of the 26th of July Movement to serve as judge and executioner.

Sori Marin was one of those responsible for applying the death penalty to ex post facto crimes; in other words, laws which made it a capital offense to have done something that was legal at the time. He had been the chief prosecutor at the military tribunals during the early phase of the Castro reign of terror. He had been the presiding judge at the subsequently famous trial of Captain Jesus Sosa Blanco, in which an Army officer was tried before television, with a howling mob demanding his blood, and sent to his death on perjured testimony. Sori Marin had drafted many of the laws of paredón and he was a prisoner with much to answer for.

We knew that he had defected in January 1961 and that he had escaped from his home in Santiago de Cuba, where he was being held under house arrest, by crawling through an air-conditioner duct. He had then gone to Florida, where we supposed he had joined the crowd of hand wringers, who claimed that the Cuban Revolution had been pure and wonderful as long as they had anything to do with it, but that unhappily Castro had betrayed it to the Communists. There were thousands of these people in Miami, those fellow- travelers of Castro Communism who had chosen freedom and fat subsidies from the CIA and had conveniently forgotten that their hands were red with the blood of patriotic Cubans. These left-wingers, who were not Communists, but were nevertheless accomplices in Castro's crimes, were the group most favored by the Kennedy Administration in the year of invasion—1961.

But Sori Marin proved to be of different caliber from the other outstanding turncoats from the Castro movement. Unlike other left-wing Cuban leaders, Sori Marin left the fleshpots of Florida to return to Cuba illegally. He was detected, wounded by gunfire, put in the military hospital and now was being transferred to Galera 14.

You can imagine how the twelve men in our galera, who had been sentenced to death under laws that this man wrote, felt about meeting him face to face. I waited expectantly for the encounter.

To my surprise, Dario Valdéz and Brigadier General Sanchez Gómez argued with us and finally convinced us that, when Sori Marin came into our galera, nobody was to accuse him, but, on the contrary, he was to be treated with the utmost respect. Regardless of the past, they pointed out, he was in prison because he had fought Fidel Castro and Castro would execute him, as he had executed Morgan and Carrera

That night, they brought him in, hobbling on a crutch. As he made his way painfully across the patio, one could feel the tension and excitement. To the Rebels, he was an almost legendary hero of the Revolution, a hero going toward trial and execution under the laws he himself had written.

"I am putting you here," Dario Valdéz said, when he entered our galera, "in the bed next to John Martino, the American. You two may have a lot to talk about."

He was nervous and edgy. Later, he told me in his adequate, but broken, English that he had been shaken because they had told him that he would occupy a galera with twelve men whom he had condemned to death.

Sori Marin was a tiny man, about five feet two, perhaps forty-five. He had a hawk-like face and wore glasses. He was the only man I ever knew who could shave himself without looking at a mirror. It was a trick; he told me later, that he had to learn (since he had no intention of growing a beard) when he was with Castro in the Sierra Maestra. He was suffering great pain, but we gave him enough drugs to ease his suffering. As soon as he was put on the bunk next to mine, Comandante Felipe Mireval, whom he had sentenced to death, walked up to him:

"Good evening. I have two sheets for you and a blanket."

When prisoners enter a galera, there are no bedclothes furnished, merely the bunk and the mattress.

Sori Marin peered at him. His expression was one of bewilderment. He did not understand what was happening and suspected an elaborate joke at his own expense.

Behind Mireval, Julio Sanchez Gómez appeared with a pillow and pillowcase.

"Make yourself comfortable," Orlando Jáuriga said. "We will make you some coffee."

He lay back on his bunk. He looked stunned. Dario Valdéz turned to him:

"Comandante, I want you to be at home here. Be at ease. Here you are among friends. Nobody has any hard feelings toward you any more. What happened is in the past. We are all here for one common cause. We know that, after you escaped to the United States, you came back to Cuba to fight. We respect that. We are one family here."

"Thank you." Sori Marin lay back in his bunk. The tears came to his eyes. He pretended to sleep, but we knew it was to hide his emotion from us. Many people came into the galera to talk to him and this included captains and lieutenants who had served under his command in the Sierra Maestra, but Dario Valdéz posted a guard at the door and barred sightseers.

Dario Valdéz approached us:

"Comandante, you will have your food brought in here like Martino and the twelve condemned men." The practice was to have the twelve facing death eat inside the galera. "You will eat with John Martino," Dario continued, "the first American arrested in Cuba and convicted under your laws."

"You see, there is still some of that feeling against me," Sori Marin said to me.

"There has to be. As for me, I am not a Cuban. Nevertheless, I hold some resentment toward you. We will try to get along as best we can."

"Can I shake your hand?"

I said, "Of course" and we shook hands.

"I want you to know one thing," Sori Marin continued, "I am not anti-American, but I was and I still am a nationalist."

Then he gave me the old story about my not being able to understand how it felt to live in a country where all the industries were owned by foreigners or controlled by foreign interests. Sori Marin was a man who believed his own propaganda.

"Yes," I said. "All of you Castro defectors tell the same story, even William Morgan. You never heard of Communism; you thought it was just us nationalists here. And a 'nationalist,' of course, is somebody who tears up decent laws and writes a law code that justifies murder. You were with Castro in the mountains. You were at his side. You had every opportunity to observe him. But you never suspected he was a Communist and you were just an innocent dupe."

"I swear by my wife and children," Sori Marin replied, "that Fidel Castro fooled me until the bitter end."

He went on to explain that, as a member of the Council of Ministers, which supposedly ran Cuba right after the Rebels took over, he had voted against every proposed law with only one exception. The agrarian reform law he had drafted provided for the distribution of government lands to land- hungry peasants and for the expropriation with compensation of part of the large estates. Castro had perverted the land reform by denying compensation, seizing land indiscriminately and forcing the peasants on collectives where they became serfs of the totalitarian state. All of this, by the way, was true, but it was not generally known in Cuba at the time. Sori Marin then proceeded to blame the United States for the fact that Castro was a Communist. He claimed that Castro had felt slighted, when he came to America in early 1959, and was received by Nixon, instead of by President Eisenhower. He conveniently forgot that Castro's visit was not official.

He alleged that the United States Government made no attempt to understand Castro or help him financially, which was also completely untrue. Then his final point was that some American Ambassadors had taken a superior attitude toward Fidel, which had enraged him. The fact was that Ambassador Bonsal had behaved in a most conciliatory Mariner toward Fidel Castro and had merely aroused his contempt.

The more I talked with Sori Marin, the less impressed I was with him as a political mind. He told me that he had known that Raul Castro and Ché Guevara were Communists and that Fidel Castro was surrounded by Communists. Yet, supposedly it came to him as a great shock to discover that Fidel himself was also a Communist and that his movement was a cat's-paw of the Soviets.

He once told me that he was "a middle-of-the-road man" and explained this by saying that he had hoped Fidel Castro would turn out to be "another Tito." In other words, as I saw it, he wanted Communism, but he wanted it to come a bit more gradually. He was not in favor of spitting on the United States the way Castro had done, presumably because he knew that Cuba could use American money. But he did have courage and dedication and we respected him for that.

One day, I asked him what his chances were. "Fidel Castro came to see me when I was in the military hospital," Sori Marin said. "What he had to say to me was this:

"'Well, cabron, I am going to see that you are cured so I can put you in La Cabana and watch you die with my own eyes. You have been against me from the beginning and you have given me nothing but trouble. You have also become a traitor and have sold out to the Yankees.'

"Therefore, I know that my days are numbered."

On another occasion, he asked me if I knew why he was in prison. I shook my head.

"There is really going to be an invasion," Sori Marin said, "and there is a possibility of a military putsch or revolt at the same time. That is one of the main reasons I came back to Cuba. I have many friends in the Rebel Army. I came back here to convince them. There are also armed groups in the hills and there are counterrevolutionary units in the cities. When the invasion starts, they will go out into the streets and there will be an insurrection. I returned to Cuba because you don't make a revolution by making speeches and writing articles in Miami. You make a revolution by coming back to your country and organizing men who are able to fight."

Meanwhile, the prison was filling up with men who were being arrested in raids, men accused of being part of the underground that was supposed to take up arms when the invasion forces landed.

On the 12th of April, which was a visiting day, we were told that the invasion would take place between the 15th and the 20th.

"My God," Sori Marin said, "if everybody knows that, then the Devil knows it too." By the Devil, he meant Fidel Castro.

I once asked him why he had signed the laws that led to paredón and his reply was essentially the old Marxist answer that you can't make an omelet without breaking eggs. The eggs, however, were human beings. He did say that he had opposed the excesses and injustices of the Castro dictatorship—such matters as my arrest and the murder of about seventy prisoners by Raul Castro in the first days of the new regime—but that he had been powerless to do anything about it.

THE BETRAYED BEACHHEAD

On the evening of Friday, April 14, we heard sirens in the streets and we were locked up in our galeras. Great flames and billows of smoke were coloring the Havana sky. We assumed that some spectacular act of sabotage had been committed and tuned in to the Key West station, which was almost always correctly informed about these matters. Sure enough, we learned that the most famous and lavish store in Havana, El Encanto had gone up in fire. The invasion was now only three days off and all counterrevolutionary activities were supposed to proceed at an accelerated tempo. The next morning, we heard explosions. Havana was being bombed. For a while, we believed that the invasion was starting.

What actually had happened was part of a tragedy of cowardice and betrayal. The explosions were from a B-26 strike against the Cuban airfields. This blow destroyed about half of Castro's air force and the plan was for a second strike for dawn on April 17, the day of the invasion. This would have sufficed to destroy Castro's few remaining aircraft. Consequently, the invaders, even with their antiquated B-26s would have had command of the skies.

Under these conditions, they would have been able to hold the airfield they had seized a dozen or so miles inland from the beachhead, set up fuel supplies there and use it as an airbase for forays and strikes anywhere on the island of Cuba. As I shall show later, there can be little doubt that, under these conditions, the Cuban patriots would have had a good chance at victory.

There is some question as to exactly who pulled the panic button and talked or pressured President Kennedy into calling off the decisive B-26 strike, in the interests of the "American image" in the United Nations and a mythical entity known as "world opinion." While the President rightly accepted full responsibility for the decision, this unknown adviser bears a terrible responsibility for drastically undermining the security of the United States and for unnecessarily prolonging the Calvary of the Cuban people.

The blame for this advice is generally placed on the shoulders of Adlai E. Stevenson, the American Ambassador to the United States. When he was first accused of having played the role of Mr. Appeasement in the Playa Girón invasion by Senator Hugh Scott of Pennsylvania, Stevenson issued a denial which few informed persons accepted at face value.

On May 10, 1961, less than a month after the disaster of Playa Girón, President Kennedy entertained a group of Florida newspaper editors and publishers and had a frank off-the-record discussion of the Cuban crisis. A statement by Attorney General Robert Kennedy in January 1963 made the Florida newspapermen consider that their off-the-record pledge was no longer valid. Accordingly, on January 24, 1968, Jack Gore, publisher of the Ft. Lauderdale News and the Sun Sentinel, declared that the President had told him that he had planned "to protect the invaders from the air, but that he had made the decision not to use the air power."

According to Gore, the President then added: "that (he) decided against supplying air cover because U.N. Ambassador Adlai Stevenson complained that any such action would make a liar out of him in the UN."

Gore's statement brought comments from other publishers present, from Senator George Smathers of Florida and from President Kennedy. None, however, questioned his charge that Stevenson was the man who gave advice that made the defeat of the Cuban anti-Communists inevitable.

I knew very little about Stevenson's political past at the time. All we knew there in La Cabana was that the explosions denoted a crisis of some sort on the verge of eruption. There was a strong possibility that the first act of retaliation by the Castro dictatorship would be to have us all murdered.

"Everybody stay in their bunks," Dario ordered. "Don't make any noise. Any demonstration of any sort could be very dangerous."

We waited. Around nine that morning, the explosions stopped. The news came over the radio that planes had bombed Ciudad Libertad, Managua, Santiago and other airfields. When I gave Humberto Sori Marin that report, he asked: "Did they bomb Columbia airport in Camaguey?"

I said there was no report of that. He kept insisting on an answer to that question throughout the day. Finally, when it was clear that no such attack had been made, Sori Marin said:

"That means we are lost."

I suppose Camaguey had been one of the fields reserved for the second strike of the B-26s—the one that had been called off in Washington.

During much of this time, we were locked in our galera. When it was finally opened, we found that the heavily armed guard detail on the roof had been reinforced.

On Sunday the 16th, we learned from the grapevine that militiamen with tanks and other armor were moving toward Matanzas, the province where the ill-fated invasion would break in the pre-dawn hours of the following day. The jeeps and halftracks stored in the dry moat of La Cabana now started moving out.

On the 17th, the guards seized all radios at conteo. We were cut off from our main source of news and had to rely during the next few days on the grapevine. There was a radio in the kitchen, however, and we managed to keep some sort of contact with the prisoners who worked there. On the 18th, we learned indirectly from Rebel officers that the invasion forces had inflicted very heavy casualties on Castro's militia. Meanwhile, the American radio was making fantastic claims, concocted by the CIA, that las Villas, Santa Clara and other key cities had fallen. None of us believed this. By the 20th, we knew that the invasion had failed. We suspected that it had failed because it had been betrayed.

On the same day, the loudspeaker called Humberto Sori Marin and his people to the office. The little Comandante was much troubled and, as he was too badly wounded to dress himself, we had to help him put on his clothes.

Two hours later, he returned with the news that he and his men were charged with counterrevolutionary offenses carrying the death penalty.

THE DRAGNET

The next morning, when we came out into the patio, we saw that the part of the courtyard reserved for visitors was filled with women of all ages. Some were pregnant. Some were unable to stand up and were lying on the bare concrete. We were not permitted to approach the railing. Several prisoners tried to send out blankets, pillows, water and cups to the women, but the guards did not permit this.

That afternoon, prisoners, picked up in a gigantic dragnet, began to file into La Cabana. The place was crowded beyond imagination. Although our galera was the elite cell, it was jammed late that afternoon with 163 men. The prisoners' part of the patio was also used for detention and was crowded and there were prisoners in the dining room and in the kitchen.

One of the men brought into my cell was Father Dario Casado. As there were only about thirty-five beds, he had to sleep on the floor beside my cot. The galera was so jammed that one could scarcely move. There was no place to walk and the patio was barred to us. It was raining hard and there had been a cold snap. The newcomers had no blankets of any sort.

The new prisoners were bank clerks, employees of the telephone company; in short, middle class and white collar elements. Probably, about half a million people had been arrested. They included everybody against whom there was any suspicion whatsoever, everybody whom the local defense committees did not trust. The arrests were also directed, more or less indiscriminately, against those who were educated, those who were successful, and those who wore neat clothes and those who belonged to the white race. These groups, with the exception of the minority among them who were Communists or Communist sympathizers, were correctly classified as potentially disloyal elements.

These dragnet raids were not a demonstration of the efficiency of the 0-2 at all, for they scooped up the innocent as well as the guilty and, in the final screening-out, some of the key men of the underground were released. It was a precautionary measure on a huge scale, designed to incarcerate the sort of people who would be most likely to hate Communism, in order to paralyze the feared uprising of the underground.

The underground had already been paralyzed by orders, issued by President Kennedy, again in deference to world opinion, preventing it from doing anything. But Castro did not know that and neither, of course, did we.

I Was Castro's Prisoner

Father Casado had been arrested on the street in civilian clothes and taken to the Blanquita Theatre, which was already full of prisoners. The Sports Palace, the Principe, the Moro Castle and virtually every other available building were used as jails. The prisoners were sometimes held for days without food and with inadequate water. I know of one group that was put in a large abandoned cistern. When they were released, two had committed suicide and one had gone mad. On the 20th, Sori Marin and his people were taken to trial. Even before the trial had concluded, the firing squad was assembled. Thus, the verdict had been decided beforehand. Beginning shortly after eleven that night, the jeep took men out of capilla every five minutes and the firing squad did its work before a horrified audience of the prisoners who had been rounded up in the dragnet.

Eufemio Fernández Ortega, who had been head of the Cuban secret police under President Prio, was next to the last to die. When they took him out of capilla and started to put him into the jeep, he fought the guards with his bare hands. When they tried to tie his hands behind him against the paredón, he charged the firing squad and fought until they bayoneted him to death. Finally, they came for Sori Marin and he hobbled into the jeep, was taken out and executed.

Among the witnesses, we learned later, were his twin brothers. These men were loyal to the regime and they attended Sori Marin's execution in the uniform of the Militia. Shortly before these events, I had another conference with my lawyer, Dr. Camargo. He told me that a new medical captain had been appointed, who had refused to do anything to get me transferred to a hospital.

"I think I will have lots of trouble with him, Martino. He is a real, fanatical Communist. When he found out who you were, he refused to sign the expediente I had brought for him and he said: 'I will take care of the American. I will take care of him personally.'"

"He might have meant that literally," I suggested.

"Not a chance. Don't forget that Dr. Dubuté is your enemy. He will never forgive your giving William Morgan that injection. There have been many cordilleras since the six Americans were sent to the

Isle of Pines and I have been fighting tooth and nail to keep you in La Cabana."

"Thank you," I said, "but if the worst comes to the worst, I will just have to go to the Island."

"If you go there, I guarantee you will die," Camargo replied. Then he shifted to another subject: "Do you remember those six Americans?"

"Of course."

"Do you know the real reason why they were convicted?"

"You understand the authorities had no proof that these men had come to Cuba for counterrevolutionary purposes?"

"That is what they told me."

"That is the truth. Do you know why the trial of those Americans was postponed? I am going to tell you. The night before the trial, a Florida paper published a photograph of these men training in a camp in South Florida. That camp belonged to Senator Masferrer. The same picture was shown on one of the Miami TV stations. Also, and I have positive proof of this, on television the night before the trial, there was a brief film sequence in which one of these boys was seen coming out of the house of Rolando Masferrer.

"Why do your newspapers do things like this? Don't they care whether people live or die? Don't they realize that thousands of lives are involved and that men are sacrificing everything to bring back freedom to their country? Isn't there anything more important to them than news?"

"I can't explain that sort of mentality," I replied. "If I ever get out of here, I will see that the American people learn about these things."

On April 23, we learned from the grapevine that Manolito Fernández, the chief of the prison, had been arrested by the G-2 and that we had a new director, a dyed-in-the-wool Communist named Espinosa.

The reason Manolito had been transferred was another tribute to the CIA. It had a radio station called Radio Swan. To our horror, we heard this station broadcasting about conditions in La Cabana, describing how good the chief of the prison was to the inmates, how he treated everybody fairly and how the requisas had improved.

By broadcasting to the world what a wonderful fellow Manolito was, this CIA station got him in trouble with the Castro authorities. As a result, he was turned over to the G-2 and, at this writing; he is in a military concentration camp on one of the Cuban cays as a prisoner of Fidel Castro. Through this operation, the CIA brought about a change in prison administration that was to cause all of us much misery and suffering.

CHAPTER 14
DOWN INTO THE ABYSS

Lieutenant Espinoza inaugurated his new administration with a savage and senseless requisa. Around three in the morning, guards armed with Russian R-2 rifles entered our galera and ordered everybody out at once. We were allowed to wear shorts only and commanded to march out barefoot. These orders were reinforced with bayonets and a few sleepy men, who had not reacted quickly enough to suit our new master, were jabbed or beaten across the buttocks.

From 1,200 to 1,500 men were packed in the little courtyard so tightly they could hardly move. Meanwhile, the guards went into the galeras, turned over the bunks, ripped the blankets with their bayonets and piled the prisoners' clothes in huge heaps.

During the day of that requisa, resentment began to build up among the prisoners. One of the results of the betrayed invasion was that the prison was swarming with students and young workmen in their late teens or early twenties. These new prisoners had not mastered the lesson that patience and inconspicuous conduct are the keys to survival when one is behind bars.

The explosion began when a group of young prisoners at the far end of the courtyard began singing the Marine Anthem. Another group responded with "Anchors Aweigh." This infuriated Lieutenant Espinoza to such an extent that he started to fire a .30 caliber machine-gun over our heads. He swore over the loud speaker that, unless the singing stopped, he would shoot to kill.

There was consternation among us older prisoners. We knew that, if firing started, we would all be killed. The young hotheads began to push against the barricade that bisected the patio and we knew that, if they broke it down, we would all be machine-gunned to death. Some of the sick prisoners fainted. We urged the new prisoners to calm down.

Meanwhile, some of the old guards, men who had served under Manolito Fernandez, formed a ring around Lieutenant Espinoza, who was raging and had apparently lost all vestiges of self-control. They apparently convinced him that, if he provoked a massacre of the prisoners, he would be held responsible for it. The immediate danger passed.

We were ordered to file outside of the barricade by galera numbers, remove our shorts and pass through a line of guards, who would search our underpants and return them to us as we re-entered our galeras. This operation proceeded smoothly.

However, there was a prisoner named David Salvador, who had been arrested the previous November when trying to escape from Cuba. He was a former Communist, whose break with the Cuban Party had not materially changed his attitudes of rebellion toward authority and hatred of the United States. This man had been the first head of the Cuban Confederation of Labor (CTC) under Fidel Castro. He had lost his job because of Castro's determination to turn over the trade union federation to the Communist minority.

David Salvador was confined in Calera 13. He never went into the patio, because he was one of the men who had started paredón and he was afraid to venture outside and face his victims.

But now he had no alternative; he was in the patio. As he crossed it, the prisoners began to jeer. He stopped before one of the guards, who told him to take off his shorts. Salvador refused. One of the guards walked up to him with a Colt .45 and said:

"Salvador, you are one of the men who started all this. You are the one who demanded firing squads. What are you trying to do? Be a leader here?"

There was a bedlam of cursing and jeering from the prisoners. Salvador's little group prevailed upon him to take off his shorts. He did so and was jabbed by the guard with a bayonet. He returned quietly to his galera, as did the rest of us. We were locked into our cells.

FILTH, SQUALOR, THIRST

On April 25, there were two cordilleras and 400 men were sent to the Isle of Pines. We learned from the grapevine that this was partly to make room for the new prisoners who were being arrested every day and partly because Lieutenant Espinoza was afraid of us. This last was confirmed by the fact that he never dared stick his head into the galeras. That day, Espinoza announced over the public address system that, if there was any danger of another American invasion, all the prisoners could expect to die. He would see to it personally that every one of us was killed.

Similar orders had been given the chiefs of every prison in Cuba. A few days later, two of my friends were returned from the Isle of Pines to La Cabana. They told us that right after the invasion they saw prison guards place plastic explosives under each of the circulares on the Island. There were standing orders that, at the first intimation of a new invasion, the entire prison was to be blown up and not a single inmate left alive. I was told that the Communists had done exactly the same thing in Guatemala immediately before the patriotic revolution under Colonel Castillo Armas, which destroyed their Red dictatorship there.

For the rest, the returned men told us that conditions were terrible on the Island. The food was abominable; there was a desperate shortage of water due to the overcrowded conditions, and they had no cigarettes for three months.

About a week later, they started wholesale releases of the men who had been picked up by the thousands immediately prior to the invasion. Most of these men had nothing to do with the underground. They had been arrested for being pro-American, but then so were most Cubans.

Their place was taken by prisoners of the G-2. These men were, for the most part, lawyers, doctors, bankers, businessmen, engineers—in short, the elite and the brains of Cuba. A group of prominent Americans was arrested at about this time.

I would estimate that there were 1,500 prisoners in La Cabana at this time and beds for only about 675. Many of the men transferred from the G-2 were in very bad physical condition and they responded poorly to the overcrowding. At this time, an epidemic of colds and flu swept through the prison. Three men died in the Fortress because of medical neglect.

During almost all of this time, water was rationed to about half an hour during the morning. The men would fill their little cans or cups and that was all they would get during the day. Consequently, these people were lousy; they stank; the whole place continuously smelled of urine and of feces and of dirt and of body odors.

When it rained, it would do so through the open grill in the courtyard. Since the galeras were underground, the rainwater from the patio would run off into them and there was no way of keeping dry. We were infested with bed bugs, lice and fleas. Many men suffered from diarrhea because of the rotten food.

There were rats everywhere. They were huge and so fierce that the cats we brought into the galera were afraid of them. The garbage was kept in open containers in the patio and this attracted swarms of flies and mosquitoes. These insects came through the open railings into the galeras. One had to fight them off continuously. During good times, they would send men with insecticides to spray the galeras.

The minute there was any trouble with the guards or the authorities, however, we would be back with the open garbage, the insects and the danger of malaria.

When you moved around at night, you didn't know what you would be stepping into. There was no toilet paper ration. This is a problem we could cope with during the occasional times when there was plenty of water. Moreover, the prison authorities would occasionally provide diarrhea pills. However, most of the time it was as I have described it.

Our food was simple, poor, with little variation. For breakfast, a demitasse portion of coffee served cold and kept in an oil drum. Also a stale roll. Lunch was around eleven. It consisted of a scoop of soybeans in water. Dinner was a scoop of macaroni. In good times, we would be able to buy powdered milk and sugar in the prison canteens and we would hoard it so we could keep alive during the bad times. It was hardest for the big men, whose food requirements were the largest.

ANOTHER ESCAPE

Four tribunals were operating now, but they were using the old paredón outside the prison gates. Men would be brought directly from the C—2 to their deaths. During the first three weeks of May, eighty-seven men were executed in La Cabana Fortress. We heard the firing squads, but did not know the names of their victims.

The ban on visits from lawyers was finally lifted and Camargo, looking much thinner and spiritually shaken, came to see me. He told me he had defended two more Americans in Pinar del Rio, men named McNair and Anderson.

"They were convicted and executed," he said. "Sometimes, I think my defense work is useless, but I have mounted the horse and now I must ride it."

I told him to stop visiting me and to get out of Cuba, because otherwise he would soon be one of my cellmates.

"I have my papers ready," he replied. "I have official permission. When the pressure mounts a bit, I will have to go."

When the men who had been picked up in the dragnet raids were to be released, the procedure was to call them to the office. There, they would be asked four questions: their father's name, their mother's name, their address and their marital status. When they had replied satisfactorily, they were set free.

A prisoner named Ignacio had become friendly enough with a gusano, as the pro-Americans swept up in the dragnet raids were called, to be able to answer these four questions. When the gusano's name was called for release, Ignacio took advantage of the fact that he was sound asleep—or else the whole thing was contrived—went into the office, impersonated him, answered the four questions and left La Cabana a free man.

This substitution was not discovered by the authorities until much later, when a cordillera was assembled to take Ignacio to the Isle of Pines to serve his ten-year sentence along with hundreds of others. Lieutenant Espinoza was unable to understand what had happened and resorted to his usual expedient of threatening everybody with physical violence. They had a roll call and the gusano was naturally the one man not accounted for. He was put in solitary confinement in capilla for three months, but, when they found they could prove nothing against him, they let him go.

Captain Contino, the man who had been the head of the legal department of the Cuban National Police and the person who had helped me in the Catillo de Atarés, was arrested together with a group of about ninety men, who were accused of waiting for the invasion in the Escambray Mountains.

They also brought in Alfredo Sanchez, the son of the Cuban leader in exile, Aureliano Sanchez Arango. With him was a man named Benito Gâlvez, a graduate of a United States military academy, in his middle thirties, who spoke excellent English. He told me that he had been betrayed to the Cuban Communists by people in the American Embassy. Communist Methods of Torture.

This was the first time we had met people who had been in the hands of the G-2 for long periods. Gálvez explained that they have little rooms, called cabanitas, in G-2 headquarters. The prisoner is thrown into one of these naked. It is so small that he must stand up and can barely turn around. There are enormously powerful lights in the ceiling and the heat is almost unbearable. The victim is kept in the hot room until he has had all he can stand and then is put into a similar cell, which is air conditioned and is kept at near freezing temperature. This treatment is continued, alternating heat with cold, until the victim loses consciousness or confesses.

They also apply mental torture. One method is to take prisoners from the G-2 blindfolded to one of the beaches. The men are tied to stakes and told they are about to be executed. A firing squad is assembled; the commands are given; the only departure from realism is that blanks are fired.

In most of these cases, there was no physical torture in the sense that the victims were not touched. At the time Gálvez was there, about 1,500 prisoners were being held in G-2 headquarters in Havana. Among them were women and children. They were given the physical and mental torture of the cabañitas to make them confess. Those who did break down and confess generally ended at the paredón.

The questioning was done by teams of interrogators who repeated their questions and charges hour after hour. The prisoners who were recalcitrant would be put back in the hot and cold cells for hours and then brought back again for questioning.

There were also G-2 "farms"—in reality, isolated houses—out in the country, where men were taken for more severe torture. Few people ever returned from these farms and hence it was not easy to find out what happened there.

One case we knew about was that of Jorge Diaz. He was blindfolded and taken at night from G-2 headquarters to one of these torture farms. Here he was imprisoned for six or seven months with no toilet paper of any sort.

When he was brought to us, he was unable to walk and his buttocks and anus were a festering mass. We had to wash him with boric acid and, by doing that continuously while he was with us, we improved his condition about 50 per cent.

Then he was shipped out to the Isle of Pines and we never learned what happened to him.

He said that six men had been taken with him from the G-2 to the torture finca. He was the only one brought back to Havana. On the return trip, the guards were joking about how one man had died of heart failure, another for a different reason and so forth. In short, all had been tortured to death or allowed to die of neglect.

"Then we were Rebels with Fidel Castro in the hills," Diaz once said, "we used to talk about how the Batista people would run red hot irons up women's vaginas. This was propaganda, of course. But in the G-2 farms, they actually do this to women and they also run hot irons up the anal openings of men. Whenever this is done, a human being is killed."

I have seen men come back from the fincas whose fingernails had been torn out. There was a man who had all the bones in his fingers smashed with a gun butt and there was another whose legs had been stretched so much to make him confess that he couldn't stand up.

A man named Segundo Prieto was kept in the hot box in G-2 headquarters and made to look into the bright light until he lost his eyesight. He is now in La Cabana and hopelessly blind. Another man, who is now serving time on the Isle of Pines, had his testicles twisted off on a G-2 torture farm. He was able to stand the agonizing pain because he is a student and practitioner of yoga.

In the G-2 farms, the torturing is usually done by Negroes. As for the Rebels who fought for Castro in the hills, almost all of them are whites and are considered unsuitable for this ghoulish business.

The supervision and direction of the tortures is in the hands of Russians. These men are generally either police officials or physicians. They never touch the victims themselves, but they give the orders for torture and decide when it is to be interrupted. They also handle the interrogations and inject sodium pentothal, the so-called truth serum. Outside of the specialized machinery of torture to induce confession, sadistic treatment and callous neglect tends to be the rule.

For example, a former corporal in the Cuban Army under Batista, named Adolfo Caballero, was sentenced to serve three years on the Isle of Pines for allegedly having mistreated Rebel prisoners. When he was sent to the Island, he was a very powerful man, slightly over six feet tall, weighing perhaps 210 pounds. On the Isle of Pines, he got into trouble during one of the requisas, was put into an isolation cell and left there to die.

At the last moment, he was transferred to La Cabana and became one of our cellmates. The ex-corporal was all skin and hones. He could hold no food. His eyes were glazed. He would cry like a baby and ask for his wife and children. During the three years he had been on the Island, he had never received a letter and did not know whether his family was alive or dead.

While Adolfo was dying in our cell, a male nurse, Manolo Blanco, who was serving four years for having tried to leave the country by plane, became furious at the fact that nothing was being done to save this man's life. The turnkey, who was also a decent human being, was persuaded to help Blanco to carry the dying man on his mattress into the prison office. There, the two put up a successful fight to have Adolfo admitted to the Military Hospital.

But it was too late. Adolfo died there the next morning. For this act of mercy, Blanco was sent to the Isle of Pines and the turnkey became a military prisoner in La Cabana.

Another case of callousness was that of fourteen elderly, retired monks, who lived in a monastery in the Havana area. Because of Castro's fierce hatred of the Catholic Church and of religion in general, I suppose, these old men were arrested and thrown into Calera 12, which was supposed to house forty prisoners and already had 180. These monks naturally had no beds and it was raining very hard. The oldest, a man of ninety-two, had to sleep on a tiny ledge by the open grating, exposed to the rain, and, when the morning came, lie was dead. I should add that, after four weeks of prison, the aged monks were released. When they left, all the prisoners cheered them.

THE LAST ESCAPE

Around this time, they brought a prisoner into Calera 14, whose name, strangely enough, was José Martino Alvarez. He told me that he had the name Martino, because generations ago his ancestors had been Italian. This man was a good friend of Dr. René Dubuté, the blackmailer, and he was to play a sinister role in my story.

The Americans who had been rounded up at the time of the invasion were released. One man remained, Robert Geddes Morton, the president of the Pepsi-Cola bottling company in Cuba. He avoided me because he was yet to go to trial and did not want to make his situation more dangerous than it already was.

Another new prisoner was a tall, handsome boy of about twenty-two with a beautiful sweetheart. Carlitos, as we called him, had burned the Encanto department store. He loved America and would sit on my bed and sing American songs. He was marked for death.

Late that spring or early that summer, Dr. Camargo came to see me for the last time. He reported that the military physician in La Cabana had issued an order that I was to receive no medical treatment, since I was an enemy of the Revolution and deserved to die, It was the end of the road for my lawyer. I told him he had done all any human being could and urged him not to take any more risks. A few weeks later, he left for the United States. I would meet him in Miami a year and a half later.

Victor Maurin, the well-known Cuban songwriter, came into our galera. He and others wrote about five songs, including Cha-

cha-cha etc la Bayoneta and Paredon. We organized a quartet of fine singers and used buckets for drums. Every day, we would put on a show for the different galeras. These songs were political and they were parodies. From a Communist standpoint, they were subversive. Our black guards did not like our singing, but they were not allowed in the patio and all they could do was stand on the roofs and glare at us.

In July, they opened the prison for visits again. At the time, there was a young man in the prison, named Iram Gonzalez, who was charged with being the head of a counterrevolutionary group in Marianao. He faced either thirty years on the Island or paredón.

This boy managed to get women's clothes, even a brassiere. I have no idea how he did it. During the visiting hour, a group of prisoners surrounded him and he made a quick change into female attire. Meanwhile, another group cut the fence that separated the visitors from the prisoners. Tram was hurried through the gap. I will never forget watching him wall out with the women visitors, blowing kisses at all the prisoners. That was the last escape from La Cabana.

Naturally, after this happened, the galeras were closed again and our treatment deteriorated. Lieutenant Espinoza was removed from command and replaced by a young militiaman, who had been trained in Russia. Espinoza had been a wild man, a person of low intelligence, addicted to rages and irrational violence. The new Communist chief was a calculating person, who planned new ways of making life more miserable for us.

Tram Gonzalez, the escaped prisoner, was recaptured on his farm two weeks later. He was taken to a G-2 detention place for interrogation and torture. However, he managed to knock out his guard and then put on the latter's uniform. He walked into the office of the Comandante in militia uniform, borrowed the Comandante's car and drove to the Uruguayan Embassy, where he was granted asylum.

CHAPTER 15

VICTIMS OF THE
BETRAYED BEACHHEAD

Conditions were abominably bad in the prison and I kept getting sicker and weaker. I could not keep my food down and was passing a lot of blood. I stayed in my bed as I could scarcely manage to walk. My weight dropped steadily.

Father Dario Casado was finally released and enabled to go to the United States, where he joined the faculty of Villanova University. This was a great relief to me, as I knew he would keep his promise to look up Florence and the children in Miami and my mother in Atlantic City. They would have definite word that I was alive.

When I asked Father Casado how Castro and his Communists had managed to conquer in a Catholic country such as Cuba, his answer was that Cuba is only nominally Catholic.

"I would estimate that only 30 per cent of the Cubans who call themselves Catholics have been baptized and confirmed," he told me. "Moreover, while most of the colored people know of God and of the Virgin, they devote them selves to the worship of various saints and use voodoo practices in their worship. They are not Catholics in the true sense. Catholic doctrine does not guide and restrain them and, for the most part, they are too ignorant to understand it."

The members of the Catholic youth organizations, however, were of very different fiber. Many were students. All understood the doctrines of the Church. Religion played a guiding role in their spiritual life and made them implacable enemies of the Communist dictatorship.

The Castro regime evidently recognized that fact. In the late summer of 1961, we had a special requisa. The objects of search this time were not weapons, but religious objects. The guards seized all the medals, rosaries, holy pictures and Bibles they could, piled them in the middle of the patio and, in the presence of the prisoners, set fire to them. The new rule was that no prisoner could possess any religious article and that no more rosaries or prayers could be said.

This did not stop the young Catholics, who by this time constituted a large proportion of the prisoners. Instead of saying rosaries openly in the mornings, we would place men at the galera door at night and say the rosaries clandestinely as the early Christians in Roman catacombs must have done. As before, prayers were invariably said for the men who were executed. The guards know of these religious practices and many of them fiercely disapproved, but they were unable to stop them.

Carlitos Gálvez, the boy who had set fire to El Encanto, used to come to my galera at least once every day to talk about American jazz. He had worked in a music store and had become a fan. In September, he was called up for trial. Like the others, he shaved and dressed very carefully for this occasion.

The reason for this was that the judges and the militiamen in the audience looked filthy. Their shirts would be open and their shoes half laced. They had no military hearing or discipline. The prisoners, by contrast, went to trial with their hair cut, their faces shaved and scrubbed and their clothes as neat and clean as possible. They sat up straight and preserved a military bearing. This contrast was one that the Rebels resented.

Carlitos came into my galera the morning before the trial and sat on my bed, while his friends came to say goodbye. We were all sad because there was no doubt of his fate.

"I don't know why all of you look so gloomy," Carlito said. "After all, I am the one who is going to be shot. The only thing I am sorry about is that I didn't have time to burn down the Palace of Justice and the Ministry of Communications building."

He had these two additional acts of sabotage carefully planned when he was arrested. That night, they took him back from the trial and executed him two hours later.

We could see that the dictatorship was preparing for a new American invasion. Anti-aircraft guns were mounted on the prison walls and the dry moat was filling with tanks and artillery.

Outside in Havana harbor, tanks, military trucks, field pieces and anti-aircraft guns called cuatro bocas (four mouths) were being unloaded almost daily. All this new materiel was of Russian or Soviet-satellite origin.

At the same time, around October, we learned from the grapevine, from our visitors and our lawyers that the Communist Party was openly taking over all across the island. They were running the trade unions, the cooperatives and the industries, supported by hordes of fellow travelers and a substantial group of former Batista people with administrative know-how who had jumped on the bandwagon.

PURCHASING AGENT FOR CASTRO

About this time, a young man named Roberto Riveroni was put into La Cabana. He was in his early twenties, slight and delicately built. Moreover, he seemed highly intelligent.

Riveroni had worked in the Ministry of Foreign Relations and had been in charge of a purchasing commission, which had traveled around the world to buy strategic materials for Cuba that the United States would not sell. I was amazed that they would entrust that amount of responsibility to anyone so young.

"Yes," Riveroni said. "Most of us in key positions in the government today are in our twenties."

Riveroni emphasized that he was not a counterrevolutionary or a political prisoner. On one of his trips, he had bought $300,000 worth of automobile parts in Canada, but they were for old models. Castro had him imprisoned for sabotage. Ignorance and inexperience might have been a more accurate diagnosis.

He claimed that he was not a Communist and had never been one. In the past, he had been anti-American, hut when he saw how the people of the United States lived and how the American system worked, he changed his mind.

"I am a Cuban," he said. "I don't think I am doing anything wrong in going abroad to try to buy food and transportation equipment for my country.

"You know, you can get anything you want in the United States, provided you have hard cash—even for a Communist government.

In Detroit, I met a group of businessmen and bought all the hard-to-get parts, motors and other strategic items I wanted. I had to hand over the cash; they had to ship the stuff to Mexico. From Mexico, we transshipped to Cuba."

He told me that there were twenty-five men with him on his first foreign mission. However, when they got to Western Europe, twenty-two of those twenty-five defected. The defection situation got so bad that, for a while, half of the technical commissions consisted of C-2 operatives. That didn't work either. Finally, they had Russian and Czech guards with the missions as soon as they left Cuban soil.

I was interested in a revolutionary Cuban's impressions of the Soviet world. Since Czechoslovakia is the most prosperous of the Iron Curtain countries, I asked him about that.

"On the trip from the airport to Prague, a distance of about ten miles, we only met about a dozen cars," he replied.

"Don't they have cars over there?"

"Yes, but you can count them on your fingers and your toes. It made a bad impression on our group. Then we checked into the most luxurious hotel in Prague. Remember we had been used to the Havana Hilton, and the Capri. When we went into this top hotel as diplomats, we found the elevator was hand-operated by cable and had room for only three people.

They assigned me to a bedroom. The toilet was just like La Cabana. You had to flush it down with a bucket of water. There was a terrible stench.

"On top of all this, when I took a shower the first night—I was using plenty of soap and lather and I was whistling— well, what do you think happened? After five minutes, the hot water stopped.

"I didn't think anything of it. I phoned downstairs and complained. The clerk told me that in Prague hotels they only have hot running water for five minutes. However, since I was a diplomat from Cuba, a friendly country, they were going to give me another five minutes. Big deal!"

"Wasn't there anything good about the country?"

"Yes, the girls. There is free love there. You can have any girl, in fact anything you want, for American cigarettes. The same goes for American lipstick, American nylons, American ties.

"The first night, I took a girl out and she suggested we go to her home and make love. I asked whether her mother and father wouldn't mind, but she said no, that everybody in Czechoslovakia believes in free love.

"However, I believe in privacy and took her in the park. In their apartments, they may have a whole family crowded into a single room."

THE BETRAYED UNDERGROUND

In La Cabana, 107 men were awaiting trial for counterrevolution. Their leader was Robert Geddes Morton, whom I have already mentioned. These men were a major component in the underground organization that was supposed to synchronize an armed uprising with the Playa Girón invasion. Most of the underground never got off the ground because of cowardice and irresponsibility at high levels of the American Government. These 107 men believed they were betrayed because of stupidity and irresponsibility of the counter-intelligence people in the CIA.

In December 1960, a Cuban named Pedro Cuella alias Sergio Alonzo supposedly fled from Cuba to Miami. He infiltrated almost immediately into the CIA-directed operation and was trained to serve as the radio operator for a large organization of the underground.

The position of radio operator is of key importance for a variety of reasons. He is one of the few elements in the organization that must be able to recognize all of its members or at least all of its group leaders. Yet Pedro Cuella was cleared for this work. His clearance seems incredible in view of the fact that he had a brother who was a well-known Communist in Cuba.

When we discussed this situation in La Cabana, the prisoners would offer one of two theories. The most generally held was that the CIA itself was staffed with leftists and badly infiltrated with Communist elements. The other theory was that the pressure that President Kennedy had applied to make the CIA choose left-wing

Cubans, and preferably disillusioned turncoats from the Castro movement, made a breakdown of security inevitable. There were many technically trained, competent, loyal Cubans available, but these men could generally be smeared as having a right-wing taint of one sort or another. The fact that a Cuban had been fooled by the democratic façade of Castro's Communist Revolution (or had later found it convenient to pretend that he had been fooled) was proof that he was "progressive" in the Alice-in-Wonderland world of the New Frontier.

Under these conditions, the CIA had to look in murky places for its personnel. It could not reject men as bad security risks merely because they had been close to Fidel Castro, merely because they had been associated with Communists or merely because they had been accomplices in the judicial murders and other moral enormities committed by the Castro dictatorship before it declared itself openly to be Communist. The leftist clique around the President argued that, if a man had been imprisoned by Castro, that was sufficient proof of his opposition. Quite aside from the Communist stool pigeons I was to know in Cuban prisons, this view was naive. Not all of those who fell out with Castro could be trusted to cooperate with the United States or to work for a free Cuba.

The imposition of these left-wing leaders by the White House made the CIA develop a profound distrust of the underground from a security standpoint. This was particularly the case when Manolo Ray, a former member of Castro's Cabinet and a sort of would-be Caribbean Tito, was put in charge of liaison with the underground. This distrust reached pathological levels and caused inexcusable decisions.

Shortly before the invasion broke, one of the key leaders of the underground slipped out of Cuba and arrived in New York with an ambitious program for massive sabotage to cripple Cuban power and transportation. He was given two tons of plastic explosives to carry this out and told to return to Cuba. Despite the vital importance of timing this wave of sabotage for the eve of invasion, he was not told when D-Day would be. Accordingly, he was still in Miami with his explosives when the Cuban volunteers hit the beaches of Playa Cirón.

Perhaps even mare inexcusable was the fact that the CIA people in charge of the Cuban operation failed to take steps to prevent the 100-or-so known Castro agents in Miami from penetrating their ranks. The names and dossiers of these people could have been obtained from the Miami police.

In this chronicle of blundering, factional feuding and irresponsibility, one of the worst incidents was that Pedro Cuella was cleared from a security standpoint and sent to Cuba as a radio operator for the underground.

A young group leader of the underground, who had been married for only three days, knew something about Cuella's background and treacherous character. Cuella silenced him. With a squad of Castro's G-2, Cuella raided his house and shot him and his wife to death in their bed. Cuella's next step was to betray 107 members of the underground to the G-2. These victims were now in La Cabana, awaiting trial.

In Castro's Cuba, when the G-2 has no further use for an informer, when he is "burned out," they throw him into La Cabana. They did this with various stool pigeons including Pedro Cuella.

Cuella was put into the patio with the rest of the prisoners, who cornered him in the back of Calera 7 and started to beat him up. The traitor managed to make the 150 yards to the office, but, when he arrived there, his skull, nose, ribs and one arm were broken.

In the office, he was patched up. Since he could not be returned to the patio or any of the galeras and live, he was held in capilla until trial. Here he waited, confident that he would be acquitted at the trial and probably rewarded for his Judas work.

In the trial of the 107, there were sixteen petitions for death. One of them was for Robert Geddes Morton, the businessman who had sent word that he couldn't talk to me, because it was too dangerous. Morton had been born in Peru and moved to the United States at the age of two. His father was English, his mother American. Although he lived on the Florida Gold Coast and had an American wife, Morton was a British subject.

The trial lasted all day, ending around nine o'clock that night. When it was over, we learned that Robert Ceddes

Morton and ten of the others facing death had been saved by the pressure of world opinion.

One of the main things in Ceddes' favor was the conduct of the British Ambassador. He went to the prison himself and demanded to see Morton. When there was objection, he took the microphone himself and called Morton to the office.

Then, he added: "If there is any other British subject in this prison, he is to come to the office immediately."

He left the line open and we heard him telling the prison director that he represented Her Majesty and insisted on the right to talk to any Englishman who was held there.

His Excellency won the admiration of the prisoners by his resolute conduct. They asked me why the United States, which wielded so much more power than Great Britain, could not be represented abroad by better men. I could only explain that I had nothing to do with the Foreign Service and had no responsibility for the appointment of the representatives at the American Embassy whom they had seen in La Cabana.

There were five death sentences and, to everyone's surprise, one of the doomed men was the informer, Pedro Cuella. Before he met death, he requested the pardon of all the men he had betrayed. They forgave him. The day after the executions, a tall, thin man, very pallid and with a pleasant smile, came into my galera. He offered me English cigarettes, which the British Ambassador had given him, and introduced himself. He was Robert Geddes Morton.

"I can finally talk to you, because my fate is determined. I am very lucky. I drew thirty years. The trial, Martino, was one of the worst things I ever saw. Pedro Cuella took the stand and denounced all of us."

He introduced me to Comandante Miranda Gonzalez, who had also been one of the leaders of the organization. They had been waiting in Cuba for the signal to strike. They had important targets and they were ready. Their mission was to seize two airports and then to take over an entire province. There were almost 3,000 men armed and waiting on the island of Cuba.

Ceddes Morton insisted on orders, but the only word he got from Guatemala was to sit still and wait. His last radio contact was the day before his arrest. He begged for permission to go into action. However, he was ordered to make no move at all because of the delicate international situation. Morton replied that, if they didn't move, they would simply be arrested, because there was no way they could get off the island.

The CIA promised help. They would send a boat to pick up some of the leaders of the organization, "but help never came and I was finally arrested because the CIA-cleared stool pigeon gave the names of all the men who were ready to fight as soon as the invasion forces hit the beaches.

"We knew the invasion force was moving into action. We knew the beaches had been struck. But the only orders we got were to do nothing, to avoid any foolish steps, because action by the underground would only cause trouble internationally."

He shook his head: "I can't understand it, Martino. If they didn't want us to strike, why did they send us down here to throw away our lives? They sent us arms. I had been to Miami, had conferences there, and returned. I had everything ready. Then we were double-crossed at the last moment. The worst of it all, from my standpoint, was that I had twenty-four hours in which I could have gotten out of Cuba, but they kept stalling and ordered me to wait. As a result of their betrayal of our people, thousands of good men have been arrested and many of the finest have died at the paredón."

Ten days before the invasion, Federal Communications Commission officials closed down a vital high-power, shortwave transmitter that was sending instructions to the Cuban underground forces and to the guerrilla remnants in the Escambray Mountains from Lignum Vitae Island in the Florida Keys. The result was that, at the most critical period, the underground units were out of contact with that command center. They waited desperately, trying to re-establish liaison for seven days, and during that time the net around them steadily tightened.

The reason given for shutting down the Lignum Vitae transmitter was that it was interfering with the more or less useless propaganda broadcasts to Cuba from Swan Island. This interference was the result of a change in frequency ordered at the last moment. The result of this last-minute change and the consequent shutdown of the station was that the underground groups did not receive their orders. They were poised to destroy bridges, roads and other key installations, to do everything in their power to slow down the mobilization of Castro's militia and its deployment to the beachhead. I do not know who was responsible for these measures, which looked like sabotage and brought about disaster.

The abandonment of the Cuban underground may have been the result of cumulative blunders, but, to the Cubans in prison and the Cubans abroad, it had the reek of treason. A thorough investigation of what happened would seem to be an elementary act of justice toward those who died because of what the CIA did and because of what the CIA failed to do.

I mentioned a prisoner named José Martino Alvarez. This man went to trial and was sentenced to nine years on the Isle of Pines.

Meanwhile, the relationship between Dr. Dubuté and me had become much more strained. He not only didn't take care of me; he didn't even come to see me. He was marked as an informer and hated by the whole prison. He had already neglected prisoners of the invasion and, as a result, three of them had died.

When the next cordillera was called in early November, I was sitting on my bunk at about four in the morning when I heard over the public address system:

"John Martino, get your things ready and be prepared to be transferred with the rest of the group."

This was it. The Isle of Pines. The end of the line for me. My old friends stood around me commiserating. They helped me pack and carried me into the patio. I was too sick to walk.

Then a strange thing happened. As I learned later, during the fifteen minutes or so it takes to get the prisoners assembled, all the chiefs of all the galeras went into the office and argued with

Franco, the officer of the day that he should not send me to the Isle of Pines.

The first I knew about this was when Franco walked to where I was, shook his head and said:

"This is not the Martino I mean. Take him back to his galera. This man does not go to the Island." I was carried back to my cell and the cordillera left without me.

Later that morning, I was called to the office. The chief of the prison and Dr. Dubuté were there. The chief turned to the informer:

"Is this man Martino sick or isn't he?"

Dubuté said that I was not sick. I was only faking. When the list had been made up, they had asked him which men were too sick to move and he had not included me among the invalids.

"We will send for another doctor and we will get Martino's records and find out the truth," the chief said. "I am going to the tribunal to see whether this name was put on the list originally."

The meeting broke up and they took me back to my galera. About half an hour later, my good friend, Raul, cornered Dubuté in the patio and gave him a terrible beating. Dubuté was taken to the infirmary and Raul was put into capilla as punishment.

The next day, Dubuté came into my galera with murder in his face.

"You are the cause of all my trouble," he said, drawing a sharp instrument from his pocket. "I am going to kill you." Felipe Socorro, who was standing about two bunks away, made a great leap, disarmed Dubuté, dragged him into the back of the galera and almost beat him to death. Now the whole prison was in an uproar. The chief called all of us back into his office and announced that this time he was going to get to the bottom of the matter. He turned to me with a question and I said that all I knew was that Dr. Dubuté was half insane.

"Who is José Martino Alvarez?" The director asked. "Send for him."

He came into the office deadly white. He said he knew nothing; only that he had been tried and convicted.

"Where are the other men in your case?"

"They left on the cordillera this morning."

We were again dismissed.

That afternoon, I was called back to the office. A military doctor was there from Camp Columbia. He examined me and glanced at my records from the tribunal.

"This man is in no condition to be sent to the Isle of Pines," he said. "I also have the list here that was prepared by the tribunal." He handed it to the chief. "As you see, the man who should have been sent was José Martino Alvarez." The chief soon discovered that José Martino Alvarez had paid $200 to one of the prisoners who worked as a clerk in the office to change his name to mine on the cordillera list. Dr. Dubuté was part of the plot and was probably paid off as well.

Raul and Felipe Socorro, who were in capilla for having beaten up Dr. Dubuté, were sent back to the patio. An order came through that John Martino was not to be sent to the Isle of Pines, but was to remain in Galera 14 until sent to the Military Hospital.

In a few days, there was another cordillera. Among those sent to the Island was José Martino Alvarez, the clerk who had forged my name and Dr. René Dubuté, stool pigeon, corruptionist, forger and blackmailer. While I would never get to the Military Hospital, I had won a decisive round in the struggle for survival.

CHAPTER 16

THE COMMUNISTS PLAN "REHABILITATION"

The prison director was changed again. The new man, a Sergeant Pedraza, had just returned from Russia, where he had studied prison systems. His first move was to have all of us fingerprinted and mugged. As I was being photographed, I read the caption on my card: "War criminal and friend of Batista."

That same week, the case of Dario Valdéz came up. After almost two years in prison, he was freed because there was no one to accuse him. Amaro Yboney was set free for the same reason and Comandante Mario Salabarrios was released on "provisional liberty" when they discovered he was suffering from cancer of the bone. The new chief of our galera was Orlando Jáuriga, the former official of the Cuban narcotics bureau.

The strategy of the new administration was to go easy on the old Batista men, to try to win them over and split them away from those who had defected from Castro when they discovered he was a Communist stooge. This move seemed intelligent, but it was checkmated by the fact that we were all united by common bonds of suffering and torture. To show us how humane he was, Sergeant Pedraza announced we could each have two women and one child as visitors on Christmas Day. We worked all night washing the galeras, decorating them and borrowing sheets, so the families would not know how bad conditions were.

When the visitors arrived, they were subjected to a violent and humiliating search. The women and children were stripped naked and forced to jump into the air three times with their legs spread apart. This search was so thorough that, although the visiting day had started at ten in the morning, women were still standing in line to be searched so they could see their husbands at eight that night.

The prison director offered us another visit in the galeras on New Year's Day. The men decided, however, that they would rather not see their families at all than have them humiliated and the offer was rejected unanimously by voice vote.

JACK PAAR'S FOLLY

Two leaders of the Student Directory, Carlos Almoina and Miguel Garcia, were tried, condemned to death and placed in capilla. To our astonishment, they were not executed that night. Instead, they were held there for three days and then returned to their galera. There had been tremendous propaganda in their favor and against the paredón system throughout Latin America. Their lives had been saved and they were given long prison sentences instead. Miguelón Garcia had been parachuted into Cuba about four months before the invasion to work with the underground. He was working effectively and keeping in constant touch with the Guatemalan center by radio. To disguise his appearance, he had grown a mustache and put on weight.

However, he made a terrible mistake. One day, he walked into a restaurant. The man behind the counter had known him since he was three years old, first as a cook in his father's house, then as a bartender in the Miramar Yacht Club. The counter man turned him in to the Militia.

Carlos Almoina had been the head of the Cuban Tourist Bureau in the early days of the Castro regime. He had gone to the United States to enlist the support of the television star, Jack Paar. "Tell me," I asked him one day, "Is Jack Paar a Communist or something? And, if he isn't, why did he go down to Cuba to put on these propaganda shows for Castro?"

"I don't think he is even a pink, John," Almoina replied. "When I was in New York, he would take me around to the different studios in the network building.

He would introduce me and show me off and then ask the various people there: "'Look at him. Does he look like a Communist?'"

"What did he think a Communist looked like?" I asked Carlos.

"I don't know, John. I could never make Jack Paar out. Perhaps he thought Communists wear badges to make it easy for the rest of us to recognize them. Frankly, I thought he was a jerk. It seemed to me very shocking that a man with that tremendous influence over tens of millions of people should be so naive."

THE COMMUNIST SCHOOL

Roberto Riveroni introduced me to a young friend of his, known as the Checo. This man was violently anti-American and an old-line Communist Party militant. He was in prison because he had a personal dispute with Ché Cuevara when the latter headed the Cuban National Bank. He was very friendly toward me. As all Communists in Cuba did, he assured me that he was anti-American merely in the sense of being opposed to the trusts and imperialism; he had nothing whatsoever against the American people.

One day, he told me that he had heard a good deal of discussion of my case. He did not want to arouse my hopes, but there was a good chance that I would be set free before very long.

"Moreover," he said, "the Communist Party has a fine plan for the political prisoners, but the Party is having trouble with Castro. This is partly because Fidel Castro tends to follow the line of Red China. He is strongly opposed to freeing political prisoners and he is equally opposed to putting them to work. He wants to keep everyone under lock and key and subject them to the worst tortures imaginable. He seems to have limitless hatred for everyone who has turned against him or opposes him."

"What do you Communists propose?" I asked.

"It is not convenient for the Party to have so many Cubans in prison. Do you know that there are from 100,000 to 150,000 political prisoners on the island? And with our large Cuban families that means that over half a million people—about a tenth of the population of Cuba—have a member of their immediate family in prison. These people hate Castro and the regime. They will hate him as long as these conditions continue."

"Castro should have figured that out," I said.

"That is the trouble, Martino. Castro doesn't figure things out. He doesn't think; he does whatever comes into his head. We have fine leaders in the Party, men like Juan Marinello, Blas Roca and Lázaro Pena. We are trying to make him see the light. You see, Martino, many things have been done wrong in Cuba and the Communist Party is trying to correct them."

"Why are you telling me all this, Checo?"

"Because I have plans for you. We are going to need you."

"I am an American. I am not a Communist. And I have nothing to do with the problems of Cuba."

"That is where you are wrong, Martino. You are part of the Cuban situation now. Things are going to get better for you, because you can be useful in the new plan."

"What plan?"

"A school will be opened in La Cabana to give the prisoners a chance to learn to read and write, to study and to do many things." I looked at him in amazement:

"Checo, you know who these prisoners are. They are doctors, lawyers, and university students. They don't need you to teach them how to read and write."

Checo waved this objection aside:

"The school is just the beginning of the plan. Pretty soon, everybody will be called into the office and they will fill out questionnaires. They will ask you about your social and class background, why you are in prison, whether or not you have been tried, how many years you have to serve, about your wife and your relatives and their social origin and whether—if you had a chance— you would be willing to be integrated into the new society and to go to work. In that way, many men will go free.

"Now as to the school. The teachers, in many cases, will be drawn from the prisoners. I will head what we call the Communist Party nucleus of the school. We will pick the teachers and try to sell the idea that the men should go to school in all the galeras. We will show them that the school is a way toward freedom."

"How will that work, Checo?"

"The prisoners will show their good intentions by signing up for the school. After they have worked in the school and been under observation for one or two months, they will be passed out of the prison compound and will live beyond the walls in Galeras 24 through 28."

"Then what?" I asked.

"There they will have better food, better beds, and a canteen where they can buy what they want and visits three times a week. They will be allowed to wear civilian clothes. But they will have to study, to work hard."

"Study what, Checo?"

"Socialism. After they have mastered the elements of Marxism-Leninism and after three months in the outside galeras, then the ones who pass that test will be sent to farms. There, they will work and study under close observation for another half year. The ones who pass that test will go free under provisional liberty."

"What is going to stop them, once they get their provisional liberty, from going right back into counterrevolutionary activities?"

"You don't understand," he replied with a condescending smile. "After they have eventually been set free, they will go on the streets, But with one proviso. A member of their family or the neighborhood Committee of Defense will have to guarantee that these men will not engage in counterrevolutionary activities, because, if they do, they will go back to prison, another ten years will be added to their sentences and reprisals will be taken against their families."

"What will stop these men from going to a foreign Embassy and getting political asylum?"

"Well" he said, "that is where the family comes in. A member or two will be held responsible and they will go to jail in place of the man who was set free provisionally and escaped."

"Checo, you have worked out quite some plan."

"It is not my plan, Martino. It is the plan they use in the Soviet Union and elsewhere in the Communist world. It is going to be put into effect here. I will be in charge and my assistant will be a good friend of ours, Alejandro Martinez Saenz, the Nicaraguan."

"So he is in the act too? That doesn't surprise me." Martinez Saenz was a Nicaraguan revolutionary who had trouble with Chi Guevara. He was one of those people who

He kept assuring me that he was a just a nationalist, not a communist.

I told him I didn't think the plan would work, as he would have trouble trying to force the prisoners to accept it.

"You will see," Checo replied. "They will be called into the office, one by one. Those that reject the plan will not just be sent to the Isle of Pines. They will be put in a concentration camp where they will have to work with pick and shovel at forced labor, you will find out where on come in later," was his parting shot.

WE FIGHT THE BRAINWASHER

The Communist faction put two men into each galera to sell the school plan to the prisoners.

However, of 1,289 prisoners in La Cabana at the time, only sixty-seven men attended the opening classes of the school. Shortly before the school opened, Checo came to me to urge that I be its English teacher.

"We are against the American system," he said, "but not against your language. Furthermore, if you join the school as a teacher, you will have the biggest class in the school."

"Why is that. Checo?"

Because you are an American and many of the prisoners will follow you.'

"Checo, the answer is no."

"But, you teach English right now in the galera, don't you?"

"That's right. I teach my friends who want to learn the language." I had acquired a dictionary and a first grade reader and I had been teaching Jose Cabanas Gonzalez, General Sanchez Cortez and a few of the others. Checo argued that, if I could teach English in the galera, I could do the same in the school. I could get better food, fresh milk, medicine and a chance for freedom.

"Checo," I said, "you know I am an American and not a Communist. You also know all about my case and that I am innocent.

I don't see why I have to sell myself to get out of prison. Moreover, if jail is good enough for my friends, I will stay here until I die."

"It is up to you," he said, shaking his head.

Soon the attempts at persuasion were resumed. This time the agent was a boy, Cesar Fuentes, who had been in the same case as Dr. Julio Yebra, the man they had shot. Cesar Fuentes, for some unexplained reason, had been kept in La Cabana instead of being sent to the Isle of Pines.

He came to the galera to tell me that he would be the German teacher in the school and that, if I cooperated by teaching English, I would have a good chance to go free. I repeated what I had said to Checo.

"If you don't cooperate," Fuentes said, "remember you have a good chance to be sent to the Isle of Pines. They are setting up these schools all over Cuba and in all the prisons. When they take men from the Isle of Pines to go to the schools, there will be room there for a few hard heads from La Cabana."

That afternoon, the prison was in great excitement because the sixty-seven men who had decided to join the school had been told that, if they did so, they would be beaten up.

Alfredo Montoto came in.

"The chief of the prison says it is very important for you to join the school, because you are looked on as one of the leaders here. Everybody respects you and, if you join, there will be no trouble. The rest will follow the lead of an American."

"In other words," I replied, "I am supposed to be a symbol of the United States. If an American goes to school to become a Communist, it will break the morale of the rest. They will feel the United States has thrown in the towel."

"That is one way of putting it," he said.

I repeated that I would not do it. When he asked me what I would do if the chief forced me to go at gunpoint, I replied that I was a prisoner and would yield to force, but that the chief would merely be making trouble for himself.

"I am sorry to say this," Montoto replied, "but you are going to be shipped out together with a lot of other trouble makers."

The school stayed open exactly thirteen days. On the night of April 23, 1962, as the students were going to school after the dinner hour, a riot started in the patio. The prisoners ganged up on the students and teachers and mauled them for about a quarter of an hour.

The prison director took a machine gun and fired over the heads of the prisoners. He then ordered all men back to their galeras.

When they had returned the prisoners to their cells, including those who were bloody and beaten, the guards took the students with them and went from galera to galera. The students were ordered to pick out the men who had attacked them.

What followed was one of the most terrible sights I have ever seen. They opened up Calera 17 and took out six or seven men who had been accused of taking part in the riot. The guards lined up in two files facing each other. They made these prisoners run the gauntlet between the two files and, as they did so, about twenty-five guards on each side jabbed them with their bayonets and clubbed them with their rifle butts. As the guards battered them, the men tried frantically to reach the safety of the office before being clubbed off their feet.

They repeated this galera by galera. The entire bloody process took nearly four hours. By night, 167 men had bayonet wounds. Some also had broken ribs and cracked skulls.

About ten that night, we were all ordered back into the patio, including the sick. Four machine guns were pointed down at us from the roof. The chief, who had fired wildly into the patio with his .45 during the disturbance, now spoke over the public address system:

"If there is another riot in the prison, if anybody tries to stop the school, if any of the prisoners tries to beat up the students, then I will kill everybody."

The prisoners who had run the gauntlet were being patched up in the office. Afterwards, they were put in an underground galera, held incommunicado and fed on bread and water. Later, they were given a special trial for starting a riot in the prison and sent to the Isle of Pines.

The night of violence ended around two o'clock and early in the morning I was called to the office and, for the first time, met the chief of the prison face to face. He asked me to cooperate with the school and again I refused.

"We are going to take care of you troublemakers," he said.

At that moment, Franco, the officer of the day, intervened in my favor. I have no idea why he wanted to help me.

"Do you know the story of John Martino?" He asked the chief.

"I don't want to know his story. He is another American. He is an enemy of the Revolution."

"Why don't you go into the office and look at his dossier," Franco replied. "There is an order from the tribunal that he must not be removed from La Cabana Fortress."

The chief asked Franco why he was defending me. The O.D. replied that he was pointing out what was in the Martino file so that the chief would not get in trouble with the tribunal.

"All right, take him back to the galera. I will see why they don't want to send him to the Isle of Pines. But he must go out of this prison, because he is the source of a lot of trouble here, because he keeps telling the prisoners that some day the Americans will come and free them."

"I don't know where you got that information," I told him.

"It is false, but I suppose it is useless for me to try to argue with you."

"I know everything that goes on in the galeras. I know you are always talking politics."

After the riot, they suspended all visits and locked us in our galeras again.

That night, when the school opened, the students were escorted out galera by galera, but instead of sixty-seven men, only forty-two went to the school.

That morning at three o'clock, we had another requisa. This one lasted for ten hours.

Because of the riot, there was an investigation of the prison by high officials of the G-2. It was rumored that Ramiro Valdéz was taking part in the probe personally.

The galeras were opened again. Three new guards were brought in. From now on, they would be the only ones allowed inside the prison area and in contact with the prisoners. These men were ardent Communists, who had just returned from Russia. The chief of the prison was removed and a young man of about twenty, whom we knew only as Pepe, took his place.

Three or four days after the change in administration, they announced that the school was closed. The 100-odd men, who had been held in the underground galera on bread and water, were brought back. The water was turned on again. They explained that the whole thing had been a mistake and that the plan for a school had been shelved, as far as La Cabana Fortress was concerned, because we were too vicious and incorrigible and had no real desire to go free.

CHAPTER 17
REVOLT IN THE VILLAGE

One day, Roberto Riveroni came into my galera to tell me that Alejandro Martinez Sáenz wanted to talk to me. Could he come in? I shrugged my shoulders.

"You know everybody in the prison wants to kill this man, and the only reason they haven't is they are afraid of reprisals; but what have I got to lose?"

Martinez Sáenz came into the galera; nobody acknowledged his existence.

"You are mad at me, aren't you, Martino?" He said, giving me a hangdog look.

"You have always protested that you weren't a Communist and yet you were one of the first to join the Communist nucleus," I replied. "You say you are such a friend of the weak and the poor, but you stood by the other night while they beat up and bayoneted the prisoners."

He hastened to assure me that things were not as they seemed. He said that he and the Checo had been working to help me and that Checo had told him the other night:

"You know, Alejandro, I admire John Martino and we must do all we can to get him out of here."

"Don't do me any favors," replied. I had no idea what his new game was.

His next statement was that he was going on trial the next day as an agent of the CIA.

"How can you be convicted as a CIA agent when you are a Communist like the rest of the collaborators?" I asked him.

The next day, Checo appeared with a similar story of how the Communists wanted to help me.

"This morning I had a meeting with the chief of the prison and the three political commissars," he said. "I told them that you made trouble by the mere fact of being an American. If they wanted the prison to quiet down and they wanted people to cooperate with the school—the school plan is really on, by the way—the first thing they should do is get the sick men out of La Cabana and have them put them in the Military Hospital. That will make the prisoners think that we are humane and want to do the right thing."

"What happened?"

"I made the suggestion. The chief of the prison and I then talked to the political commissar of the G-2, who said he would take it up with the Minister of the Interior."

"That sounds too good to be true," I said.

TROUBLE IN THE COUNTRYSIDE

There had been riots in numerous villages all over Cuba. Two of the places where the people had protested against brutality and food shortages were Artemisia and El Cano. Some of the people taken during the suppression of these popular protests were imprisoned in La Cabana.

One of them was a man of about sixty-five, named Jose Licaso, who had lived in the United States for twenty years, was the father of three and a grandfather. I was curious about how a man could spend two decades in the United States and then wind up in a little Cuban village. I got to know him and soon heard his story.

He had been in the export-import business in New York, representing a Japanese radio and appliance firm. Then in 1961, he had become one of the Cubans who voluntarily repatriated themselves and thus had lost his American citizenship.

"That was when I made the biggest mistake of my life. Martino, I never really knew what propaganda was and so I became one of its easiest victims."

When he was in his late thirties, he had gone to the United States to make a better living. By hard work and good luck, he had built up a thriving business and acquired three apartment houses in the Bronx. He had educated his family in America and was living happily there.

When Castro came to the United States in April 1959, Licaso was one of the Cubans who welcomed him at the airport. He had been one of Castro's most ardent supporters, had given money for the 26th of July and was proud to be meeting the man whom he considered Cuba's savior.

Then the American press became increasingly critical of the executions and other unsavory features of the Castro regime. Licaso, who was regularly receiving Bohemia and other Cuban periodicals, gradually became convinced that the United States was persecuting Fidel Castro. This rankled in his mind.

'When Castro came to the United States a second time for a meeting of the United Nations, Licaso was again at Idlewild. When Castro accused the police at the airport of pushing him and later when he moved to the Hotel Theresa in Harlem, Liecaso interpreted this as further evidence of persecution.

Fidel Castro appealed to all good Cubans to return to their country and help rebuild it. Licaso then sold all his belongings, put his property up for sale and prepared to return and stand beside the man victimized by the American press and the American Government.

"I was taken in hook, line and sinker. I didn't go directly to Cuba. I went to Mexico. The reason for this was that I had to deceive one of my daughters, who was absolutely adamant against my going back. I told her I was taking a trip to the West Coast.

"Back in Cuba, when the newspapers found out what I had done, they made a great deal of propaganda out of my case. Like a fool, I went along with this. I turned over everything I had, including all my cash, to the Banco Nacional, which gave me pesos in return.

"They also gave me a home, but I lived there for only three months. After that time, they were through with the propaganda and they moved me into a little house that was a thousand times worse than I was used to in the States. "But I was still dazed by their propaganda. Before I finally woke up, I sent for my family and, since I was its head, they all came to Cuba.

"One day, I got a letter from INRA the National Institute of Agrarian Reform, to the effect that all repatriates would have to go to work and that they had found a job for me. They put me in charge of a duck farm in the little town of El Cano. I had never lived on a farm and knew nothing about ducks, but I had to go.

"They assured me that they had skilled agronomists who knew all about ducks and that I would be the overall boss and would have no trouble. It turned out that their so- called agronomists didn't know what they were doing. We had an epidemic; most of the ducks died, and, of course, I was blamed.

"I tried my best to explain and they seemed to have forgiven me, for I was kept on as interventor, or mediator, on the farm."

"And how about your family?" I asked.

"Well, my daughters are school teachers."

"And what are they teaching?"

"You know what they are teaching. They are teaching Communism."

He had tried to leave the country on three different occasions, but had been refused. To keep on asking would be dangerous. And where could he go? To the United States after he had renounced his citizenship?

I asked him about the riot.

"Trouble was developing all over the island. There was great discontent over the rationing system, largely because the stores didn't have the goods corresponding with the ration coupons.

"One Saturday night, a couple of militiamen killed a fifteen-year-old boy. This caused a scandal in our little town. The townspeople were incensed. The next day, about 1,500 people turned out for the funeral.

"The grumbling continued and, after much discussion, the businessmen decided to close their stores for one day—that Monday—as a protest against the murder of the boy.

"Monday morning, the local G-2 phoned Havana for orders. They were directed to open the stores, but the merchants refused. Two or three hours later, 15 truckloads of militia and roughnecks arrived. They broke open the stores and declared that all businesses that had shut down were confiscated. The owners were arrested."

"But you didn't have a store, did you?"

"No, but I happened to be in the house of one of the men whose shop was closed down. He had a feed business and he sold articles to the campesinos under INRA direction. Every business in our little town and all the stocks of goods were confiscated. When the men were arrested their houses and cars and personal belongings were taken. 'Their women and children were left to shift for themselves.

"This caused a terrific riot in the village. Eleven men were killed in the streets of El Cano that day and Cod knows how much property was destroyed. As a result, the citizens who protested were arrested and charged with counterrevolutionary activities and I am part of that group."

"I am sorry for you," I said. "Let me tell you that you will be a very lucky man if you get less than ten years."

Around July 10, a group of about forty men were arrested for illegal dealings in foreign exchange. They had tried to profit from the fact that the workers on the Guantanamo Naval Base were paid in dollars. Castro, of course, wanted to get that payroll of over $500,000 a month for the regime and any private enterprise that tried to muscle in would be pounced on.

The foreign exchange ring had been trapped by a man named Santiago Lopez and another, both of whom had families living on the naval base. We learned within twenty-four hours that both men were old-time Communists who worked for G-2. It seemed to me disturbing that American counterintelligence had tolerated the presence of the families of these veteran stool pigeons and Communists on the Guantanamo base for years.

THE COMMUNIST VIEWPOINT

In mid-July, a prisoner who did electrical work brought me a message from Riveroni, the Checo and Martinez Sáenz. There was a lot of activity on my behalf. I was to be especially careful not to alienate the prison authorities. There was a plan to get José Cabanas Gonzalez, the cripple in the bed beside mine, and me removed from the prison. This was confidential and I was not to tell anybody.

Shortly after this, Raul Martin came to see me, the man who had worked in the Banco Nacional and had been a close associate of

Ché Guevara. He was a hard-core Communist and boasted that he had been a member of the Party for twenty years.

"If Fidel would only listen to the Party," he told me, "we wouldn't have this trouble. We would be friendly with the United States and the Americans would be buying our sugar."

"You mean to tell me that the Communist Party could have taken over Cuba without any trouble from the United States?"

"Yes, because you Americans are incredibly naive. We would have had to call ourselves nationalists or neutralists for a while. But words hurt nobody. Our people in the United States and their dupes would not only have proclaimed that Castro is not a Communist, they would have urged massive aid to our regime to prevent Cuba from falling into the hands of 'the real Communists.'"

I told him I thought he was possibly right, but I didn't understand why he was talking to me this way.

"Because I feel like it. To satisfy my curiosity about your reaction. This is our farewell anyhow. I don't think you will ever get out of prison and, if there is another invasion, you will be finished."

"Go ahead and talk," I said. "I have nothing better to do than listen to you."

He told me that he had been one of the Communist agents who were sent to Caracas to organize the demonstrations against Vice President Nixon and the attempted assassination of Nixon and his wife. "The amusing thing is that I was in Caracas as an accredited correspondent and I even got an interview with Nixon, the man we were planning to destroy.

"Another thing. You read about the Caryl Chessman case here, didn't you, Martino?"

"I heard Castro sound off about it," I said.

"We were behind that. A year before he was executed, we sent people through Latin America, getting hundreds of thousands of petitions to save Chessman. We had books written about the case. We circulated petitions among the poor and the oppressed. We used Chessman as our unconscious tool. And we were responsible for his death, because we put the American authorities on the spot with so much publicity that to have pardoned him would have been yielding to pressure. We attained our real objective. It was to convince the ignorant and stupid masses, the people who can't think, that you Americans are the real oppressors of liberty, the real assassins.

"You have read our literature, haven't you, Martino?"

"Some of it," I said.

"Most of it is for the birds. Our real objective is to take what you of the West have. We are not going to give it to the masses, the imbeciles and dupes. We, the cadres, intend to be the ruling class. Don't think for a moment that I have anything against air-conditioned cars, good wines and expensive women. But we have to put a different show on the road and believe me, Martino, we put on a good show."

"Yes, it is a good show," I agreed. "But you Communists can't deliver. We in the Free World produce abundance and you in the Soviet World produce hunger. People are waking up.

"They never really wake up. I have lived in America and you Americans always amaze me. We are going to take you over because of the nature of your system and its weaknesses. We use civil rights and freedom of speech, that you give us, in order to destroy you. We manipulate the misguided people—and above all the misguided intellectuals—who have vague desires to do good or to seem important, but who never have the brains to ask themselves where they are going.

"We exploited the Little Rock affair. We even had our agents in the racist groups, urging them to take action that would create more conflict and a greater international scandal. We are knee-deep in the Black Muslim movement and, in a few years, that organization is going to spread terror in the streets of your cities on a scale that you can't imagine. Your authorities won't dare to crush the Black Muslims because the one thing they are afraid of is being branded as racist or anti-Negro. And we have infiltrated into the other militant organizations of Negroes too.

Part of this plan of wooing the blacks, by the way, was to have Fidel Castro leave his New York hotel, when he was in your country for the UN meeting, make a great scandal and then move to the Hotel Theresa in Harlem. The Party planned that. The first idea was to have him sleep in the park, but we decided that to have him fraternize with the blacks was a lot better.

"I went to Bolivia in 1960. The Party has done a tremendous job there. In both Bolivia and Ecuador, the poor peasants and other ignorant creatures were told that they could go to the Cuban Embassy and get free food. We were distributing this food, we said, because our agrarian reform had been a huge success and we had enormous surpluses." He laughed a bit hysterically. "You can make ignorant people believe anything."

"It has been instructive," I said. "I suppose you are getting out or you wouldn't talk this way."

"Yes, I expect to be free very soon."

CHAPTER 18

BLACK SUPREMACY

Jose Cabans Gonzalez and I were called into the office to be interrogated by Captain Oliva, the head of the medical department of all the prisons of Cuba. He proceeded to ask me when I had first been registered as a patient by a Cuban physician and what the nature of my illness was. After querying Cabanas in similar fashion, he dismissed us and we were returned to our galeras. We noticed that Captain Oliva had treated us with a courtesy rarely displayed by Cuban Communist officials toward political prisoners and were told that this was an omen of our forthcoming freedom.

About five days later, approximately August 15, 1962, we were again called to the office. We were told that we would be taken to the military hospital in Marianao for a two-day check-up. Under strong military escort, we were driven through the city of Havana.

This was not the city I had once known. The streets had been torn up by tank treads. There were trenches in the Malecón. The once-splendid residences, hotels and apartment houses were run-down and shabby. The paint was peeling off. Wherever you turned, the hypnotic eyes of Fidel Castro and the porcine face of Nikita Khrushchev would stare at you from gigantic photographs. Placards and signs displayed the monotonous Communist slogans, patria o muerta (fatherland or death) and venceremos (we shall conquer).

The buildings displayed more Russian than Cuban flags. Another strange thing I noticed in my brief tour of the city was that there were very few people to be seen on the streets. In fact, they were almost deserted. In the old days, lovers and other people would parade against the background of the sea wall, while others would sit at the water's edge and fish. The city had been crowded and vivacious; now it was a ghost town.

As we drove past the beautiful Havana Riviera Hotel, I looked up and saw lingerie and other garments hanging from the windows.

The city was going through a process of accelerated decay, of transition from order and cleanliness to disarray and squalor.

This city-of-the-dead aspect was somewhat modified by the cars of the G-2, always Impala Chevrolets, which raced through the streets on their various errands.

THE RISE OF THE NEGRO COMMUNISTS

At the time of the Revolution, there were very few Negroes in the hills with Castro. I was in Havana when the victorious Rebel forces entered in triumph and I would say that only about one in ten was black, whereas about one person out of every three in the island is colored. The old Communist Party had made a prodigious effort to attract Negroes to its ranks and boost them into the leadership. Bias Roca, the general secretary of the Party, and Lázaro Pena, its outstanding labor leader, were both colored.

When I was first brought into the Catillo de Atarés as a prisoner, the officers and garrison were almost entirely white. And in El Principe, about nine-tenths of the officials and guards connected with the Rebel regime were of the Caucasian race.

In the summer of 1960, when Lumumba became Prime Minister of the Congo, Castro began to take the side of the Negroes, of the new African republics and of the colored people all over the world. The killing of Lumumba was treated by the Cuban propaganda machine as if a latter-day Christ had been crucified or a 20th century Lincoln done to death. The Cavadongo Hospital was renamed for Lumumba.

All the fine hotels, such as the Hilton and the Riviera, and the various nightclubs and casinos had to give popular dances which anyone could attend free of charge. When the Negroes attended, the whites tended to stay away. Previously in Cuba, the two races had lived amicably side by side, but at a distance.

The changeover to Negro control was part of Communist policy and it proceeded relentlessly without regard to the wishes of the Cuban people. We could see the change everywhere. It was noticeable on television. The actors got darker; one saw more and more black faces.

As prison guards left and were demobilized, they were replaced and the replacements were almost always black. I would say 90 per cent of the new guards were Negroes. When I was confined in the infirmary of El Principe, I could see the hordes at the great mass meetings Castro held in the central park. The activists, the organizers, even those who simply carried the banners, were almost all blacks.

NEGRO RACISM

As the guajiros, who had been fighting the Castro regime in the countryside, were brought into La Cabana, they told us that the same racial transfer of power was taking place in the rural areas as in the cities. The blacks were being put in charge of the trade unions, the expropriated businesses and the cooperatives. These people were for the most part untrained for such jobs. The interventor or mediator of one industry, for instance, was a former car washer.

At the time the invasion cracked up and the mass arrests occurred, we were able to talk to hundreds of prisoners who had been recently living on the outside and who were therefore up-to-date on conditions in Communist Cuba. They said that the police outside were almost entirely black. The refugees, who constituted the cream of Cuban intellect and ability, were overwhelmingly white. Their houses had been confiscated and turned over to Negroes. Most jobs involving power were being given to black men.

There is an organization known as the brigadistas. They are uniformed youth of fifteen to twenty, who are sent on a government stipend to go into the countryside and teach the common people how to read and write. These shock brigade teachers are also almost entirely Negro.

Scholarships were being awarded all over the island of Cuba by the Castro Government. The recipients of these awards, despite their poorer preparation, were almost invariably Negroes.

All the schools had been taken over by the state, and in the process educational standards had been debauched. It used to take six years of higher education to become a doctor in Cuba. When I left the island, it was taking four. Of these four years, two were devoted to political education. In other words, Marxist-Leninist nurses with a few courses of medicine behind them passed as doctors.

The hospitals I had been in or was familiar with—such as the Calixto Garcia—were staffed exclusively with doctors who were either Iron Curtain imports or Negroes. All the nurses were black. This applied to the Committees of Defense and to all the Communist and repressive organizations upholding the dictatorship.

BATISTA AND THE MILITARY

Because Batista was popular among the Negroes, his chivatos and many of his police were black. All the former Batista soldiers who never reached the grade of non-corn— the privates and privates first class—were offered jobs by the Castro regime as soldiers, bus drivers and policemen. These elements were happy to be taken over.

The Batista army had consisted of white officers and Negro ranks. Perhaps 80 per cent of the non-commissioned officers were blacks. This force had fought against Castro and had proved itself miserably inadequate. The troops suffered from marihuana and cocaine addiction. They were easily corrupted and they ran away under fire.

Castro now had all these people back in uniform. This was the ragamuffin militia force that broke at the Playa Girón. In addition to Negroes, Castro had the frustrated whites and the perennial revolutionary intellectuals of the Orthodox and Autentico parties. For years, these people had wasted their brains and their training in conspiracies, political murders, grafting and playing demagogue. They had helped bring instability to the country and disrepute to its educated classes. They had stood in the way of the intelligent and constructive elements that wanted to do something for the nation.

Castro issued an order which was still in effect when I left Cuba. Titles of rank were abolished in all military and civilian organizations. Superior officers were to be addressed as corn panero (comrade). The chief of our prison was known to us only by his nickname, Pepe.

Miscegenation and Venereal Disease

In the early days of his regime, Castro was violently opposed to sexual laxity and vice. He closed down night spots and gambling casinos. He orated against prostitution and urged all couples that were living together in Cuba to get married. Then, at some point in its development, the regime made a volte-face and endorsed free love.

In June 1962, we received a distinguished visitor in La Cabana Fortress, Dr. Rafael de la Palma, who had been the head of the Public Health Department in the early days of the Castro government. He said that one of the most terrible problems in Cuba was the explosive growth of venereal disease, both syphilis and gonorrhea. He said this was accentuated by the lack of Penicillin, Aureomycin and other antibiotics. Moreover, the Russian supplies of these drugs were inferior and often resulted in massive adverse reactions from the patients.

The basic trouble, however, was race mixing. The Negroes were thoroughly infected with venereal diseases and the Russians and Chinese, sent to the island by the Communists, were almost as badly off.

If a white girl refused the advances of a Negro in Cuba, she could immediately be accused by him of white chauvinism or counterrevolution. Then she would be taken before a Committee of Defense, which was almost sure to be black.

I talked to prisoners in La Cabana, and I know of some on the Isle of Pines, who were there for no other reason than that they tried to protect their women—wives, daughters and sisters—against the advances of Negroes, Russians and Chinese.

The Blacks and the Prisons

During the entire time that I was in La Cabana Fortress, they executed only one Negro. I would estimate that of the 10,000 or so prisoners who passed through the prison during my time there, not more than fifteen were Negro. In other words, a large segment of the white upper and middle classes was behind bars, with the Negroes guarding them there. The

I Was Castro's Prisoner

colored garrison of La Cabana included young Negro kids taken off the streets at fifteen or sixteen and put in the militia and taught how to handle a gun. The theory was that they had been unable to get jobs because of race discrimination. Their being placed in the militia was regarded as an act of compensatory justice.

As long as the prison guards were white men, there was a certain amount of cleanliness and a certain effort to keep order and behave with some degree of justice. But when the blacks took over, the prisons became pigpens.

The Negro guards took out their resentment of the whites by sticking them with bayonets, by jeering at the men who were being executed and by displaying bestiality and sadism. These Negroes are different in culture and appearance from most American Negroes. They seem more primitive; they are credulous and ignorant and they believe everything Castro tells them. They have no stable direction and can fluctuate from one mood to its opposite without any apparent reason.

THE NEGROES AND THE UNDERGROUND

Nevertheless, at the time of the Playa Girón invasion, a fairly large number of Cuban Negroes were in the underground. We were told that the problem of organizing them had at first seemed insuperable, since most of them were uneducated and uninformed. The key to the problem was the almost universal Negro interest in sports and in jazz. A representative of the underground might ask a group of Negroes how many champions in the seven boxing divisions were American Negroes. The answer would come right back: Five. The next point would be to ask how it is possible for the American Negroes to be as badly treated as Castro says they are, if they have five Out of seven boxing championships. Then the underground representative might talk about Negro ball players in the United States and about such outstanding colored basketball teams as the Harlem Globe Trotters. In addition, even the most ignorant of the Cuban town Negroes, knew about Nat King Cole.

"When Castro first started changing conditions here, I believed it was a social revolution," one underground leader told me. "Now it has become a race revolution. Fidel has the majority of the blacks on his side. They are sitting on the heads of the whites and they like it. The main reason the streets of Havana are deserted today is that there is a race terror in addition to the other terrors. The white people are not safe on the streets. The Committee of Defense, which is almost always Negro, can arrest you on the spot and give you a so-called popular trial before a black People's Tribunal. That generally means you are shot then and there."

THE NEGROES AND PAREDÓN

The changeover to Negro guards, Negro militia and Negro Defense Committees brought a continuous development of viciousness in the mode of execution. For example, in September 1962, there was a night when twenty-one men were put in capilla for execution. These men had been brought up from underground galeras, where they had been held incommunicado. They were probably part of a military conspiracy against the Cuban Communist regime.

Around eight o'clock that night, we heard a lot of automobiles coming into the Fortress. The man in the back of our galera announced that floodlights were already illuminating the paredón.

Then I heard a chilling sound—women's and children's voices. The word swept through the prison that there would be lots of spectators to the executions that night because many army men and policemen were to die. The Rebels were treating the executions as a sports spectacle.

We also learned that, as the result of a direct order from the MINFAR, or Cuban War Department, the women and children of the prisoners were being forced to attend the executions. The authorities wanted them to see how men who had become "traitors to the Revolution" died, and in that way intimidate them.

Around nine-thirty, the firing squad came in. An hour later, the jeep arrived with the first victim. The firing squads were busy until after midnight. Every five minutes, they would lash a man to the wall; we would hear the commands being shouted to the firing squad, the discharge of rifles, and then the fateful thud of the .45 bullets smashing the victim's brain.

We could hear the spectators on the roof, laughing, shouting, jeering, cursing the doomed men, and calling them traitors to the Revolution. I asked myself: What has Cuba come to? Who are these people out there in the dark? They seemed to me demonic creatures unlike the gentle and gay Cubans I knew. As a boy, I used to read about Roman mobs, watching Christians being torn apart by wild animals and I wondered whether we had really made any progress since that time. The spectators were having a wonderful time.

You could hear expressions like:

"Look at the way he fell; he was afraid." They would argue about whether a man had died bravely or as a coward. They would jeer at him and tell him to pray to his God:

"Where is your God now? Why doesn't he help you?"

The taunted, dying men were former Rebels. They had helped create this monster that was both destroying them and trying to rob their deaths of dignity and meaning. Yet, they died like men, all of them with the same cry on their lips:

"Viva Cuba Libre! Viva Cristo Rey! Abajo Fidel Castro!"

Twenty-one human lives were extinguished that night before the jeering, howling mob of blood-crazy spectators.

CHAPTER 19

ORDEAL OF THE INVADERS

When I arrived at the militia hospital, I was put in a room with two veterans of the Playa Girón invasion, both of whom had been wounded. Their names were José de Leon from Santiago de Cuba and Carlos Manzanilla from Santa Clara. These were the first men I had met who had been in the initial assault wave and had been captured on the beachhead. Consequently, I was anxious to talk to them.

Both were extremely bitter. Their resentment was not directed at the American people or at President Kennedy, but almost exclusively at the CIA, which they believed had betrayed them.

When I asked for specifics, de Leon said that it was hard to know where to begin.

"For instance, if I told you the things that happened in our Guatemalan training camps, you would feel ashamed of being an American."

"What things?" I asked.

"One of my friends was in charge of the books," de Leon said. "He told me that the CIA was paying eight dollars a day for the expenses of each man in the camps. This included food, other necessities and money for their families in Florida. According to my friend, the bookkeeper, the actual expenditures per man were only three dollars a day. They were reporting fake expenditures and somebody was grafting on us to the extent of five dollars a head daily. The total take on that operation was about $6,000 a day.

"We were promised fine, modern weapons. Then when we were ready to go, the instructors apologized and explained that they were not able to give us the good arms that we had been promised. However, we were not to worry. The invasion couldn't fail, because the American Government would go in there if necessary to be sure it was carried through to success."

"Did you men believe that?"

"We had no choice. We had to believe what they told us."

"What was your training like?"

"It was excellent, first class. But only the men who had been in the camps a month or more had it. When we were committed to battle, we took 600 to 700 men with us who had just arrived at the camps and scarcely knew how to fire a rifle.

"When the invasion hit the beaches, it was no surprise to Fidel Castro. That was because of the poor security measures taken by the CIA. We were allowed to move freely in the little Guatemalan towns, which, of course, were crawling with Communist spies. We complained about this to our superiors, but after all we were just soldiers and they didn't listen to us. It was like talking to a tree."

I asked him if he thought the invasion would have succeeded, given air cover and real American backing.

"Martino," he replied, "I want to tell you what Fidel Castro said to us in the Sports Palace. He said before two or three thousand people that, if he had us with him, well supplied and with good arms, he could have conquered South America. That was the comparison he made between our brigade and the rag tail army he had with him at Playa Girón.

"Moreover, when our first prisoners were captured, Fidel Castro asked one of them how many of us there were.

"When the prisoner said, 'about twelve hundred,' Castro struck him.

"'Don't lie to me,' he said. 'I know you have at least 15,000."

These prisoners had been at sea on the same craft for four days. During that time, they had only two hot meals. The rest of the time, they lived on canned beans. Yet it is an elementary rule of logistics that men must be fed as well as possible with high-energy food before going into battle.

When they were on the beaches, the enemy commanded the skies and one of the main supply ships was sunk. Landing craft could not bring supplies from transports to the beaches because they were sunk from the air. The supply line was cut, despite the fact that an American carrier stood off to sea with jet planes that could have pulverized Castro's T-33s and Sea Furies. The Navy airmen and carrier commanders were awaiting the order to strike, but the word from Washington was to hold back.

The men fought until they were out of ammunition. They held their positions for three days, despite the fact that no food could be brought to them and, during this time, they subsisted on the rations they had carried ashore with them. Their mortars had no shells. The parachute troops lacked the mines necessary to interdict the approach roads to Castro's militia. At one point, the only ammunition that reached them was for .45 revolvers.

Although they were outnumbered more than fifty to one, although the enemy commanded the skies, although they were not supplied with the ammunition they needed and were forced to fight on empty bellies, they held their positions for three days and inflicted an estimated 5,000 casualties on the enemy, suffering only 250 combat losses themselves. The inner weaknesses of the Castro dictatorship were revealed by the fact that militia units surrendered en masse without firing a shot. The beach area was destined to benefit from a grandiose Castro reclamation project and its inhabitants had been subjected to intensive propaganda and were supposedly loyal to the regime. Yet they fraternized with the invaders. Many asked to be allowed to fight in their ranks, but had to be refused because of lack of arms.

Talking to these men and to other veterans of the invasion before and after, the analogy that came to my mind was the Alamo. Both were heroic actions by small bands of soldiers, who fought because of deep conviction and who were superior to the enemy in physique, management of weapons, resourcefulness, intelligence and morale. The men at the Alamo died under enemy fire. The men at Playa Girón were the victims of stupidity, cowardice and betrayal in high places. The Alamo is one of the glories of our past as a nation. Playa Girón is a stain on our national reputation for courage and integrity. I believe that at some future date April 17 will be set aside by the American people as a day of national shame.

This is not the place to argue whether President Kennedy pledged air support to the Cuban patriots and then withdrew it at the last moment, thus condemning them to capture and death, as most of them believe, or whether he never contemplated an air commitment, as he stated at a press conference on January 24, 1968. Regardless of what the President did or thought, the Cuban invaders, with scarcely a single exception, were given to understand that they would have the air support necessary for domination of the skies. The creation and perpetuation of this sort of misunderstanding concerning a matter of life and death is not an error, but a crime.

The veterans of the invasion I talked to had heard that Adlai Stevenson was the American chiefly responsible for their defeat and betrayal. I would be asked whether Stevenson was a Communist or a Communist dupe and why a person of his character was tolerated in the American Government. I told them that, whatever Stevenson was, I was sure he was not a Communist. But the hatred they concentrated on him was amazing.

There was also an attitude of bewildered disappointment toward Ernest Hemingway, who had turned into such a vociferous propagandist for Fidel Castro and his Communist state. Hemingway had greeted Castro when the latter returned from the United Nations. They appeared on television together on several occasions and Hemingway even appeared on a program with Juan Marinello, the nominal leader of the Cuban Communist Party. This great figure in world literature would tell his radio and TV audiences in fluent Spanish that the American people were being hoodwinked by their capitalist exploiters, that they were being told lies about Cuba by Wall Street and that there was real freedom under Castro.

In short, it was the unadulterated Communist Party line. The Cuban Communists were planning to build a Hemingway museum at the time I left prison. And the Cuban press characteristically reported Hemingway's suicide (or perhaps accidental death) as murder by the American Government and the American political police.

These Cubans felt that they had been betrayed by Hemingway and by a well-known American publicist, and correspondent. These two, I was told, had been part of the inner group that Castro had generally consulted before making big decisions during the years of the struggle for power. The other members of this group were Ché

Guevara, Raul Castro, General Alberto Bayo, the veteran Spanish Communist, and General Enrique Lister, one of the top Communists on the General Staff of the Spanish Republic during the Spanish Civil War. These people, my informants believed, could not possibly have been dupes. They were insiders. This inside group, by the way, did not include the roughnecks and criminal elements, such as Almeida and Almeijeiras.

During the last phases of Castro's struggle for power, Raul Castro had kidnapped 45 Americans. Fidel was very worried about the impact of this proposed action on American opinion. The American publicist, who was part of his inside group, reportedly told him:

"Don't worry about American opinion. I make American opinion."

To return now to the Cuban veterans of the invasion and their ordeal. I asked de Leon, who had been confined in El Principe, what it was like there these days?

"You can imagine our situation," he said. "During the day, everybody would try to put on a bold front. Then the lights go out at night. Each man is alone with his own thoughts, his own emotions. He is alone with his bitterness, his resentment, his hatred . . . I don't know how this experience will ever be erased from our minds and hearts. You are an American and, like most Americans, you have no conception of what happened. But I can say to you that we were double- crossed from start to finish. Some people made a lot of money, some of them Cubans, I am sorry to say. Others maneuvered our defeat either because they were Communists or because they believed in appeasing Communism. The only thing we can't understand is why the Government of the United States permitted it."

THE TRIAL OF THE INVADERS

He told me that, when they were prisoners in the Naval Hospital, Fidel Castro and his political commissars would go there to indoctrinate them. They would try to win them over with the promise of farms.

"They opened up a school in the Catillo del Principe."

"Okay, doctor. What is the treatment and where do we go from here?"

"Treatment? There is no treatment. I have made my investigation and you will go back to La Cabana Fortress."

"Why was I taken here in the first place?"

"American, you ask too many questions. You will get some good food while you are here. Tomorrow you will return and the Ministry of Interior will take up your case from there."

I was dumbfounded. I had been given the red carpet treatment merely so they could confirm what they already knew about my illness. I still had the naive notion that people went to hospitals to get medical treatment.

Later that day, five Russian doctors came into my room. They had a brief talk with the invaders, examined their wounds, then left. That night, I could hear them talking and laughing on the veranda. I knew they were Russians because of their guttural Spanish accents.

The next morning, a young girl came to clean the room. "When are the Americans going to come to free us?" was her first question.

"Little one," I replied, "be careful. Don't you know that the guards can understand us?"

"It doesn't matter. Like everybody else in Cuba, they hate the Russians. You don't know what is happening here. At one time, this was a very fine hospital. Now that the Russians have taken over, we Cubans are treated like dirt under their feet.

"Look at this hospital now. It is run down. We have hardly any medicines. Antibiotics are high priority and the only people who get them are big shot government officials.

"You remember that last summer we had an epidemic of gastroenteritis. You have no idea of how many babies died in Marianao. It was because we had no drugs. If somebody gets sick, the best we can do for him is aspirin and maybe Russian penicillin, which is no good."

"What do you mean it is no good?"

"There is something wrong with it. It has very bad side effects. The American medicines are infinitely superior to the Russian junk we are getting now.

That afternoon, I was taken out of the military hospital. I had the bad fortune to fall into the hands of a really nasty guard. My papers said that I was to be returned to La Cabana, but he announced that he was going to drop me off at the G-2 headquarters at 5th Avenue and 14th Street instead, because there was a cordillera leaving for the Isle of Pines from the G-2 that night. I tried to reason with him, but it was hopeless. This was a nightmare. With freedom close to my grasp, it looked again as if I was going to be sent to a place where I would surely die.

The G-2 consists of two city blocks of homes, which had once belonged to Batista people, in the center of Miramar, a fine residential section. The G-2 has connected all of these homes by a series of tunnels. The rooms had been transformed into prison cells, the worst of which were the two car garages, which had only a water spigot and no toilet facilities.

"This man belongs in La Cabana Fortress," the receiving clerk said when he looked at my papers.

"He is an American spy," the chief of my escort said.

"What we should do is take him out and shoot him."

The clerk shook his head. I was waved into an air-conditioned waiting room with a television set.

"You will wait here until we get orders from the Ministry of the Interior," the admitting clerk said.

"But I belong in La Cabana."

"You have been delivered here," the clerk said. "Once that happens, it takes a lot of red tape to get you out."

After an hour or two, I was practically carried through a series of tunnels to Galera 2. Here I was welcomed by a man known as El Checo, because he was from Czechoslovakia. He had been a prisoner of the G-2 since the spring of 1959 and was no relation of the other Checo I knew in La Cabana.

As head of the galera, El Checo cleared a bunk for me. The others looked at me in amazement. I had been taken from the hospital in a very weakened condition and looked emaciated as well as terribly sick.

In this cell, there were fourteen bunks and forty-one prisoners. The heat was so appalling that the men wore only shorts and sweat poured off their bodies.

On the cell wall, I saw a list of names, headed by that of Dr. Julio Yebra, the young man whose execution I had witnessed in La Cabana. The prisoners told me that they kept a record of everybody who had ever been in this cell and, when he was executed, they carved his name on the wall. This apparently went on in all the cells of the G-2.

They explained to me that there had been a big roundup of suspects when the Alpha 66 organization of Cuban exiles had launched its successful hit-and-run raid on the Rosita Hornedo Hotel. Moreover, during the two days that I had spent in the hospital, the G-2 had broken up a conspiracy to destroy all the tanks at Camp Managua. Some 400 military men were prisoners.

Checo called one of the guards, demanding that a doctor be sent to the galera as I was in no condition to stand that terrible heat. That started wheels moving and, in less than an hour, a male nurse arrived with an official document from the Ministry of the Interior. I was taken back to La Cabana and was with my old cellmates and friends about two o'clock that morning.

The next day, my friends told me that almost 200 prisoners had been taken from Camp Managua and placed in an underground dungeon. Five lieutenants from the military installation and a Colonel Alvarez Margolla had been placed in Galera 14.

THE ANDRES VARGAS GÓMEZ CASE

The day after my return, they called Andres Vargas Gomez, the former Cuban Ambassador to Switzerland, to trial He was a fragile gentleman, mild, soft spoken, highly educated and with thirty years in the diplomatic service behind him. I shook hands with him and wished him luck.

"Well, Martino, I am on my way to paredón, but you may go free. If you ever get back to the United States, please go see my wife and tell her that I love her very much and am sorry that I caused her all this trouble. Cuba is my fatherland and I had to come back. Here I am on my way to execution, but that is the way fate dealt the cards. I don't look like a fighter, but I did what I had to do."

I promised. He hugged me and thanked me, then walked away. That night, his trial ended and he was put in capilla. We now knew he would die that evening. Almost two dozen men were put in death cells and we knew that we were facing a night of blood.

We waited tensely. To tell the truth, we were somewhat worried about Andres Vargas Gómez, because, as I have said, he was frail, delicate and gentle. In our whole time at La Cabana, nobody had ever broken down or begged for mercy. We hoped that Vargas Gómez would not break that record.

The firing squad came in. Fifteen minutes later, they took Vargas out of capilla and returned him to another galera. We learned almost immediately that his sentence had been commuted to thirty years imprisonment. Everybody breathed a sigh of relief.

Later, Vargas Gómez told us about it.

"Martino, I would be a liar if I said that I was not afraid. When they put me in the death cell, I went down on my knees and prayed. I kept thinking of my wife and my grandfather, the general, and I said to myself: 'Be brave; be strong.' I knew that, if I broke down, I would disgrace my grandfather and my family. I prayed to the Holy Mother for strength. If they had shot me, I would have gone the same way as everybody else."

He was sitting on my bed. Everybody was questioning him or congratulating him. He sat there, this frail man, smiling to himself because he knew that, if the ordeal had come, he would have met it in a way worthy of his grandfather, General Maximo Gómez, one of the great heroes of the War of Cuban Independence.

CHAPTER 20

AN AMERICAN
BRAINWASHER IN CUBA

We were still feeling the backlash of the Playa Girón betrayal. From a prisoner, I learned about the men who were supposed to have been alerted by the CIA so they could leave Havana immediately before the invasion and proceed stealthily to the Escambray Mountains, there to organize guerrilla warfare.

There were only two things wrong with this operation. They were never told that the invasion was coming and somebody, presumably somebody inside the CIA, betrayed the names of these Cubans to the G-2. The result was wholesale executions. In one instance, three brothers were shot.

In another instance, a man had been dropped into Cuba by the CIA to organize an underground. He recruited a guerrilla band and went into action. Then his radio contact with the United States evaporated into thin air. He was given no orders, no arms, no supplies, and no contacts with other groups. Isolated in a hostile police state, he tried to encourage his men and to rely on prayer. He too was captured.

Conditions in the prison were getting worse. The food was deteriorating and we were being rationed on water. In the hot, sticky weather, this meant that we could neither wash ourselves nor shave. Tempers were becoming frayed. Fights would break out among the prisoners for no reason at all. The guards were also on edge. The prison was like a forest in the dry season filled with campers too lazy to put out their fires.

Castro had unleashed another campaign of hate against the United States. We had learned that these rages were more than the explosions of a disturbed personality. They were invariably the harbingers of blood and of paredón. The long-delayed trial of the

MRP (the underground organization which had been led by Manolo Ray) was about to take place and there were twenty-eight petitions for death. Men waited anxiously for the juggernaut of death to start rolling again at full speed.

A TYPICAL REVOLUTIONARY TRIAL

By this time, the trials before the revolutionary tribunals had lost even the semblance of legality which my own had possessed. They would begin by calling the prisoner to the office, where he would be presented with an indictment, a mimeographed sheet, listing the acts he was accused of having committed against the state and specifying the law he was supposed to have violated. Law 988 meant that the prisoner was charged with espionage, with being a CIA agent or being a traitor. The punishment was death.

These impersonal looking sheets turned out by a mimeograph machine, told men their fate. With only a very few exceptions, the number of the law determined whether the accused would be alive or dead a week hence.

After the indictment, the prisoner is brought to trial within a day or two. There is no time to prepare a defense. There will be no confrontation of witnesses. The defense is a matter of ritual anyhow.

In the usual trial before a revolutionary tribunal, the only spectators allowed in the courtroom are militiamen and young Rebels. However, if the prisoners are very important or come from prominent families, a father, mother or wife may be allowed to attend. The prisoners are brought in handcuffed. They are not permitted to talk to their families or even to look at them, despite the fact they may know they will be executed that night. Sometimes, men who know they are about to die will try to break through the cordon of guards so they can touch their wives or children, but they are quickly beaten down with rifle butts or jabbed with bayonets.

The trial starts. There is only one tribunal in La Cabaña that has the power to pass out death sentences in political cases. There are two judges who preside over this tribunal; they serve on alternate days. These two, who are among the most bloodthirsty figures in the history of Cuba are Pelayo Fernández, nicknamed Pelayito Paredón, and Flores Ybarra, whose nickname is chorro de sangre (stream of blood). The way they alternate is that one day Pelayo will be the presiding judge and Flores Ybarra the prosecutor, and on the next day these roles will be reversed. There are five men who comprise the tribunal.

The prosecutor reads the indictment and makes the accusatory speech. Then the defendant, with the guidance of his lawyer, tells his side of the story and attempts to speak in his own defense.

The accusing witness in La Cabana trials is always the same—a lieutenant in the C-2. The prisoner is informed that the reason there is only one witness for the prosecution is to prevent the counterrevolution from learning the identity of the G-2 agents, provocateurs and spies who have infiltrated the subversive groups. The G-2 lieutenant, who is a complete stranger and has had nothing to do with the investigation of the case, then proceeds to state the evidence accumulated against the prisoner. He will testify that the prisoner performed the following acts at the following times.

If the defense attorney asks him for proof of these accusations, he will reply:

"The investigators told me that the prisoner performed these acts on these dates and that he is suspected of these other counterrevolutionary acts."

Since no evidence is presented, there is no opportunity for cross-examination. The prisoner may have been accused by the worst men on earth, but there is no possibility of impeaching them, as their identity is kept secret. The justification advanced for this procedure is that, if the agents who infiltrated the counterrevolution were forced to testify, their identity would be exposed and they would be killed.

As a rule, material evidence is not presented. Thus, the prosecutor may state that bombs were found on the prisoner's premises when he was arrested, but these bombs will not be produced in court. Since men can be held by the G-2 for six months or more before being sent to La Cabana for trial, every effort is made to break them down by torture. When this has been achieved, the trial generally begins with a reading of the prisoner's confession.

Ordinarily, the court will take about five minutes to reach a decision that the prisoner is guilty. If this had not been already settled, the man would not have been brought to trial in the first place. As a rule, within an hour of the verdict, the prisoner will know his sentence. If a man is doomed to die, his lawyer may appeal. The appeal must be made in the same courtroom before the same tribunal that passed sentence. Usually, it is filed immediately and the court decides on it in a matter of minutes.

Where powerful pressure is exerted, either through diplomatic means or by world opinion, death sentences may be commuted. This can occur on appeal or when the man is in capilla, awaiting execution. The decision to commute a death sentence has nothing to do with the merits of the case, but is based on foreign policy considerations.

These trials are even greater travesties of justice than this summary of the procedure reveals. The charges may be so vague that it is almost impossible to answer them. Thus, I saw a copy of the indictment of Captain Melitón, an electronics engineer, who had worked for many years in the Hershey Refinery and who had fought with Castro in the hills. The exact words of the charge were:

"The investigators from the G-2 had the moral conviction that he was counterrevolutionary because he hadn't joined the Militia and various other organizations and because he hadn't volunteered for work brigades." This was the only evidence they had against Melitón, but it was enough to get him a sentence of thirty years imprisonment.

There are also non-military tribunals. These have Communist judges. As a rule, the Batista people are tried before these courts. However, since most of them haven't done anything, they cannot be brought to trial and hence must be kept in prison indefinitely. During 1962, the regime made many overtures to the Batistianos, promising them freedom if they would integrate themselves into the Communist society. During my whole time in prison, I know of only five men who accepted this proposition.

At this time, the grapevine informed us that the Russians were taking over openly all over the island of Cuba. We learned from a transferred prisoner that there had been riots and hunger strikes in the Isle of Pines prison and that no visits had been permitted the prisoners for the past three months. We were told that all the people living on the north end of the Isle of Pines had been evacuated. The area has been declared restricted and Russians and Chinese moved in. Only the top brass of the Castro dictatorship was allowed there. Fidel himself had made many visits. The guards were becoming cocky and arrogant. The prison director would make speeches on the public address system, telling us that we would never leave La Cabana alive and that the United States would be destroyed.

We knew that rockets and missiles were being brought into Cuba. We assumed that the United States must know about them because of U-2 surveillance. Yet, the American radio was saying nothing. We were puzzled.

In the last week of August, we heard more executions. One morning, a boy who worked in the kitchen told us that they had taken eight men from the streets in their civilian clothes, herded them behind galera 14, lined them against the wall and shot them all at once. This was a departure from the standard procedure of individual executions at five-minute intervals. We also learned that they had a "popular trial" on the street. That is to say, the same militiamen who arrested them condemned them to death.

There was an epidemic of paredons started all over Cuba. The armed forces were being purged again and Fidel was boasting over the radio that the Russians would back Cuba to the hilt and that the United States would be totally destroyed. We gathered from relatives of the prisoners that the people lived in the grip of terror. If you were caught on the streets late at night, you were lucky if you weren't shot then and there. It might depend on whether the militiamen who stopped you were in an ugly or a pleasant mood.

DIALOGUE WITH A COMMUNIST

On September 3, I was called into the office. Dr. Oliva came in and sat down. He offered me a cigar and then assured me that the guard who had taken me to the G-2 would be punished.

"What did the report from the military hospital say, Doctor?"

"It confirmed your statements. We are investigating your case. There are some very strange things about it. I would like to have a talk with you."

"Go ahead."

"Tell me, Martino, what do you think of us Cuban Communists?"

I decided this was going to be another political fencing match and another effort to get me to make a deal.

"Everybody has a right to his own political ideology," I said. I added that, since I had been kept in prison since July 1959, I was poorly informed on the subject of Cuban Communism.

"Come now, John. I know you are highly intelligent. We know a great deal about your life and I have taken charge of this investigation personally. Now I want you to talk to me man to man. Do you think our Revolution is honest and just?"

My mind was racing. I knew that this discussion would have a lot to do with my political future. The wrong move might set me back to the almost hopeless condition I had faced a few months before.

"Well, doctor, the only news we get here is from the official press and radio and that is just a bit one-sided."

"That is what I like about you Americans, you speak your minds. . You know Cuba was not ready for this Revolution. We made many mistakes and your case was one of them. But we are trying to correct these mistakes."

He then asked my opinion of the thousands of schools Castro was building. He conceded that most of them were just one-room shacks and I said that I could agree with him that one-room schools were preferable to no schools at all.

Did I think the Cubans had the right to defend themselves? Yes, I replied, it is an American principle that everyone has the right of self-defense.

The doctor then expounded the Communist line that the American Government and monopoly capitalism were their enemies, but that they had nothing against the American people. Did I agree?

"If I told you I agreed with you, Doctor, you would know that I was a liar," I replied. "Do you recall that I replied to one of your questions a few minutes ago with the statement that I believed everyone has a right to choose his own form of government, raise his family and live a normal, healthy life?"

"That is absolutely right," he said. "Then why is the American Government so much against us?"

I hedged. I said that I was not very well versed in politics, that I had not read much about Marxism-Leninism in prison because my Spanish was so poor and that I thought our two trends of thought were entirely different.

"Tell me one thing, Martino. I have gone over your case thoroughly and there is one part of it I don't understand. You were in the American Embassy on October 5, 1959. Why did you leave the Embassy and deliberately go to prison?"

"Dr. Oliva, I was asked to do this by the American Government. Since I am an American, I tried to do the right thing for my country. When the matter was put to me that way, I really had no choice, did I?"

He said that he liked my answers to his questions, that he always appreciated frankness.

"Martino, we have fine doctors in Russia. I am going to make you this offer: We can send you to Russia and you can get your health back there. Meantime, you can go through a period of training in the Soviet Union. You could come back here after a year of study on the other side and then you would have your freedom. You could bring your wife and family to Cuba and, with your electronics training, you could make a very nice life for yourself here. I am offering you this opportunity."

This took me by surprise. The Communists emphasize winning the youth. They generally assume that a man of fifty is not worth re-educating. Therefore, I concluded that they wanted me for some special purpose, which Oliva was not disclosing.

The type of electronics in which I am a specialist would be most useful to an espionage service and I surmised that this was the real reason for the proposal.

"You want me to be frank with you, don't you, Doctor?" He said that he did. "There is no way on earth you could get me to go to Russia. You must remember my age and the fact that my mind is so set in a certain mold that there is nothing you can do to change it. I have been indoctrinated in the ways of democratic life. Also I consider myself a loyal American. I have no wish to change my political ideology. Hence, I am afraid I will have to turn down your offer."

"You know you have a little bit more than nine years to go to finish your sentence?"

"If that has to be," I replied, "then it must be."

"What do you have against our Revolution, Martino?"

"I have nothing against the Revolution itself, but I have a great deal against some of the people of the Revolution, who, to my mind, are counter revolutionaries."

"Please explain yourself."

"In the first place, I was framed and unjustly jailed."

"That we are investigating."

"Secondly, I was convicted illegally. My case went to the Supreme Court, which agreed that I was illegally convicted, but refused to free me. I am told it did so because the authorities did not want to set a precedent, which would free not only me, but many other people."

"You know a lot about your case, don't you, Martino?" I replied that I did.

"Thirdly, I have been held here incommunicado. I am not allowed to write letters and I have not received a letter from my wife since I was transferred to La Cabana Fortress."

He stood up abruptly: "That is impossible."

"Dr. Oliva, I am telling you the truth. If you want to verify it, call the officer of the day to this office. The whole prison knows it."

He took a notebook from his pocket and made notes:

"What other complaints do you have?"

"After the Playa Girón invasion, all medical treatment was withdrawn from me.

"That I know and am investigating. As a doctor, I cannot understand that decision."

"These are things I hold against whoever in the Cuban Revolution did them to me," I concluded.

"Your mother lives in Atlantic City, doesn't she?" Oliva said. It was a strange remark. I wondered whether pressure for my release was building up from that quarter. It would not be wise to ask. Oliva asked me to change my mind about his offer, but I refused. We shook a hand, which is definitely not usual between officials and prisoners in Cuba, and I was taken back to my gal era.

The trend toward complete Communist control was soon evident in a subtler way of dealing with the prisoners. We had a mild requisa, one without bayonets, and the public address system announced that John Martino and any other very sick men were to stay in their galeras while it occurred.

The men had been ordered to dress completely before going into the patio. Then a group of young Rebels came into the galera and confiscated all extra clothing. There was a great deal of protest. Some of the prisoners had got permission to have extra clothing and their families had sent them khaki trousers and shirts with the letter P in big black letters.

The next day, we were informed that new uniforms would be issued. Each man was given a shirt and a pair of trousers. They were khaki American Army uniforms which had been made very recently. The shirts did not have the letter P on their backs.

This seemed to confirm the rumor that Castro was now manufacturing American Army uniforms in quantity. The grapevine told us that, if an invasion took place, the prisoners would be sent out in front of the Rebel Army, to be used as cannon fodder and a shield. The theory was that the American invasion forces would hesitate to fire on us.

The next day, we noticed that all of Castro's military prisoners in galera 22, who had been wearing olive drab uniforms, had to change into blue trousers and light blue shirts. The garrison had also changed into blue.

Olive green was disappearing from the island of Cuba. This tied in with the report that Fidel Castro was creating a new Communist army—and that he was getting rid of olive drab because it was the symbol of the Sierra Maestra and the Revolution. Blue, I remembered, was the color, not of the Soviet Union, but of Mao's Chinese brand of Communism.

CASTRO'S PLANS FOR INVASION

I have already stated that all the prisons in Cuba were mined with dynamite or plastic explosive charges sufficient for the total extermination of the prisoners.

Moreover, Fidel Castro had acquired two American jets, in Italy, I believe, and his plan was that, in the event of a second invasion, these planes would fly over La Cabana and bomb it. Men on the ground would be taking photographs of the attack so that later the killing of the prisoners could be chalked up as an American Air Force atrocity.

One of Castro's pilots told a prisoner in La Cabana that the Cuban dictator had eight Russian jet 53s. The pilots said that Castro had told him that it was inevitable that the United States would wake up eventually and invade Cuba a second time. He said that he wanted to go down in history as the first Latin American to attack U. S. soil. He boasted that he would send these jets out with nuclear warheads on suicide missions against New York, the Panama Canal and the Maracaibo oil fields in Venezuela. Moreover, he personally would be in one of them. Those prisoners who had known Castro well and considered him a physical coward— not all of them, however, were in agreement as to this— thought that the attack might be carried out, but that Fidel would never sacrifice his life on a suicide mission.

AN AMERICAN BRAIN WASHER

Around this time, they brought Luis Alfaro, the leader of the students who had staged the January 1961 hunger strike, back to La Cabana from the Isle of Pines. I was surprised to see him. He came in with a group of six other boys.

"You must have good connections to get off the Island," I said.

"No, we are returning from the so-called rehabilitation farms."

I was shocked. I told him he was one of the last people on earth I would have picked to turn collaborator.

"You have to try to get out of prison one way or another," he replied, "but these people turned out to be too smart for me. We are running up against Russian methods here."

He told us that, when they were on the Isle of Pines, all the men who wanted to be rehabilitated were put in circular 3, which was known to the prisoners as Moscow. He said that, at the time he left, there were about 15,000 to 20,000 prisoners on the Isle of Pines: that conditions were indescribably bad, that they suffered most from the water shortage and lived in a morass of human excrement. Tuberculosis and fungus were slowly killing the prisoners and it was a place worse than death.

Very cautiously, he had gotten together a group of men who had no ties and no family in Cuba and who were willing to do anything to escape to the United States. They decided to join the school, take part in the rehabilitation program and, at the first opportunity, try to escape.

"How many prisoners on the Island would you say have joined the school?"

He gave me a wan smile: "About 300 or 350."

"Out of fifteen to twenty thousand?"

"It was very dangerous to join the school," Alfaro explained, "because, unless your group really knew your plans, you had an excellent chance of getting killed. Eight or nine men had been killed in the prison because they wanted to join the school and become collaborators.

"It was dangerous in two ways. To keep from getting murdered, you had to let a few people know your real purpose. But if too many knew or the wrong people knew, the authorities would find out and you would be put in punishment cells or sent to torture farms. We lived in an atmosphere of suspicion, fear and terror. Everyone looked on me as a traitor, a traitor to the other prisoners and to the cause of Cuba.

"We finally convinced the political commissar and his five assistants that we were sincere. We joined the school and studied there for three months. Then they moved us from circular 3 (Moscow) to one of the outside galeras, which was much safer.

"There they buttered us up. We had lessons and studied Marxism-Leninism ten hours a day. Living conditions were much better. They gave us plenty of water and we even had clean beds.

"After two months in the outside galera, we were sent finally to the farm in Pinar del Rio.

"Now, Martino, do you know who ran this farm?" I shook my head.

"He was one of your paisanos. Yes, an American. His name is Stanley Mitchell and he is the boss of the rehabilitation farm. He does all the political screening. He is a brilliant man. In fact, he is so brilliant that we wound up back here in La Cabana Fortress. They gave us another ten years yesterday."

Luis Alfaro was moved to the farm with a group of thirty other prisoners. They were met by Mitchell, who lived there with his wife. He was affable, always smiling or laughing. He spoke Russian, Spanish and English fluently.

According to Luis, Mitchell is about forty-five and originally from California. In World War II, he had claimed to be a conscientious objector, but his claim had been rejected and he had been compelled to go into the Army.

He deserted, was caught and sentenced to serve two years in Leavenworth. There he became a Communist. He traveled to various parts of the world to learn about Communism and studied the Soviet system. After working in the United States, he was sent to Cuba by the Communist after Castro took power. He was put in charge of setting up rehabilitation farms in Pinar del Rio Province.

"What were conditions like on this farm?" I asked.

"They make it very inviting for you, John. You get clean bunks and good food. You wear blue pants and light blue shirts."

"The same uniform as the guards wear?"

"Yes. There are thousands of Russian and Chinese technicians around, Martino, large numbers of them in Pinar del Rio. They are supposed to be working on farms, but I guess you heard that there are missile bases being built all over Cuba—particularly in Pinar del Rio.

"These Russians wear blue pants and light blue shirts also. This is the new uniform in Cuba for the workers. The workers in factories and in the militia are to wear the same uniform.

"To get back to my story, we thought we had this man, Mitchell, fooled. We even had permission to go to the adjoining village twice a week with only one guard. We were getting visits and money from friends. Finally, they sprung the trap on us."

"What was the trap?"

"We were doing light work on the farm, tending chickens and that sort of thing. One day, Mitchell got the six of us and five others together. He told us we were all honor prisoners. He had decided to allow all of us to go home and visit our families in Havana the following Saturday and Sunday. He said that we were on parole. We were honor-bound to be back at the farm on Monday.

"This was just the opportunity we had been waiting for. We had made all our plans to go into hiding in Havana and then try to get to the United States. But we made the same fatal mistake everybody else makes."

"What was that?"

"One of my group had been on the other side all the time. Mitchell and the G-2 were completely informed about our plans. We had arranged to meet some people and escape in a boat. I had spent $2,000 of my own money to arrange the getaway for the six of us.

"We went to the rendezvous point and stepped into the boat. Then, one of my men pulled a gun on us. We waited there with our hands up until other members of the G-2 arrived. And here am I, Luis Alfaro, the leader of the students, the man who thought he was so smart, right back in La Cabana."

"You mean, Luis, you never suspected that this man was an agent?"

"How could I? I hand picked the men myself. The terrible thing is that this is what is happening all over Cuba.

"I will never underestimate the Communists again. These men are determined and dedicated. Can you understand a man allowing himself to be sent to the Isle of Pines so he can work there as an informer among the prisoners? These informers suffer the same way we do. They go through the requisas. They thirst. They live in filth and feces. They have to endure everything we do. But there it was, when the chips were down, this man belonged to the G-2."

Luis is a man of strong character. Yet, in the middle of his story, he broke down and cried. He became so hysterical; we had to send for the doctor. I realized that it was the hard core of dedicated Communists that enabled Fidel Castro to do the seemingly impossible.

Once, Checo had said to me: "You know, Martino, the difference between a Communist and you people who believe in democracy? We work twenty-five hours a day at being Communists. The ruthless dedication of our people—especially the young ones—is something frightening to see."

CHAPTER 21

I FIND FREEDOM

I have already mentioned that one of the new prisoners was Alvarez Margolla, a former Colonel in the Cuban Army. He had been implicated in the Managua military conspiracy, for which thirty-five men had already paid with their lives. I had a long and frank talk with him two days before his execution. He told me that he was certain to go to paredón and predicted that the court would hand out from thirty to forty death sentences to men in his group. He was wrong; the court doomed fifty-one of them.

"You know I am an agent?"

"I understand, Colonel, that you are fighting to free your country."

"That is entirely correct. I want to talk to you at length, Martino, because you have a chance to go free. If you ever get back to the States, I want you to tell the American people the things I discovered on my return to Cuba."

I promised that I would do that. "You know that I am a regular army man and I am proud to say I am a graduate of a first-class military academy. In other words, I am not some tin soldier who got his rank by playing politics with revolutionaries of one sort or another . . ."

"I understand that, Colonel."

"Therefore, when I tell you about the military situation in Cuba today, I am speaking as a professional soldier."

"Yes."

"The army in Cuba today, Martino, is under Russian command. Its hard core consists of young Rebels who have been sent to Russia and Czechoslovakia over the past three years for indoctrination and training. Do you realize that every month 2,000 young Cuban boys go behind the Iron Curtain? This has been going on for close to three years. After having been carefully screened, on their return to Cuba, they are made political commissars. These are the men who have been training and indoctrinating the Castro youth. These men, together with the hordes of Russian technicians, are building a powerful, armed force on completely Soviet lines.

"Fidel Castro today has three different armies in Cuba. One is nominally commanded by Ché Guevara, another by Raul Castro and the third by Fidel. But actually, of course, Soviet generals command. "Each of these three armies has its own bases, armaments, tanks, air arm, helicopters, medical corps, hospitals and food supply. In case of a second American invasion, a single, pulverizing blow will not do the trick. Each of these three armies will have to be beaten.

"Castro today has a fleet of fast, heavily armed torpedo boats for anti-invasion defense. All Cuban beaches are protected by modem radar installations. Most areas of access are heavily mined.

"The old Rebel Army has been purged and re-purged until all unreliable elements are believed to have been eliminated. There is also the Russian system of political control. There are the Communist Party cells and the Communist underground apparatus, the identity of which is known to only the highest Communist echelons in Cuba. Finally, there is the secret Party consisting of men whose Communist commitment is not known to anybody on the island of Cuba.

"The army of ragamuffins that could have been knocked out with two or three jet planes at Playa Girón is a thing of the past. The new Cuban Army can be beaten, but only at a considerable cost in American blood. "Let me tell you for a fact that there are missiles in Cuba. They have IRBM's capable of delivering a nuclear strike at the United States."

"What? You mean those rumors are true?"

"Absolutely. They have mobile units. They have been bringing in rocket equipment for over a year now. Castro also has jet bombers that can make runs with nuclear bombs over American cities.

"I have always had the greatest respect for the American armed forces and its leaders. But I cannot understand why this has been permitted. And nobody can tell me that the United States does not know these facts. If your military leaders were given a free hand, they would crush this threat to your national security. But they are not allowed to do anything. Something is radically wrong.

"Another thing. They have been using the port of Mariel for submarine fueling. I know there are U-boat pens and supply depots on the island.

"I can also tell you that Fidel Castro knows that the Russians are proceeding with the military occupation of this country. He plans to double-cross them by striking against the United States on his own initiative. He plans to hit the American mainland, the Panama Canal and the Maracaibo oil fields. He has plenty of ideological support from Red China for his plan to touch off nuclear war.

"I only hope that if you get back to the United States, you will try to get this message across." He looked at me dejectedly. "But they will just say that you are embittered and that you are exaggerating. They won't believe you, but tell them just the same. Somebody must give the warning. Your Government is playing with the fate of the whole Hemisphere."

"One of my reasons for thinking there is something wrong with your Government is that they had the intelligence reports of Fidel Castro's previous record of Communist activities. And yet they supported him." He went on.

"Castro has been receiving foreign students from many countries. God knows how many thousands of young embittered boys and girls, who have been filled with the poison of anti-Americanism and Communism, will fight to defend this Russian satellite we have here in Cuba. You would not have had this problem if you had squashed Castro when it was easy. "

"I don't like to say this, Martino, but you must have some very bad Americans in your Government who permitted this disaster to happen."

I told him he was talking rather drastically.

"I am not bitter," he replied. "I knew the odds. Most of the damage has already been done. It will take years to roll these Communists back. And unless it is started very soon, it will be too late.

"I am talking to you as a man who is about to die," he said. "Please try to warn your countrymen. And be careful how you do it.

The same forces that helped Castro and his Communists take power in Cuba will try to muzzle and discredit you.

I thanked him; we shook hands. Two days later, I am sorry to say, he died at paredón.

The day after his death, they brought four boys into our galera, whom they had caught in the mountains. They had been running so long in inhospitable places like the Cienaga de Zapata, a vast swamp, that they had no shoes when they were brought into the Fortress. We scraped around and found them wooden sandals and a pair of sneakers. The boys came in at four o'clock one afternoon. They were put on trial at seven and executed at ten-thirty. One of them was sixteen and another seventeen. I don't know the ages of the other two.

THE ROAD TO THE SUNLIGHT

On September 20, I was called into the office again and interrogated by three men. This team was under Captain Ayala, the chief interrogator of the G-2. We went over the same ground again and again. This, I may say, was typical, for time is seemingly of no importance to the Communist bureaucracy.

Ayala told me that the G-2 had taken an interest in my case. People told me that I would be free soon. I assumed that powerful forces were working on my behalf, but I did not know who they were or their motives. I was skeptical about my release. Hope is a poor staple for the prisoner, for its salt is disappointment.

But the other prisoners had confidence in my future. They kept coming into Galera 14 with messages for their families. I don't know how many names and addresses I had to memorize. I also memorized the messages and promised to deliver them. All this had to be arranged in whispers because of the informers. I could not write anything down because, if it were found on me, I would be suspected of carrying coded messages and engaging in espionage. Many of the prisoners refused to give me messages because they did not want to jeopardize my chance for freedom.

Between October 1 and 4, twenty-seven men had died at the paredón behind my galera. Trials were taking place every day and the mills of death were grinding more furiously than ever.

On the morning of Saturday, the 6th, there was an announcement over the loudspeaker that I was to be helped to the office. This was auspicious; since it was the first time the authorities had recognized that I needed help.

The officer of the day told me to sit down and make myself comfortable, as I would be having visitors. Santiago, one of the two guards who made conteo, sat down beside me and told me "pretty soon you will be there."

The other G- guard, known to us as Gasolina, smiled, patted me on the shoulder, and then walked away with his comrade. This was not only unusual; it was unprecedented.

At six-thirty, I was given coffee and a roll and (another shattering of precedent!) invited to eat my breakfast at the table in the back of the office.

As soon as I had finished, Captain Ayala and two assistants came in.

"I have a little surprise for you, Martino."

"What is it, Captain?" My face was getting red. I was nervous and I knew I was sweating.

"Don't get excited. Just take it easy. I don't want anything to happen to you now."

He then asked me if I could read Spanish and I answered that I could do so haltingly.

"Then get a friend who can read and translate for you." At that moment, Dr. Laraldi came into the office and I called him over. He agreed to translate for me.

The first document was a petition from my wife, Florence to Oswaldo Dorticós, the President of the Republic, asking for a review of my case. She pointed out that I had been convicted unjustly, that I was sick and that I had already served three years and three months. She implored them to let me go home to my family. The petition had been sent on August 8, 1962. It was signed by her and by my three children.

"Do you understand that one, John?"

I felt too weak to answer, but I nodded assent.

"All right, now read him the next one, Laraldi."

The doctor translated a letter from President Dorticós to Comandante Ramiro Valdéz, enclosing the petition and suggesting that, if I had been unjustly convicted, I be deported to the United States. The third letter was from Ramiro Valdéz to Fidel Castro, stating that he had reviewed my case and recommended, considering my weakened physical condition, that I be sent home.

After these documents had been translated, Captain Ayala turned to me:

"John, the Revolution made a mistake in your case. Comandante Fidel Castro, Comandante Ramiro Valdéz and the President of the Republic, Oswaldo Dorticós, have discussed the matter and decided that you should be given your freedom and returned to your family. In this way, the Revolution corrects the injustice that has been done to you."

When I was able to speak at all, I thanked Ayala and said:

"When?"

"These things take time. Two or three weeks. What size suit do you wear?" I told him. "I will see that you have clothes to go home with. When you go home, I know you are going to talk to the newspapers?"

I sensed a trap.

"The newspaper reporters are going to talk to me," I replied.

"Forget it," Ayala said abruptly. "What you say to the newspapers is up to you . . . Would you like to give your thanks to the President of the Republic? I think you should write him a letter, thanking him for your release."

"I can't write Spanish that well, Captain."

He called over a clerk with a typewriter. I was instructed to dictate the letter to President Dorticós in English. Accordingly, I thanked the Cuban President in my own name and that of my family for having given me my freedom.

MY FRIENDS, THE CONDEMNED

The prison learned almost instantly of my good fortune. Everybody wanted to congratulate me, to shake my hands and to give me more messages for family and friends in the United States.

Mestre and some of the others saw that I was exhausted and shaken. They managed to persuade the visitors to leave the galera. I explained that there would be plenty of time to say goodbye as the paper work would take two or three weeks.

To my amazement, about an hour later, the loudspeaker ordered me to pick up my belongings and report to the office. This was it!

Prisoners were pumping my hand. Others were giving me abrazos and kissing me. One man was crying. He put his arm around me: "No matter what happens, John, you must tell the American people the truth. They must come here and save our country. Fidel Castro will kill all of us at the first sign of invasion, but that makes no difference." All the time he was telling me this—I cannot mention his name—he was crying.

Mestre and another friend got me to my feet. Ronny and Mestre took me by the arms and helped me out of the galera. So many people were crowding in, pounding my back and wishing me luck that I could hardly move.

When we got to the patio, the prisoners were cheering. My fifty- or sixty-foot walk from the galera to the prison office was one of the most dramatic moments of my life. There was pandemonium.

Voices said: "Go see Kennedy. Tell him we are waiting. God bless America." Men started singing the Marine Anthem. Hands grabbed my arms and shook me. One man gave me a bear hug and lifted me off my feet. It was a blurred, confused scene. Jáuriga was laughing. Ronnie and Ernesto gave me abrazos. There was a great surge of happiness because of my good fortune and what was completely absent was any expression of envy or spite. These men were among the most selfless people it has ever been my privilege to meet.

The loudspeaker came on. The office of the day ordered the prisoners to keep quiet if they wanted John Martino to go free. There was absolute and immediate silence. They were waving at me. There was a sea of faces, blurred before my eyes because I was crying. I knew that I would never see many of these dear friends again. Many would die. I could hear their words ringing in my ears:

"Don't forget. Tell the world what we are suffering here."

I was taken into the office. The chief of the prison turned to me:

"We are finally going to get rid of you and I am glad. We are getting rid of a headache. Maybe we can do something with the prisoners now."

I didn't answer. I put on the pants and shirt they gave me. They didn't even search me. As they were putting me into the car, the chief of the prison said:

"Martino, do you know President John Kennedy?"

"I do not."

"Make it your business to know him. I have a message for him. Tell him that the Russians and the Chinese will be seeing him soon, because we are going to take the United States of America."

I stared at him in frank amazement, but he was not joking. The officer of the day shook his head, as if to indicate that the chief was crazy. The chief was a young Rebel—Moscow indoctrinated, about twenty years old. As he slammed the door of the car, he said: "Hasta luego."

Until then! If there is another meeting, I thought with quiet satisfaction, it will take place in a liberated Cuba and not in Washington or New York. And you will not enjoy the meeting, my friend.

I was taken to an infirmary of the Department of Immigration. A doctor examined me to see if I was strong enough to tale the trip. Then a friendly guard assured me that I would fly home the first thing the next morning. My wife and children had been notified by telegram.

To the Land of the Free

The day dragged along on crippled feet. By seven o'clock the next morning, I was being driven under military escort to the Rancho Boyero Airport. There, my guards presented my papers to a representative of Pan American Airways.

"Can you prove you are an American?" He asked me in excellent English.

"What?" I was thunderstruck.

"If you can't prove your citizenship, I can't put you on the plane."

"Are you playing some sort of joke? I have been in prison for three years and three months. You can see these documents here. I am a resident of Miami Beach."

"I am sorry, sir. If you don't have a passport or other proof of citizenship, I can't let you on the plane. If it turns out that you are not a citizen, Pan American would have to pay a thousand dollar fine."

The chief of my escort argued with the ticket agent, but it was useless. The other passengers boarded the plane. I watched it rise from the ground and disappear into the sky.

I felt sudden panic. I might be taken back to La Cabana. I was returned to the cell in Immigration where I had spent the previous night. There I lay on my bunk, smoking, feeling black despair.

Then the chief of my escort burst in:

"Hurry up. Get ready. Everything is fixed. The Pan American man cabled for instructions. You are going home today."

We drove to the airport and I was put aboard the plane. The Cuban authorities instructed the captain that I was not to get off the plane on Cuban soil. Two armed guards stayed aboard until the last moment to prevent my escaping and rushing back to my cell in La Cabana. The purpose of this, I suppose, was to preserve the fiction that I was being punished by being deported to the United States.

The other passengers were Cuban refugees. When we were airborne and a few minutes later over the Keys, we shared silently the great experience of returning to freedom.

At Miami International Airport, newsmen and photographers were waiting on the balcony. I was the last to leave the plane. I could hear my wife and children screaming from somewhere in the middle of the wildly emotional, shivering crowd. A man from Pan American took me aside:

"You are John Martino, aren't you? Come in here. Thank God, we have you back safely."

He took me through Immigration and now I was face to face with Florence and the three children, whom I hadn't seen for over two years. She was crying and hysterical, laughing and also in tears. Flash bulbs were exploding around me. Through a daze, I saw my son, Edward, bigger and manlier, and the twins, Vincent and Stefanie, who had spent more than a third of their lives away from me while I was in prison. My lawyer, the faithful Dr. Camargo, was also there.

For a day or two, there was a stream of newsmen, radio and television interviews. After that, I was able to be alone with my family.

I told her about her petition and asked her how she had come to send it.

"I got an anonymous letter," Florence said. "It advised me to petition President Oswaldo Dorticós. I had tried everything but that. So I did it. I have seen so many people. I have tried so many different ways. I don't know the truth about how or why you were freed."

I have thought about this many times since. Was it the Checo and Roberto Riveroni? Was I set free because the Communist cell thought they would have a better chance to sell the rehabilitation program to the prisoners if the American was out? Or was I helped by a Latin American government? My wife has friends in one such regime and these friends had indicated that they would see what could be done for me.

I was soon visited by American Government representatives who wanted to know the magic formula that I had used to obtain my freedom.

Two months after I was set free, the United States Government ransomed over 1,100 Playa Girón invaders. Apparently they forgot all about the two dozen or so Americans who were also in Cuban prisons on political charges. I made as vociferous a campaign on that issue as I could, with results that are now a matter of history. It amused me to find out that, when the United States Government was asked what it was doing to free these Americans, it assured the public it was doing everything possible.

The press was then presented with an official list of the Americans held in Cuban prisons by the Castro regime. Although I had been happily at home with Florence and the children for two months by that time, the name, John Martino, was on that list!

Florence never stopped praying. She prayed to God and she prayed to the Holy Virgin. I do not know whether I was set free because of God's will or because of accident or because of causes hidden from me. I know only that I am home and out of the nightmare.

I am one of the fortunate few. Tens of thousands of Cubans suffer the unspeakable conditions I have described. They are as deserving of a human existence as I am. They are in prison because they stood up for freedom and, if we are genuinely dedicated to freedom, then they are our brothers.

Index

Gustavo Alemán 28, 29, 44, 48, 49
Gustavo Estevez 2, 8

H

Herbert L. Matthews 4, 8, 42, 96, 136
Hernández 36
Miranda Hernández 25, 25–38
Heroin 98, 100
Hotel Deauville 1, 2, 7

I

Idlewild 192
Ignacio 134, 162
Infirmary 73, 82, 83, 85, 86, 87, 89, 90
INRA 192, 194
Interpol 99
Iram Gonzalez 167

J

Jack Gore 152
Jack Paar 181, 182
Jacobo Arbenz 122
James Buchanan 79, 80
James D. Beane 123, 128
J. Edgar Hoover 2
Jesus Carrera 143
John Kennedy 88, 236
John Martino 1, 2, 3, 4, 6, 7, 8, 12, 19, 26, 43, 108, 147, 148, 177, 179, 188, 190, 223, 235, 237, 239
Jorge Diaz 164
Jorge Rosell 94
José Cabanas Gonzalez 194, 198
José Castaño 2, 8
José de Jesus Castano y Quevedo 2
José de Leon 206
Jose Licaso 191
José Martino Alvarez 166, 177, 178, 179
Juan Alegria 94

Juan Almeida Bosque 56, 57
Juan Marinello 183, 209
Juan Más Machado 94
Jules Dubois 4, 97, 136
Julio Garcia 3
Julio Sanchez Gómez 116, 147
Julio Yebra 107, 111, 112, 113, 115, 186, 213

K

Kammerer Perez 58, 60, 63, 73
Kremlin 31

L

La Cabana 4, 5, 9, 26, 63, 68, 74, 76, 78, 83, 85, 90, 92, 93, 96, 102, 103, 104, 106, 112, 113, 119, 121, 123, 124, 128, 130, 131, 132, 133, 135, 150, 152, 153, 154, 156, 160, 162, 164, 165, 166, 167, 170, 171, 172, 174, 175, 183, 186, 188, 189, 191, 200, 202, 203, 211, 212, 213, 214, 216, 217, 219, 222, 224, 226, 227, 237
La Cabana Fortress 63, 68, 92, 93, 96, 128, 132, 162, 188, 189, 202, 211, 212, 222, 226
La Cabana Prison 9
La Coubre affair 75
La Lorna 23
Law 425 45
Lucky Luciano 97
Luis Alfaro 126, 224, 226, 227

M

Major Huber Matos 122
Major Pedro L. Diaz Lanz 61
Manolito Fernandez 159
Manolito Fernández 102, 113, 127, 156

V

W

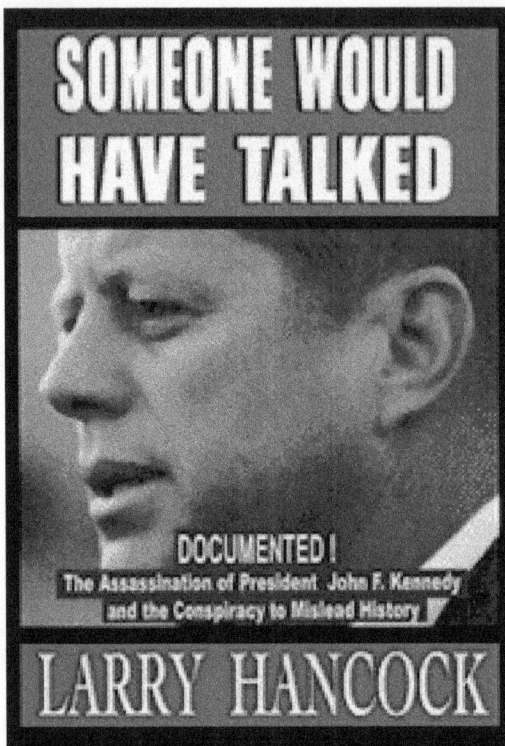

SOMEONE WOULD HAVE TALKED

DOCUMENTED!
The Assassination of President John F. Kennedy
and the Conspiracy to Mislead History

LARRY HANCOCK

"They're going to kill him. They're going to kill him when he gets to Texas."

John Martino,
Former Cuban prisoner and
anti-Castro activist

John Martino knew that President Kennedy was going to be killed in Dallas. He didn't know the details but he knew the people that were doing it – and he had helped them in small ways during his trips to Dallas that fall.

Martino was nervous that day, wanting to distance himself from what was going to happen and knowing that he couldn't. He announced to his family that he would paint the breakfast room in his house. But he had also asked his son, Edward, to stay home from school that Friday. No reason given and no explanation offered. During the morning, John asked Edward not to help paint but instead to watch television and to notify him immediately of any special news or bulletins.

Later, while catching a piece of coverage of the President's travels on the radio, John Martino exclaimed to his wife, "Flo, they're going to kill him. They're going to kill him when he gets to Texas."

Excerpt from *Someone Would Have Talked*

SOMEONE WOULD HAVE TALKED: THE ASSASSINATION OF PRESIDENT JOHN F. KENNEDY AND THE CONSPIRACY TO MISLEAD HISTORY identifies people who talked about a personal prior knowledge of the conspiracy to murder President Kennedy: including a veteran of multiple Castro assassination projects and two senior CIA's officers of the JM WAVE station in Miami, Florida. A fourth man, John Martino, was a three year prisoner of Castro and organizer of the most explosive Cuban penetration mission ever conducted.

Gaeton Fonzi, author of *The Last Investigation* and Former Staff Investigator for the US House Committee on Investigations states:

"There have been two official US Government investigations of the assassination of President John F. Kennedy; the first resulted in the Warren Commission Report. Rank with distortions and manipulations of the evidence, its conclusion that Oswald was the lone assassin quickly disintegrated under objective scrutiny.

The public's distrust of the Warren Commission's Report produced political pressure for a new investigation and the subsequent formation of the U.S. House Select Committee on Assassinations. Unfortunately, the HSCA was intimidated and manipulated by the very government agencies it was investigating and its final report emerged as misleading as the Warren Commission's.

Now, with his experience and analytical acumen, Larry Hancock has identified and detailed culpable conspiratorial associations. Among the most respected researchers of the JFK assassination, Hancock has produced SOMEONE WOULD HAVE TALKED, an awesomely comprehensive and impressive work of compelling validity and a 'must-read' in the field."

Someone Would Have Talked is available at www.jfklancer.com and www.larry-hancock.com

UPDATED VERSION TO BE
RELEASED IN 2009

www.ingramcontent.com/pod-product-compliance
Lightning Source LLC
Chambersburg PA
CBHW020607270326
41927CB00005B/215